A WORLD OF
BREADS

A WORLD OF
BREADS

DOLORES CASELLA
ILLUSTRATED BY LORETTA TREZZO

DAVID WHITE COMPANY · NEW YORK

PRINTING HISTORY
HARDCOVER EDITION

FIRST PRINTING, OCTOBER 1966
SECOND PRINTING, SEPTEMBER 1968
THIRD PRINTING, AUGUST 1970
FOURTH PRINTING, MAY 1971
FIFTH PRINTING, SEPTEMBER 1972
SIXTH PRINTING, JUNE 1974

PAPERBACK EDITION
FIRST PRINTING, JUNE 1974

LIBRARY OF CONGRESS CATALOG CARD NUMBER: 66–25620
SBN 87250–028–4 (HARDCOVER)
SBN 87250–041–1 (PAPERBACK)

Grateful acknowledgment for permission to use material is made to the following organizations and individuals:
For permission to reprint recipes first published in periodicals—*Gourmet* (Arabic Bread, pp. 62-63; Sfeeha, Fatayir, pp. 288-89); *The National Observer* (Orange Doughnuts, Sweet Potato Doughnuts, pp. 117-18; Basic Date-Nut Bread, pp. 162-63).
Mr. and Mrs. Clive McCay, Englewood, Florida, for use of material and recipes on Cornell Breads (pp. 85-88).
The Stephen Greene Press, for material from *Peter Hunt's Cape Cod Cookbook*, copyright 1954 by Hawthorne Books, Inc.; copyright © 1962 by The Stephen Greene Press, 120 Main Street, Brattleboro, Vermont (Portuguese Easter Bread, p. 245).
John R. Braue for material from *Uncle John's Bread Book*, copyright 1961 by The House of Rahn, P.O. Box 3276, Midland, Texas (My Good Father's Shepherd's Bread, p. 65; Pumpernickel, pp. 82-83; No Excuse Quick Bread, p. 282).
Whittier Home Economists in Homemaking, Whittier, California, for material from *From Our Kitchens to Yours* (Cheese Bread, p. 53; Banana Date Loaf, Teatime Slices, pp. 155-56).

DAVID WHITE COMPANY
60 EAST 55TH STREET, NEW YORK, N. Y.

PRINTED IN THE UNITED STATES OF AMERICA

This book is
affectionately dedicated
to
WAYNE CASELLA

Contents

Foreword

The history of bread begins with wheat, and wheat originated as a grass, in the fertile valleys of the Middle East before history began. The first known written reference to baked bread was found on a clay tablet from Sumer about 2600 B.C. Wheat growing and bread baking figure largely in Egyptian tomb paintings and carvings, and it was the Egyptians who discovered the secret of leaven and invented the first oven. The Greeks improved the arts of milling and baking and the Romans learned from the Greeks, as they did in many areas. The Romans also improved the cultivation of wheat, developing many varieties.

With the discovery of the New World came the discovery of maize, or Indian corn, which had been cultivated for centuries by Indians in every part of the Western Hemisphere in which agriculture flourished. Except for corn flakes, every popular corn dish known today was known and prepared in both Americas. The North American colonists learned the cultivation of corn from the Indians, following Indian methods completely. The earliest American cookbooks abound in recipes for cornbreads of various kinds.

The nineteenth century brought to the United States a great influx of immigrants from all parts of Europe, and the immigrants brought with them an amazingly rich heritage' of culinary lore. The American table today is laden with the wealth of breads of many countries, adapted to American materials, methods, and tastes. The recipes in this book represent that wealth. Here are breads from all over the world—both Americas, all of Europe, the Middle East, the Far East. The ingredients, shapes, and methods are as varied as the origins. Every recipe has been made in my kitchen many times and approved by an enthusiastic family. Many are quick and easy; others time-consuming but rewarding in proportion. All reflect my belief in the immemorial satisfactions to body and spirit that only homemade bread can provide.

Bon appetit!

DOLORES CASELLA

[ix]

1. *What Breadmakers Should Know*

The information in this section is basic for the making of truly good breads. I recommend that every user of this book read it carefully before starting to try the recipes, and refer to it again whenever problems arise. Many of the questions that perplex the novice are answered, and even the most experienced breadmaker should find this compilation helpful and convenient.

INGREDIENTS

Yeast

One cake of compressed yeast, or 1 package of dry yeast, will raise as much as 8 cups of flour. However, if you wish to make bread quick-on-the-double, use 1 cake or package of yeast to each cup of liquid in recipe, or 1 cake or package of yeast to each 3 cups of flour. With this proportion of ingredients, bread can be made from start to finish in less than 2½ hours.

Cake yeast is perishable and must be kept refrigerated. Use within 1 week for best results.

Packaged dry yeast is now more commonly used than cake yeast, and is very convenient. Some good cooks claim to find a difference between the bread made with cake yeast and that made with packaged dry yeast, but I have never noticed any difference. The packaged dry yeast will keep for several weeks on the cupboard shelf, or indefinitely under refrigeration. It can also be bought by the pound at health food stores, at a substantial saving over the individual package price. I keep mine in an airtight plastic container in the refrigerator. One tablespoon of dry yeast equals 1 cake of compressed yeast, or 1 package of dry yeast. When you wish to use dry yeast in a recipe calling for compressed yeast, remove ¼ cup of liquid from the ingredients to dissolve the dry yeast in.

Liquids

Milk, water, or potato water may be used in making bread. Each gives a different result. Water provides a crisper crust, and more of a down-to-earth bread flavor. I find it significant that in the world's greatest dinner breads—French, Italian, and similiar breads—water is the only liquid ingredient. Bread made with milk is more nutritious, has a browner crust, and will keep longer. Potato water produces a coarser bread and a slightly larger loaf. Milk or potato water must always be scalded and cooled before using, to prevent souring.

Skim-milk powder may be used in place of regular milk, to provide more nutrition and for convenience. Instant Milk Crystals can also be used but only if they have been reconstituted into liquid form; used as crystals they will make the baked product gummy. As an equivalent to 1 quart milk, use ½ to ⅔ cup milk powder, or 1½ cups milk crystals. To provide greater nutrition, I simply use double the amount of milk powder necessary; for example, in a recipe calling for 2 cups milk, I use 2 cups water and ½ cup milk powder. For convenience in mixing, use water for the liquid, and stir the milk powder in with the sifted dry ingredients. If your grocer does not carry skim-milk powder, it can be bought at a health food store.

Flour

Bread flour (hardwheat flour) that is unbleached makes the best yeast dough. This flour is available in many supermarkets, or may be bought from a local miller, or at a health food store. All-purpose flour can be used in any recipe in this book that calls for white flour, but in my opinion it won't give the same results.

Unless otherwise specified, white flour should always be sifted. The coarser whole-wheat, graham, rye, and other whole-grain flours are difficult to sift, and need only to be lifted carefully with a large spoon or a scoop into a measuring cup. With this method the flour won't pack; if it packs, or settles, several extra tablespoons will be needed to fill a cup and this proportion, multiplied by 4 or more cups of whole-grain flour, may add just enough flour to ruin a good recipe. Whole-wheat flour and graham flour may be used interchangeably.

I cannot overemphasize the importance of good flour, especially with cornbreads or with any bread using whole-grain flour. The quality of the flour used will make the difference between a good loaf of bread, and a mediocre or even downright bad one. I buy all my flour at a health food store (I am not in their pay, but unfortunately these stores are among the few places where a city person can buy good flour). And I keep all flours, except unbleached white flour, under the necessary refrigeration. As I bake all of our bread and use fairly large quantities of different flours, I found it convenient to purchase a small, inexpensive refrigerator for storing various flours and cereals. If you do a lot of baking and can purchase flours in quantity, you won't notice any appreciable difference in cost. Whether or not you believe the claims of the health food stores, the excellent flavor of breads made with natural whole-grain flours is reason enough for their purchase.

Remember that different brands of flour, or the same brand at different times, will absorb varying amounts of liquid. The usual proportion is 1 cup liquid to 3 or 4 cups flour.

Sugar

Sugar helps to brown the crust and also helps the yeast to work properly. You may use granulated sugar, light brown or dark brown sugar, or raw sugar, interchangeably.

Salt

Salt gives flavor and stabilizes the fermentation. The usual proportion is 1 teaspoon salt to each 2 cups flour.

Shortening

I use butter in most recipes because I prefer the flavor. However, margarine, shortening, bacon fat, or lard can be used. In dinner breads, where a relatively small amount of shortening is required, a liquid shortening may be substituted if desired.

Eggs

Eggs add flavor, color, and delicacy to yeast doughs. Egg yolks make the finest dough for sweet breads and coffee cakes, but in any recipe calling for egg yolks alone, whole eggs can be substituted—simply use 1 whole egg for each 2 egg yolks called for. The opposite also holds true. If you have a lot of egg yolks (a problem that cake decorators always seem to have), simply use 2 egg yolks for each whole egg called for. This is very handy when a recipe calls for an odd number of eggs and you wish to cut the recipe in half. If, for example, 5 whole eggs are called for, to cut the recipe in half simply use 5 egg yolks, or 2 whole eggs and 1 egg yolk.

Special Ingredients

The usage of the following ingredients may seem complicated at first but in a very short time it will come naturally to you. These ingredients are important because by using them in the proportions suggested you can add enough protein, vitamins, and minerals to make your bread a real staff of life. If you are feeding your family on a limited budget, these additions are even more important. They all can be bought at health food stores. All should be kept refrigerated.

WHEAT GERM. Wheat germ is the embryo of the wheat, which is almost universally removed from "enriched" flour. The packaged wheat germ on the grocer's shelf usually has had the oil removed, and with it the valuable vitamin E, and preservatives added. So once again you must find a local miller or a health food store to get the real thing. Out of each cup of flour called for, replace 2 teaspoons flour with wheat germ. Some recipes call for larger amounts of wheat germ, in which case stir the wheat germ into the dough after the rest of the flour has been added.

WHEAT GERM AND MIDDLINGS. This makes an excellent quick-cooking cereal and can also replace up to 1 cup flour in any standard bread recipe.

RICE POLISH. This inner bran of brown rice, which is removed from white rice, contains important vitamins and minerals. Use it as you would wheat germ, replacing any amount of flour up to 2 tablespoons for each cup of flour called for.

SOY FLOUR. This flour provides important protein and can replace up to 20 per cent of the flour used in any bread recipe.

Onion-Soup Mix

Where called for, onion-soup mix should be stirred into the sifted dry ingredients.

Sour Cream

Sour cream, as specified in the recipes in this book, means commercial sour cream, not the home-soured kind. However, if you live in an area where commercial sour cream is hard to come by, the following recipe makes a truly excellent substitute.

HOMEMADE SOUR CREAM

1 pint heavy cream	5 teaspoons commercial buttermilk

Combine the ingredients in a container. Cap and shake for a minute just to blend ingredients. Let stand at room temperature for 24 hours. Refrigerate another 24 hours before using. Will keep for a month.

TECHNIQUES

Kneading

Except when otherwise specified, kneading is essential to a good loaf of bread. In general, turn the dough onto a lightly floured board and knead with the hands until the dough is smooth and elastic, approximately 7 to 10 minutes. If you bake a lot of bread, a home Breadmaker, which is sold in large department stores for from $9.00 to $14.00, is a good investment. Instructions for using come with it.

Rising

When the dough has been kneaded, it should be placed in a lightly buttered bowl and the top spread lightly with melted butter or margarine. This keeps a crust from forming on the dough. Cover the bowl of dough with a clean cloth and set aside to rise until doubled.

When the dough has risen enough it will have a full, smooth look to it. But to be certain, press one or two fingers into the dough. If the dough has not risen enough, the depression made by the fingers will fill quickly. If the holes in the dough remain, then it has risen enough. Then punch the dough down, and follow the particular recipe. However, if you cannot continue with the recipe at that moment, the dough can rise a second, and even a third or fourth, time with no detrimental effect. Be certain, however, to punch the dough down each time it rises, to keep it from souring, and don't forget that the dough will rise more quickly each time.

Shaping

Standard cookbooks often give what seems to me a fairly complicated and unnecessarily time-consuming method of shaping the dough into loaves. I find it just as convenient to turn the dough onto a lightly floured breadboard, divide it into as many pieces as you want loaves, cover it with a clean towel, and let it stand for 10 minutes. This resting period allows the dough to "loosen" enough so that it can be easily shaped into nice, smooth loaves. At the end of 10 minutes, use your hands to pat and roll each piece into a loaf shape. Place the loaves in buttered pans, cover, and let rise again before baking.

Pans

Standard loaf pans are 9 by 5 by 3 inches. Glass pans are usually slightly smaller, averaging 8 by 4 by 2½ inches. For any recipe calling for loaf pans either standard loaf pans or glass loaf pans can be used, with a slight difference in the size of the finished loaf. A Bundt pan, which is called for in many recipes, is a fluted, cast-iron pan (it can now be bought with a Teflon coating), patterned for the German Bundt cake. It holds the same amount as a 10- by 4-inch tube pan and the two may be used interchangeably. Pans should always be greased with shortening, butter, or margarine. Never use oil, as dough seems to absorb oil and will invariably stick.

Freezing Bread

To freeze bread, put the shaped, unbaked dough in a greased pan. Spread the top with softened or melted butter. Wrap and store in the freezer. The dough will keep 1 week. When ready to use, unwrap, let the dough stand at room temperature until doubled, and then bake as usual.

To freeze baked bread or coffee cakes, first cool them—it is best to let them cool overnight so that they are *thoroughly* cooled. Then wrap and store in the freezer. They can be kept for up to 6 months. Before using, thaw, wrapped, in a preheated oven at 300° for 30 minutes. If they are unwrapped before thawing unwanted moisture may form.

Ready-to-Serve Rolls

To make your own ready-to-serve rolls, use a French or Vienna type of roll dough. Follow the recipe up to the point of baking. Bake the rolls at 275° until the dough is firm but uncolored, about 30 minutes. Remove from oven, cool thoroughly, wrap and store in refrigerator or freezer. When ready to use, brush rolls with slightly beaten egg and bake in a 400° oven until browned.

Baking

Yeast breads in loaf form are usually placed in a hot oven (425°) for 10 minutes, to stop the growth of the yeast and to set the crust. The temperature is then reduced to 350° for the remainder of the baking time. However, many cooks prefer to bake the bread for a slightly longer period of time, at a steady temperature, usually 375° or 400°, but sometimes at a slightly lower or higher temperature.

In recent years the cold-oven method of baking has gained in popularity. Before the dough has doubled in bulk, the loaves are placed in a *cold* (unheated) oven. Then, the oven temperature is set at 350° or 400°, depending on the type of bread. The bread finishes rising as the oven heats. The method may be used with any loaf breads; hard-crusted breads, such as French, Vienna, or Cuban breads, should be started at 400°. With this method of baking, do expect a slight difference in texture.

In all bread recipes, *unless* the cold-oven method of baking is used, the oven must be preheated to the desired temperature before the dough is put in.

Bread, when baked and done, will be an even rich brown. However, if you are just not sure, turn the loaf out of the pan onto a breadboard. Tap the bottom of the loaf lightly with a knuckle. If the bread is done there will be a distinctly hollow sound; if you do not hear this, turn the bread back into the pan and bake a short time longer.

Freshening Slightly Stale Bread or Rolls

Place in a paper bag, sprinkle with water, and place in 350° oven until bag is dry.

2. *Biscuits, Muffins, Popovers*

BISCUITS

Biscuits have come a long way since Mary Stuart Smith, in her *Virginia Cookery-Book* of 1885, stated: "Nothing can be more inelegant than a large, thick biscuit. . . . Occasionally a person is found who likes a soft white biscuit; if so, special directions may be given to that effect, for this may be considered an idiosyncrasy of taste. A biscuit should be cut not more than three inches in diameter, and not more than a third of an inch in thickness."

An assortment of biscuit recipes and variations can be an invaluable addition to any cook's repertoire. But first, a good standard biscuit recipe is required.

STANDARD BISCUIT RECIPE

Any standard recipe makes good biscuits, but to make them even better use butter for the shortening and/or cut the milk to ⅓ cup and use 2 large eggs. The addition of eggs to a biscuit recipe makes a tremendous difference.

2 cups flour	¼ cup butter or margarine
3 teaspoons baking powder	about ¾ cup milk
½ teaspoon salt	

Combine the flour, baking powder, and salt. Cut in the butter with a pastry blender or a fork. When the mixture is the consistency of coarse cornmeal, stir in the liquid ingredients, using enough so that the dough holds together and can be kneaded. Turn the dough onto a floured board and knead lightly, no more than 10 times. Roll out to a thickness of approximately ½ inch. Cut into 2-inch rounds and bake on an ungreased cookie sheet in a 450° oven for 12 to 15 minutes. Makes approximately 12 biscuits.

VARIATIONS

1. Make the basic recipe, adding 2 eggs and ¼ cup sugar to dough. Divide the dough in half and add ¼ cup walnuts to one half and ¼ cup golden raisins to the other half. Knead each half into a ball and let rest for 10 minutes. Roll or pat each round to fit a 9-inch pie tin. Butter 2 tins, place a round in each, and score the tops into 6 wedge-shaped pieces. Brush tops with lightly beaten egg and sprinkle with sugar. Bake in a 400° oven for 15 to 20 minutes, or until done.

2. Brush unbaked biscuits with slightly beaten egg whites and sprinkle with poppy seed or sesame seed.

3. Add a cup of mashed bananas to Standard Biscuit Recipe, substituting whole-wheat flour for white. You may add nuts or raisins if desired.

ONION BISCUITS. Make Standard Biscuit Recipe and add 2 cups minced onions and 2 eggs. Roll dough to a thickness of ¼ inch and cut into 2-inch rounds. Placed on greased cookie sheets, brush with beaten egg, and bake in 375° oven until brown, about 15 to 20 minutes. Sprinkle with coarse salt before serving.

MINT BISCUITS. Add ¼ cup minced fresh mint to Standard Biscuit Recipe. Use to top a lamb stew or lamb pie.

WATERCRESS BISCUITS. These are excellent on or with meat stews. Add ¼ cup minced fresh watercress to Standard Biscuit Recipe.

OATMEAL BISCUITS. Replace 1 cup of the flour with 1 cup uncooked rolled oats in Standard Biscuit Recipe.

PARTY BISCUITS. Stir 1 can condensed mushroom soup and ¼ cup melted butter into biscuit recipe using 3 cups flour. Roll the dough to ½-inch thickness and cut. Bake on greased cookie sheet, in a 450° oven for 10 to 12 minutes.

BISCUIT HINTS

1. To reheat biscuits, place them in a wet paper bag, tie it up, and place in a 350° oven for about 10 minutes.

2. When making biscuits, cut out an extra panful. Cover with waxed paper and refrigerate until you wish to use them. Use within 48 hours.

3. For crusty biscuits, roll the dough thinner and cut biscuits smaller. Place far apart on cookie sheets.

4. For flaky biscuits, roll the dough thicker, cut biscuits larger, and place them close together on cookie sheets.

5. Biscuits cut very small and sprinkled with a cinnamon-sugar mixture before baking are fine for children's snacks.

CHEESE BISCUITS

1 Standard Biscuit Recipe	1 tablespoon grated onion
1 cup grated Cheddar cheese	1 tablespoon prepared mustard
¼ cup minced olives	¼ cup mayonnaise

Make Standard Biscuit Recipe, rolling the dough out ¼-inch thick. Cut into rounds. Mix all the other ingredients. Spread the mixture on half of the rounds and top with the remaining rounds. Cut into the top of each. Pinch the edges to seal. Place on a buttered cookie sheet, brush with butter, and bake in a 450° oven for 12 to 15 minutes, or until browned and done.

SOUTHERN BUTTERMILK BISCUITS

Not Beaten Biscuits, but very good.

4 cups flour	½ teaspoon soda
1 teaspoon salt	¾ cup butter or margarine
1 teaspoon baking powder	1¼ cups buttermilk

Sift the dry ingredients. Cut the butter or margarine into the dry ingredients as for pastry. When the particles are about the size of small peas, add the buttermilk, and stir just until thoroughly moistened. Turn out onto a lightly floured breadboard and knead 10 times—no more. Roll or pat to a thickness of ½ inch. Cut into rounds with a large cutter and bake on an ungreased cookie sheet in a 450° oven for 15 minutes, or until browned and done.

NOTE. You may substitute ⅓ to ½ cup bran flakes for the same amount of flour. Or add ½ cup grated Cheddar cheese to dry ingredients. Or use sour cream in place of buttermilk and decrease butter or margarine to ⅓ cup.

CORNMEAL BISCUITS

2 cups flour
1 tablespoon baking powder
1 teaspoon salt
½ teaspoon soda

¾ cup coarsely ground corn-
    meal
½ cup butter or margarine
1 cup buttermilk

Sift the flour, baking powder, salt and soda. Combine with the cornmeal. Cut in the butter or margarine until the particles are the size of small peas, and then add the buttermilk, stirring until well dampened. Turn out onto a lightly floured breadboard and knead gently for a few seconds, or about 10 times. Roll out the dough, cut with a biscuit cutter, and place on an ungreased cookie sheet. Bake in 450° oven for 12 to 15 minutes, or until browned and done.

TETERTOS POGACSA
(Bacon-Scrap Biscuit)

This and the following recipe are examples of the excellent Hungarian breads.

1 cake yeast
½ cup warm water
4 cups flour
1 cup sour cream

4 eggs
¼ teaspoon salt
½ pound bacon, cooked until
    crisp and then crumbled

Dissolve the yeast in the warm water. Combine the flour, sour cream, eggs, and salt and mix until well blended. Stir in the yeast. Cover the dough and let rise until it is doubled in size. Flour a board and spread the crumbled bacon. Punch the dough down and roll it out on the board. Fold the dough into quarters and let it rise. Roll the dough out again, fold into quarters again, and let rise. Repeat for a total of 4 times. After the dough has risen the last time, roll it out and cut into biscuits. Arrange on a lightly buttered cookie sheet, brush with beaten egg, and let rise again. Bake in a 350° oven until browned and done—20 to 30 minutes.

KRUMPLIS POGACSA
(Potato Biscuit)

Similar to Scones, but richer. If desired, roll the dough out and cut into biscuits without folding into quarters. Brush the biscuits with beaten egg yolk. Tradition requires making a crisscross on each biscuit with a fork.

1 teaspoon salt	2 tablespoons sour cream
2 cups flour	1 cup cold mashed potatoes
1 cup cold butter	3 egg yolks, or 3 whole eggs

Sift the flour with the salt. Cut the cold butter into the flour. Add the sour cream, potatoes, and egg yolks or whole eggs. Stir and knead. Roll the dough thin and fold into quarters. Now chill the dough for 30 minutes. Roll dough out again, and fold into quarters again. Chill the dough another 30 minutes. Repeat procedure for a total of 4 times. Then roll the dough to a thickness of ¼ inch. Cut into biscuits, brush with beaten egg yolk, and sprinkle with caraway seed. Bake in a 400° oven for 15 to 20 minutes, or until done.

CAMPERS' BISCUITS

Even out in the wilds there is no need to be without hot homemade bread!

2 cups flour	1 cup milk
2 teaspoons baking powder	a peeled green stick
¼ teaspoon salt	flour
2 tablespoons shortening	

Sift the dry ingredients ahead of time at home and keep in a plastic bag until needed. Cut the shortening into the presifted dry ingredients. Add enough milk to make a stiff dough. Heat the stick and sprinkle it with flour. Twist approximately one-eighth of the dough around the stick. Hold the stick about 6 inches away from hot coals until the inside is done. Then hold the stick a little closer to the coals, turning it constantly, until the outside is browned. Remove from stick and repeat until dough is all used.

Dried herbs may be added to the dough, if desired.

MARYLAND BEATEN BISCUITS

The American South's most famous contribution to the roster of breads.

4 cups flour, sifted	½ cup lard
½ teaspoon salt	1 cup milk
½ teaspoon baking powder	

Sift the dry ingredients together. Work in the lard with the fingertips. Stir in the milk and turn the dough out on a lightly floured breadboard. Beat with a wooden mallet, fold the dough over, and beat again. Continue this procedure until blisters appear on the dough. Pinch off pieces about the size of small walnuts and work with the hands. Press them flat and prick each with a fork. Bake on an ungreased cookie sheet in a 450° oven for about 20 minutes.

The cookbook authors of an early day tended to be quite opinionated and quite free in expressing their opinions. In Miss Leslie's New Cookery Book, *1857, Miss Eliza Leslie had this to say about Maryland Biscuit (Beaten Biscuits):*

"This is the most laborious of cakes, and also the most unwholesome, even when made in the best manner. We do not recommend it; but there is no accounting for tastes. Children should not eat these biscuits—nor grown persons either, if they can get any other sort of bread.

"When living in a town where there are bakers, there is no excuse for making Maryland biscuit. Believe nobody that says they are not unwholesome. Yet we have heard of families, in country places, where neither the mistress nor the cook knew any other preparation of wheat bread. Better to live on indian cakes."

BUTTERMILK HAM BISCUITS

2 cups flour, sifted
4 teaspoons baking powder
2 tablespoons butter

¾ cup milk or buttermilk
½ cup ground ham

Sift flour and baking powder. (No salt is needed as the ham usually supplies enough.) Cut in the butter until the dough is of the consistency of coarse cornmeal. Add the milk or buttermilk and ham and stir until dry ingredients are dampened. (If you use buttermilk add ½ teaspoon soda to the dough.) Turn out onto a lightly floured board and roll or pat into an oblong. Cut into circles and bake on ungreased cookie sheet in a 425° oven until brown, about 15 minutes.

RICH TEA BISCUITS

2 cups sifted flour
1 tablespoon baking powder
1 teaspoon salt
2 tablespoons sugar

½ cup butter or margarine
¾ cup milk
1 egg
½ cup diced candied pineapple

Sift the dry ingredients. Cut in the butter or margarine. Combine milk and egg, add, and stir until dry ingredients are dampened. Add pineapple. Roll out the dough, cut into rounds, place on an ungreased baking sheet, sprinkle with sugar, and bake in a 450° oven for 12 to 15 minutes, or until done.

SWEET BISCUITS

1 cup sugar
4 cups sifted flour
4 teaspoons baking powder
1 teaspoon salt
½ teaspoon cinnamon or
  nutmeg

1 cup butter or margarine
¾ cup milk
3 large eggs
1 teaspoon vanilla extract
1 or 2 teaspoons grated orange
  rind or lemon rind

Combine in a large bowl the sugar, flour, baking powder, salt, and spice. Cut in the butter or margarine until the particles are the size of small peas. Combine the milk, eggs, vanilla extract, and grated rind, and stir into dry ingredients just until moist. Roll out on a lightly floured board and cut with a biscuit cutter. Bake on an ungreased cookie sheet in a 450° oven for 15 minutes, or until browned and done. Serve hot.

AUSTRALIAN SWEET BISCUITS

This one hails from Australia and makes an excellent sweet biscuit. Serve it, in true British style, for tea, with lime, grapefruit, or orange marmalade.

½ cup plus 2 tablespoons milk	3 cups flour
1 cup white or brown sugar	½ teaspoon salt
1 teaspoon soda	1 cup butter or margarine

Combine the milk and sugar in a saucepan. Bring to a boil over medium heat and then stir in the soda. Remove from heat immediately, stir until the soda dissolves, and let cool until warm.

Combine the flour and salt in a bowl. Cut in the butter or margarine until the particles are the size of small peas. Add the milk mixture and stir to moisten the dry ingredients. Turn out onto a lightly floured breadboard, knead 10 times, and then roll out to a thickness of about ⅓ inch. Cut with a biscuit cutter and place on a buttered cookie sheet. Bake in a 400° oven for 10 to 12 minutes, or until browned and done.

HONEY BISCUITS

1 Standard Biscuit Recipe	½ cup raisins
soft butter	½ cup chopped nuts
2 tablespoons sugar	honey

Make Standard Biscuit Recipe. Roll to a thickness of ½ inch and spread with soft butter. Sprinkle with the sugar, raisins, and chopped nuts. Roll as for a jelly roll and cut into ½-inch slices. Butter a baking pan and cover the bottom with ½ inch of honey. Place the slices, cut side down, in the pan. Bake in 400° oven for 15 minutes, or until lightly browned. Remove at once, and pour any remaining honey over the biscuits.

VARIATIONS

Honey, molasses, or maple syrup may be used for these, combined if desired, with 2 tablespoons melted butter. Or use ¾ cup orange, lime, or lemon marmalade combined with 2 or 3 tablespoons melted butter. Or ¾ cup brown sugar, ¼ cup honey, and ¼ cup butter may be combined, heated until butter melts, and used instead.

CREAM BISCUITS

No shortening is used in this recipe, as the whipped cream takes its place. Sprinkle the top with brown sugar, or shaved maple sugar, before baking.

2 cups sifted flour	½ teaspoon salt
1 tablespoon baking powder	1 cup heavy cream, whipped

Combine dry ingredients and mix thoroughly. Sift again. Pour in the whipped cream and fold in thoroughly. Turn the dough out on a lightly floured board and knead for 30 seconds. Pat or roll to ½-inch thickness. Cut and place on an ungreased baking sheet. Bake in a 425° oven for 12 minutes.

CREAM-CHEESE BISCUITS

2 3-ounce packages cream cheese	½ teaspoon salt
	2 tablespoons chopped nuts
1 cup butter or margarine	2 tablespoons candied fruits
2 cups sifted flour	

Mix the cream cheese with the butter or margarine until creamy. Add the salt to the flour and sift twice. Add the cream cheese and butter mixture and blend thoroughly. Stir in the nuts and fruits. Turn out onto a lightly floured board and knead for 30 seconds. Roll and cut. Place on an ungreased baking sheet and bake at 425° for 15 minutes, or until done. Serve hot.

RICH SOUR-CREAM BISCUITS

These are actually dinner biscuits, but if you add ½ cup sugar, they become rich, sweet tea biscuits.

3 cups flour	¾ teaspoon soda
1 teaspoon salt	1½ cups sour cream
1½ teaspoons baking powder	1 large egg

Sift the dry ingredients. Stir in the sour cream and the egg. Knead very lightly. Turn out onto a lightly floured board and roll to a thickness of ½ inch. Cut into rounds with a biscuit cutter. Place on a buttered cookie sheet and bake in a 450° oven for 15 to 20 minutes, or until browned and done.

IDEAS FOR USING CANNED BISCUITS

You may prefer, as I do, to make all your breads from scratch, in which case these ideas may all be adapted to the Standard Biscuit Recipe. For working wives, however, canned biscuits may often be a lifesaver. The following suggestions add immeasurably to the flavor.

COFFEE BISCUITS. Place biscuits on a buttered baking sheet with sides. Combine: 1 teaspoon cinnamon, ½ teaspoon nutmeg, ½ cup chopped walnuts, ½ cup sugar, ½ cup raisins, and 3 tablespoons melted butter. Sprinkle on tops of biscuits. Bake at 400° for 15 to 20 minutes.

SPICED PECAN BISCUITS. Combine 1 cup sugar, ½ cup melted butter, and 1 tablespoon cinnamon. Take out biscuits from 2 cans and roll them in the sugar mixture. Place in a well-buttered cookie sheet with sides. Sprinkle with chopped pecans and bake at 400° for 20 minutes.

HERBED BISCUITS. Roll or dip biscuits in melted butter. Place on a slightly buttered cookie sheet and sprinkle with any desired herb, or with sautéed chopped onions.

SEED BISCUITS. Roll or dip biscuits in melted butter. Or else pat them out with the fingers until they are thin and brush with melted butter. Sprinkle liberally with sesame seed or poppy seed. Or, if you are of Middle Eastern extraction, sprinkle the biscuits with Zahter, a spicy mixture of thyme and sumac, available in specialty food stores.

BISCUIT PEACH SHORTCAKE. Dip biscuits in melted butter and then in a mixture of brown sugar and cinnamon. Place, overlapping, in a well-buttered, shallow casserole. Arrange sliced fresh or canned peaches around and over the biscuits. Bake in a hot oven until biscuits are done. Serve with cream. Delicious.

BANNOCKS AND SCONES

Bannocks and scones, which are similar to our biscuit, are typical Scottish breads. Traditionally, the only difference between a bannock and a scone is the size. The bannock is baked in a large round the size of a dinner plate, and then cut into quarters; the scone is cut into pieces which are baked separately. In Scotland, bannocks and scones are "baked" on a "girdle" (griddle). If you prefer this method, flour both sides and place on a hot unbuttered griddle. Cook over a slow fire until the bottom is browned, and the bread is risen. Then turn over to brown the other side.

SCOTTISH BANNOCKS

These are a perfect accompaniment to fried chicken, barbecued spareribs, or roast beef.

1 cup cornmeal	2 tablespoons melted butter
1 cup oatmeal	2 tablespoons honey
1 cup buttermilk	½ teaspoon ginger
grated rind of 1 lemon	1 teaspoon baking soda
pinch of salt	

Mix all ingredients in the order given. Heat bacon drippings in an iron frying pan. When grease is hot, pour in the batter. Fry on top of the stove for 10 minutes, then place in a 375° oven for 20 minutes. Cut in wedges and serve hot.

BRAN SCONES

2 cups flour	2 cups bran flakes
½ teaspoon soda	3 tablespoons butter, melted
1 tablespoon baking powder	¼ cup sugar
1 teaspoon salt	about 1 cup buttermilk

Sift the flour, soda, baking powder, and salt. Add the bran flakes, melted butter, sugar, and enough buttermilk to make an easily handled but not too firm dough. Roll out on a floured board, cut into shapes desired (the traditional shape is a triangle), and place on buttered cookie sheets. Bake in a 450° oven for 15 to 20 minutes.

MASHLUM SCONES

2 cups white flour	1 teaspoon salt
2 cups rye, barley, or whole-wheat flour	1½ cups buttermilk or sour milk
1 teaspoon soda	¼ cup melted butter
1 teaspoon cream of tartar	

Sift the dry ingredients and then add the buttermilk or sour milk. Stir in the butter last. Divide the dough into 4 parts on a floured board and pat each part into a circle. Cut each circle into quarters and place on buttered cookie sheets. Bake in a 450° oven until done, about 15 to 20 minutes.

DROP SCONES

To any Scone recipe add 1 egg and enough milk to make a soft dough which can be dropped from a spoon, as for drop biscuits. These may be baked in the oven, but they are especially good "baked" on a griddle.

POTATO SCONES

The potato cakes that so many housewives make out of leftover mashed potatoes are in reality Potato Scones.

Combine leftover mashed potatoes with half as much flour and, if desired, 1 teaspoon baking powder. If you make the dough too thick, thin it with an egg. These are best baked on a griddle in butter.

CREAM SCONES

These are fine with tea. You may add ½ cup of any candied or dried fruit that you prefer, or add 1 or 2 teaspoons vanilla extract to the dough.

1 tablespoon baking powder	½ cup butter
½ teaspoon salt	2 large eggs
3 tablespoons sugar	½ cup cream or evaporated
2 cups flour	milk

Sift the baking powder, salt, sugar, and flour. Cut in the butter as for pie crust. Add the eggs and cream and stir to blend as in Standard Biscuit Recipe. Turn out onto a lightly floured board and knead very lightly. Divide into 2 parts and roll each part into a circle. Cut the circles into quarters and place on buttered cookie sheets. Brush the tops with egg yolks beaten with a little cream. Bake in a 450° oven until done, about 15 to 20 minutes.

SODA SCONES

1 teaspoon soda	1 tablespoon sugar
1 teaspoon cream of tartar	2 tablespoons butter
1 teaspoon salt	2 large eggs
4 cups flour	about 1 cup milk

Sift the dry ingredients. Cut the butter into the flour mixture as for pie crust. Add the eggs and enough of the milk to make a stiff biscuit-like dough. Roll out as in the preceding recipe. Cut into triangles and place on buttered cookie sheets. Brush with melted butter and bake in a 450° oven until done, about 15 to 20 minutes.

MUFFINS

Muffins for breakfast, lunch, or dinner are always well received. And not to be overlooked is the fact that muffins are even more quickly and easily made than are biscuits. There is no kneading, rolling, or cutting required, the batter being simply dropped into a well-buttered muffin tin and baked.

Once you have the Basic Muffin Recipe firmly in mind, you have the foundation for any number of culinary treats, limited only by your own imagination.

The single most important item to remember is to stir—never beat—the batter. The ingredients should be moistened, but still lumpy. The muffin tins should be filled no more than two-thirds full, to allow for expansion.

BASIC MUFFIN RECIPE

2 cups sifted flour	1 beaten egg
2 teaspoons baking powder	1 cup cold milk
½ teaspoon salt	¼ cup melted butter
2 tablespoons sugar	

Sift the dry ingredients. Add the liquid ingredients all at once. Stir just to moisten the dry ingredients; the batter should be lumpy and rough. Fill greased muffin tins only two-thirds full. Bake at 400° for 20 to 25 minutes. Serve hot with plenty of butter and jam.

A FEW SIMPLE VARIATIONS

1. To the dry ingredients add ½ cup to 1 cup of any well-flavored cheese, grated.

2. Substitute ½ cup of any fruit juice for half the milk, increase the sugar to ½ cup, and you have a fine, sweet treat, good with tea or coffee.

3. Use pineapple juice in place of the milk, increase the sugar to ⅓ cup, and place a cube of drained canned pineapple, rolled in sugar, on top of the batter in each tin.

4. Increase sugar to ½ cup and fold in ½ cup to 1 cup of any well-washed and well-drained fresh fruit.

5. Add crumbled cooked bacon to the batter.

6. Lay a cooked sausage link in the bottom of each muffin tin before you spoon in the batter.

7. Substitute ⅓ cup peanut butter for the butter and, if desired, add ¼ cup chopped peanuts to intensify the flavor.

8. One cup of any other flour may replace an equal amount of white flour. Use brown sugar in place of the white sugar.

9. For dinner, brush muffin batter with slightly beaten egg white, and sprinkle with poppy seed or sesame seed.

BANANA BRAN MUFFINS. Use only 1½ cups flour and add 1 cup bran flakes and ½ cup mashed bananas. Substitute brown sugar for white.

DATE ORANGE MUFFINS. Substitute ½ cup orange juice for ½ cup milk and add 1 cup chopped dates.

DRIED-FIG MUFFINS. Pour boiling water to cover over ¾

cup dried figs. Let stand for 10 minutes. Drain, clip stems, and slice the figs. Add to batter. Substitute brown sugar for white.

HALF-AND-HALF MUFFINS. Combine ½ cup brown sugar, 2 teaspoons cinnamon, ½ cup chopped nuts, and 2 tablespoons melted butter. Add half the mixture to the muffin batter. Fill greased muffin tins half full and top with the remaining sugar mixture. Bake as usual.

JAM GEMS. Increase butter and sugar to ⅓ cup each. Prepare batter as usual and bake for 10 minutes. Pull pan to front of oven but do not remove from oven. Drop 1 teaspoon of any jam, jelly, or marmalade from the spoon into the center of each muffin. Work quickly and the muffins will not fall or be heavy. Finish baking.

LEFTOVER MUFFINS. Scoop out the insides of leftover muffins and fill them with any desired creamed chicken, fish, or vegetable mixture. Sprinkle with grated cheese and heat for 10 minutes in a 350° oven.

OLIVE MUFFINS. Use the liquid from canned ripe olives in place of the milk, and add ½ cup sliced olives, any kind. Omit the sugar and salt. These are very good.

DELICIOUS CREAM MUFFINS. Use heavy cream in place of the milk. No other substitutions needed.

WHEAT-GERM MUFFINS. Substitute 1 cup wheat germ for the same amount of flour, use ½ cup brown sugar in place of the 2 tablespoons white sugar, and add ½ cup chopped dried fruit and another ¼ cup melted butter. Very good.

RICE MUFFINS. Add 1 cup cold cooked rice and 2 beaten eggs.

CRANBERRY MUFFINS. Grind together ¾ cup each raisins and fresh whole cranberries. Mix with ¼ cup sugar and fold into muffin batter.

GRAPE-NUTS MUFFINS. Use 1 cup Grape-Nuts in place of the same amount of flour.

WHOLE-KERNEL CORN MUFFINS. Replace ½ cup flour with the same amount of cornmeal. Add ⅔ cup well-drained canned whole-kernel corn or grated fresh corn.

ORANGE-COCONUT MUFFINS. Fold in 2 tablespoons grated orange rind, ½ cup coconut, and ¼ cup chopped toasted almonds.

MACADAMIA MUFFINS. Add ½ to ⅔ cup chopped macadamia nuts to the batter. Spoon batter into muffin tins. Drop a spoonful of pineapple, poha, or papaya jam into the center of each. Bake as usual.

APPLE MUFFINS

These are sweet and rich, fine with tea.

¼ cup soft butter	½ teaspoon salt
⅓ cup sugar	4 teaspoons baking powder
1 beaten egg	1 cup milk
2½ cups sifted cake flour or bread flour	1 cup peeled and diced apple

Cream the butter and sugar. When mixture is light and fluffy add the beaten egg. Sift the dry ingredients. Add the dry mixture to the sugar mixture alternately with the milk. Fold in the apple and fill greased muffin tins two-thirds full. Sprinkle with sugar and cinnamon and bake at 400° for 25 minutes.

EXCELLENT SOUR-CREAM MUFFINS

I've tried many recipes for sour-cream muffins and this is our favorite.

½ cup butter	2¾ cups flour, sifted
1½ cups sugar	pinch nutmeg
½ teaspoon salt	4 eggs, beaten
1 teaspoon soda	1½ cups sour cream

Cream the butter, sugar, and salt until light. Sift the dry ingredients and add alternately with the eggs and the sour cream starting and ending with flour mixture. Mix lightly but surely. Pour into buttered muffin tins and sprinkle with sugar. Bake in a 450° oven for 15 minutes, or until browned.

NOTE.   Sugar may be decreased to 1 cup if desired.

BUTTERMILK MUFFINS

1 teaspoon soda	2 large eggs, beaten
1 teaspoon salt	2 tablespoons brown sugar
¼ cup cornmeal	3 cups buttermilk
4 cups flour, sifted	

Add the soda, salt, and cornmeal to the sifted flour. Beat the eggs and brown sugar into the buttermilk. Stir into the dry ingredients just to moisten. Fill greased muffin tins two-thirds full. Bake for 20 minutes at 400°. Serve very hot with jam and butter.

CRUMB MUFFINS

A very old recipe for muffins, and very good.

1 cup dry breadcrumbs	1 tablespoon sugar
1 cup milk	½ teaspoon salt
1 large egg	1 tablespoon baking powder
1 cup flour	¼ cup melted butter

Combine the breadcrumbs, milk, and egg in a mixing bowl. Stir with a fork to blend. Set aside. Sift the flour with the sugar, salt, and baking powder. Fold into the breadcrumb mixture. Add the melted butter and fold in. Stir until the dry ingredients are thoroughly moistened, but no longer—the batter should not be stirred too much. Fill buttered muffin tins two-thirds full and bake in a 375° oven for 25 minutes, or until browned and done.

VARIATION. A delicious sweet muffin can be made by adding to the preceding batter 1 cup chopped dates and 1 tablespoon grated orange rind. Bake as in the basic recipe.

PEANUT-BUTTER MUFFINS

This should up the sales of peanut butter.

½ cup peanut butter, crunchy or smooth	1 egg, beaten
3 tablespoons butter	1½ cups milk
½ teaspoon salt	1¾ cups sifted flour
3 tablespoons sugar	1 tablespoon baking powder
	¼ cup wheat germ

Cream the peanut butter, butter, salt, and sugar until light and fluffy. Combine the egg and milk. Sift the flour with the baking powder and add the wheat germ. Add the liquid mixture and the dry mixture alternately to the creamed mixture. Fill greased muffin tins two-thirds full. Bake in 400° oven for 20 to 25 minutes. Makes 12 muffins.

BEST BRAN MUFFINS

Even people who don't like bran muffins will like these.

¼ cup sugar	½ cup flour
1 cup butter or margarine	2 cups bran flakes
1 teaspoon soda	½ cup raisins
1 cup buttermilk	1 egg

Cream the butter and sugar. Dissolve the soda in the buttermilk and add. Stir in the rest of ingredients. Spoon into hot, greased muffin pans. Bake in 400° oven for 20 minutes. Let muffins cool in pan for 5 minutes before removing, as these muffins are exceptionally light.

REFRIGERATOR BRAN MUFFINS

A very delicious recipe, and very convenient, as the batter may be made at any time and stored in the refrigerator until ready to use. If you have a large family the recipe is easily doubled. If there are only two or three of you, the batter will keep for a week to 10 days, enabling you to have a few *fresh* muffins whenever you wish. If you wish sweet muffins you may add to all or part of the batter one of the following combinations: raisins and grated lemon rind; chopped dates and grated orange rind; frozen blueberries and chopped nuts.

⅔ cup soft butter	2 teaspoons salt
1¼ cups sugar	1 cup warm water
4 eggs	4 cups bran flakes
3 cups flour	2½ cups buttermilk
1 tablespoon soda	

Cream the butter and sugar. Add 1 egg at a time and beat in until blended. Sift the flour, soda, and salt. Add to the creamed mixture alternately with warm water. Stir in the bran flakes and buttermilk. Place in covered container and store in refrigerator. When ready to bake, spoon into buttered muffin pans and bake in a 375° oven 20 minutes if batter is at room temperature, and 30 minutes if batter is straight from refrigerator. Entire amount of batter makes from 36 to 40 medium-sized muffins.

MAPLE BRAN MUFFINS

1 cup sour cream	1 teaspoon soda
1 cup maple syrup	1 cup bran flakes
2 eggs	⅓ cup raisins
1 cup flour, sifted	⅓ cup chopped nuts

Combine the sour cream, maple syrup, and eggs. Sift the flour and soda together and add the bran flakes, raisins, and nuts. Stir in the liquid ingredients. Spoon into greased muffin tins. Bake in a 400° oven for 20 minutes.

ORANGE BRAN MUFFINS

⅓ cup soft butter
½ cup sugar
1 egg, beaten
½ cup bran flakes
½ cup orange juice
2 tablespoons grated
  orange rind

1 cup flour, sifted
2 teaspoons baking powder
½ teaspoon salt
¼ teaspoon soda
¼ cup milk

Cream the butter and sugar until light and fluffy. Add the beaten egg and mix thoroughly. Stir in the bran flakes, orange juice, and grated rind. Sift the flour, baking powder, salt, and soda together and add alternately with the milk. Spoon into paper cup-cake cups, or into well-buttered muffin tins and bake for 30 minutes at 400°.

NOTE.   To increase the flavor in any recipe calling for grated orange rind add ¼ teaspoon grated lemon rind.

DATE AND BACON MUFFINS

¼ cup butter
2 tablespoons sugar
1 egg
1½ cups flour
½ cup cornmeal
5 teaspoons baking powder

½ teaspoon salt
1 cup milk
¾ cup cut-up dates
4 strips bacon, fried and crumbled

Cream the sugar and butter. Add the egg. Sift the dry ingredients and add alternately with the milk. Fold in the dates and bacon, and mix until the dry ingredients are moistened. Bake at 400° for 20 to 25 minutes. Serve with orange-flower honey.

HIGH-PROTEIN MUFFINS

These are as delicious as they are healthful. The orange juice and dates mask the taste of the soy flour, yet each muffin contains 19 grams of complete protein.

2 cups soy flour	3 slightly beaten eggs
1 cup skim-milk powder	3 tablespoons melted butter
1 teaspoon salt	grated rind of 1 orange
1 tablespoon baking powder	¾ cup orange juice
1 cup chopped dates	3 tablespoons honey
1 cup chopped nuts	

Sift the dry ingredients into a bowl. Add the dates and nuts. Combine remaining ingredients and stir into the dry ingredients just until moistened. Fill buttered muffin tins two-thirds full. Bake in 350° oven for 25 minutes.

BERRY MUFFINS

A delectable summer muffin. The berries listed are only suggestions—the muffins are also delicious with blackberries or loganberries.

1 to 1½ cups strawberries, raspberries, or blueberries	1 teaspoon salt
3 cups flour	½ cup brown sugar
½ cup granulated sugar	½ cup melted butter
1 tablespoon baking powder	3 large eggs
	1 cup milk

Wash, hull, and dry the berries of your choice. If large berries are used they should be halved. Sift the flour, granulated sugar, baking powder, and salt into a bowl. Add the brown sugar and stir to blend. Combine liquid ingredients and stir into the dry ingredients until just blended. Fold in the berries very lightly and carefully. Spoon into well-buttered muffin tins until they are two-thirds full. Bake in a 400° oven for 20 minutes, or until browned and done. Sprinkle with powdered sugar while hot. Makes 20 to 24 medium-sized muffins.

ORANGE-CRANBERRY MUFFINS

When unexpected company arrives and you have nothing to serve, remember that muffins take only 30 minutes from mixing bowl to serving.

¼ cup soft butter
⅓ cup sugar
2 large eggs, beaten
2 cups flour
1 tablespoon baking powder
1 teaspoon salt

1 tablespoon grated orange rind
⅔ cup orange juice
1 No. 1 can whole-cranberry sauce, drained

Cream the butter and sugar. Stir in the eggs. Sift the flour with the baking powder and salt; add to the creamed mixture alternately with the orange rind and juice. Fill buttered muffin tins one-third full, add 1 teaspoon cranberry sauce to each, then fill until two-thirds full with the remaining batter. Bake in 400° oven about 25 minutes.

WALNUT-COFFEE MUFFINS

Coffee lends a cheery flavor to many things—pies, cakes, pot roast, cookies, and breads. These coffee-flavored muffins might make an appearance at Sunday morning brunch with tender scrambled eggs, sausage links with apple rings, and of course plenty of steaming hot coffee.

2 cups flour, sifted
1 tablespoon baking powder
⅓ cup sugar
1 teaspoon salt
½ cup chopped walnuts

½ cup double-strength coffee
½ cup cream
1 egg
¼ cup melted butter

Sift the dry ingredients and add the walnuts. Combine the liquid ingredients and stir into dry ingredients all at once, but carefully. Pour or spoon the batter into buttered muffin tins and bake in a 400° oven for 20 minutes.

POTATO-CORNMEAL MUFFINS

Very good, and an excellent use for leftover mashed potatoes.

2 tablespoons butter
1 tablespoon sugar
2 large eggs
¾ cup milk
1 cup leftover mashed potatoes

1 cup coarsely ground cornmeal
1 tablespoon baking powder
½ teaspoon salt

Cream the butter and sugar. Stir in, blending well, the eggs, milk, and mashed potatoes. Blend the dry ingredients together and then stir into the liquid mixture all at once, but carefully, just until the dry ingredients are thoroughly moistened. Spoon into buttered muffin tins, filling them two-thirds full. Bake in a 400° oven for 20 minutes, or until browned and done. Makes approximately 12 medium-sized muffins.

POTATO MUFFINS

A delicious muffin. These are especially good served with chicken, in which case I use rendered chicken fat in place of the butter.

2 egg yolks
3 cups grated, drained raw potatoes
¼ cup grated onion
½ cup sifted flour

1 teaspoon salt
½ teaspoon baking powder
¼ cup melted butter
2 stiffly beaten egg whites

Beat the egg yolks and stir into the potatoes. Add the grated onion, flour, salt, and baking powder. Stir in the melted butter and then fold in the stiffly beaten egg whites. Fill buttered muffin tins no more than two-thirds full and bake in a 400° oven for 20 to 25 minutes.

POTATO-FLOUR MUFFINS

A time-honored basic muffin, too good to be forgotten.

½ cup potato flour	2 tablespoons sugar
1 teaspoon baking powder	4 eggs, separated
½ teaspoon salt	2 tablespoons ice water

Sift the potato flour with the baking powder and salt. Add the sugar. Beat the egg yolks. Beat the egg whites until stiff and fold into the yolks. Add the flour mixture very slowly, folding it in gently. When all the flour is added, sprinkle the ice water on top and fold in. Spoon lightly into pans and bake at 375° for 20 minutes.

SOUTHERN MUFFINS

Wonderful with fried chicken and barbecues.

1½ cups sifted flour	5 tablespoons melted butter
1 cup cornmeal	1 tablespoon chopped green
5 teaspons baking powder	pepper
1 teaspoon salt	1 tablespoon minced onion
1 tablespoon molasses	

Combine the dry ingredients. Stir in the molasses and melted butter just until the mixture is moistened. Add very finely chopped green pepper and onion. Fill greased muffin tins two-thirds full and bake at 400° for 20 minutes.

SALLY LUNN
(Baking-Powder)

According to tradition, Sally Lunns originated in Bath, England, and were named for the young lady who made them popular. They were mentioned frequently by Carlyle, Dickens, and other nineteenth-century writers. Thackeray described a meal of "green tea, scandal, hot Sally Lunns and a little novel reading." (For yeast-raised Sally Lunns, see page 67.)

2 cups flour, sifted	¼ cup butter
1 teaspoon salt	3 large eggs, separated
2 tablespoons sugar	1 cup milk
4 teaspoons baking powder	

Sift the dry ingredients three times. Cut the butter into the dry ingredients as for pastry. Beat the egg yolks thoroughly and add the milk. Stir into the dry ingredients. Fold in the stiffly beaten egg whites and pour into buttered muffin tins. Bake in a 400° oven for 30 minutes.

POPOVERS

Popovers are good for breakfast, lunch, or dinner, and any of the sweeter variations may be served as a sweet treat with tea or coffee. The basic Popover contains eggs, flour, and milk. The addition of salt, a bit of sugar, and melted butter, bacon fat, or oil—or in the case of Yorkshire Pudding, beef drippings—does much for the flavor but is not necessary to the basic product.

The two most important things to remember in making Popovers are to beat the batter until smooth, and *never* peek while they are baking. An electric mixer does the best job of mixing, but a strong arm will do quite well. Just remember that the batter must be *smooth,* not lumpy. Unless you are using Teflon the cups must be buttered. Any cups will serve— muffin pans, iron popover pans, custard cups, or pottery cups are all equally good. The cups should be filled no more than half full, as the batter *always* doubles.

We have found that it is not only not necessary to have the cups hot but that we didn't like the crust as well, if they were. And as to the baking, one constant temperature is much better than changing the temperature during the baking.

We prefer Popovers baked a longer time at a lower temperature and usually bake ours at 375° for 50 minutes. However, they may be baked in a 400° oven for 35 to 40 minutes. Or—and this works surprisingly well—you may put the batter-filled cups into a *cold* oven, set the temperature at 425°, and bake the Popovers for 45 to 50 minutes. These times and temperatures are for large Popovers; smaller ones take about 10 minutes less. You can safely peek during the last 10 minutes.

The batter may be baked immediately upon mixing, or it may be mixed when convenient, poured into the cups, and then stored in the refrigerator for a matter of hours, or overnight. Bake as directed. This makes it a simple matter to have hot Popovers for any meal, no matter how rushed the cook. When I make Popovers in this manner, I put the cold batter into the cold oven as suggested above. This is a real time-saver.

For breakfast, hot Popovers make excellent containers for scrambled eggs. The Shellfish Popovers are excellent when filled with creamed shellfish, or with a salad made with the same shellfish that is used in the batter. Popovers also make good containers for just about anything creamed. These are good for a light lunch, or for a late evening snack. Any sweet Popover is very good when filled with sugared fresh fruit, and topped with whipped cream. We prefer popovers with strawberries and cream to a conventional shortcake. We also like sugared peaches with Popovers.

If desired, you may add a teaspoon or two of sugar, or honey, to the basic batter.

BASIC POPOVER RECIPE

1 cup flour

½ teaspoon salt

2 or 3 large eggs

1 cup milk

1 tablespoon melted butter,
     bacon fat, or oil

Sift the flour and salt into a bowl. Beat the eggs and add to the milk and fat. Pour into the flour mixture and beat until smooth—about 2 minutes with an electric mixer. Pour into buttered muffin pans or any ovenproof cups. Bake as directed above: large Popovers, a 400° oven for 35 to 40 minutes, or a 375° oven for 50 to 55 minutes, in a *cold* oven, set the control for 425° and bake 45 to 50 minutes; smaller Popovers about 10 minutes less. Serve hot with plenty of butter and jam.

CHEESE POPOVERS. Add 1 cup grated cheese, and use 4 large eggs. Very good with a main meal, or luncheon.

GARLIC POPOVERS. To serve with a roast. Mash 2 cloves garlic and add to batter. Also good in Yorkshire Pudding.

GRAHAM POPOVERS. Use ½ cup graham or whole-wheat flour and ½ cup white flour.

NUT POPOVERS. To the basic batter add ½ cup ground nuts —any kind. Very good.

RICH POPOVERS. Increase eggs to 4 or 6, and add ½ to 1 teaspoon vanilla extract. These make very good containers for sugared fresh fruit. If desired, the cups may be sprinkled with sugar before the batter is poured in.

SHELLFISH POPOVERS. To the basic batter add ⅓ cup of any preferred flaked shellfish.

WHOLE-GRAIN POPOVERS. Use all whole-wheat flour and 3 large eggs. Add 1 or 2 teaspoons of honey. If desired, ½ cup rye meal or rye flour may be used in place of the same amount of flour in this or the basic recipe. Add 1 teaspoon of honey.

YORKSHIRE PUDDING

Make the basic recipe for Popovers and pour into a pan with ¼ cup hot beef drippings. Or cook in the roasting pan along with a roast of beef; set the meat on a rack or trivet and pour the batter into the bottom of the pan about 45 minutes before the roast is done. Cut into squares and serve hot.

ORANGE POPOVERS

2 cups flour
½ teaspoon salt
2 teaspoons sugar
2 or 3 large eggs

1 cup milk
1 cup orange juice
1 tablespoon grated orange rind

Sift the dry ingredients into a large bowl. Beat the eggs and add to the milk, orange rind, and juice. Pour the mixture into the dry ingredients and beat thoroughly. Pour into buttered cups and bake as directed.

Bread is a generous gift of nature, a food that can be replaced by no other. When we fall sick, our appetite for bread deserts us last of all; and the moment we recover the appetite we have shown a symptom of recovery. Bread is suitable to every time of day, every age of life, and every temperament. It improves other foods, is the father of good and bad digestion.

—ANTOINE-AUGUSTE PARMENTIER

3. Cornbreads and Other Quick Breads

For well over a century the only bread the American colonists had was that made with cornmeal. It was in the South that cornbreads reached a peak of culinary perfection, and there are certainly as many recipes for cornbread as there are Southern housewives. To the Southern housewife the type of cornmeal used is of great importance, the preferred type being the white water-ground meal. And you'll have to look long and hard to find a teaspoon of sugar in any Southern cornbread recipe. Unless it's been added by a Northerner.

During the eighteenth and nineteenth centuries hot breads, mostly biscuits and cornbreads, were served at every meal in the South.

Thoreau wrote in *Walden*, "Bread I at first made of pure Indian meal and salt, genuine hoe-cakes, which I baked before my fire out of doors on a shingle or the end of a stick of timber sawed off in building my house; but it was wont to get smoked and to have a piny flavor. I tried flour also; but have at last found a mixture of rye and Indian meal most convenient and agreeable. In cold weather it was no little amusement to bake several small loaves of this in succession, tending and turning them as carefully as an Egyptian his hatching eggs."

JOHNNYCAKE

In early America this was called journey cake. This recipe in rhyme is easy to follow. The "Indian" referred to is cornmeal, and the "wheat" is white flour, although you could use whole-wheat flour. I don't know how old the recipe is, but it is a very early one. Use a buttered 9-inch square pan, and bake in a 425° oven 25 minutes.

Two cups of Indian, one cup of wheat
One cup of sour milk, one cup of sweet,
Two good eggs, that well you beat,
Two tablespoons of butter new,
Salt and soda, each a spoon.
Mix up quick and bake it soon.
Then you have cornbread complete,
The best of all cornbread to eat.

EARLY AMERICAN CORNBREAD

My children thrive on this bread. Whole-wheat flour may be used in place of the white.

1 egg	¾ cup flour, sifted
1 cup milk	1 tablespoon baking powder
2 tablespoons honey or maple syrup	1 teaspoon salt
	3 tablespoons melted butter
⅔ cup cornmeal	

Beat the egg until light. Add the milk and the honey or maple syrup. Mix the dry ingredients and add gradually to the liquids. Add the melted butter. Stir briskly and pour into buttered 8-inch square pan. Bake in a 425° oven for 20 minutes.

SOUTHERN RICH CORNBREAD

2 cups boiling water
4 cups white cornmeal
4 large eggs, well beaten
¼ cup bacon drippings

1 cup evaporated milk
1 cup hot water
1 teaspoon salt

Pour the boiling water over the cornmeal and stir until smooth. To the eggs add the drippings, evaporated milk, and hot water. Stir in the salt, blend well and then add the cornmeal mixture. Turn into 2 8-inch square pans, well buttered. Bake in a 425° oven for 18 to 20 minutes.

MEXICAN SPOON BREAD

A perfect go-together with fried chicken or barbecues.

1-pound can cream-style corn
¾ cup milk
⅓ cup melted butter, bacon fat, or chicken fat
3 large eggs
1 cup coarsely ground cornmeal

½ teaspoon soda
1 teaspoon salt
1 cup grated Cheddar, Jack, or Mozzarella cheese
1 medium onion, minced and sautéed (optional)

Combine the cream-style corn, the milk, melted butter or fat, and the eggs in a large bowl. Blend thoroughly. Stir together the cornmeal, soda, and salt to blend, and then stir into the liquid mixture, blending thoroughly. Pour half the batter into a buttered 9-inch square pan. Spread with the grated cheese, and the onion if used. Cover with the remaining batter and, if desired, sprinkle with more cheese and onion. Bake in a 400° oven for 45 minutes, or until browned and done. Cool slightly before cutting.

SOUR-CREAM CHILI BREAD

1-pound can corn, or the ker-
    nels from 3 large ears of fresh
    corn
1 cup sour cream
½ cup melted butter
2 large eggs, beaten
1 cup coarsely ground corn-
    meal

1 teaspoon salt
1 tablespoon baking powder
¼ pound finely diced Jack,
    Cheddar, or Mozzarella
    cheese
4-ounce can green chilies,
    rinsed of their seeds and
    chopped

Combine in a large bowl the corn, sour cream, melted butter, and eggs.
Blend thoroughly. Stir the cornmeal, salt, and baking powder together to
blend. Stir the dry ingredients into the liquid ingredients, blending well.
Stir the cheese and the chilies into the batter last. Pour the batter into a
buttered 9-inch square pan. Bake in a 350° oven for 50 minutes to an
hour, or until bread is browned and done.

NOTE. Up to ½ pound finely diced cheese may be used if desired. This
bread can also be made without the chilies.

DEEP SOUTH CORNBREAD

1 cup coarsely ground corn-
    meal
1 tablespoon sugar
1 teaspoon salt
⅓ cup butter

1 cup boiling water
4 large eggs, separated
1 cup milk
3 tablespoons flour
2 teaspoons baking powder

Combine in a large bowl the cornmeal, sugar, salt, and butter. Over this
pour the boiling water and blend well. Cover and let mixture stand for
several hours, or even overnight. When ready to use, stir the egg yolks,
milk, flour, and baking powder into the batter and blend well. Beat the
egg whites until firm, and fold into the batter last. Turn the batter into a
buttered 8- by 12-inch pan. Heat the oven to 350°. When heated, turn
the heat off. At this point place the pan in the oven for 5 minutes. Then,
leaving the pan in the oven, set the heat again to 350°. Bake for 20 minutes. There will be a thin layer of custard through the center.

NOTE.   If the eggs are not beaten separately, but simply beaten into the batter, the cornbread will be just as delicious, but there will be no layer of custard.

CHEESE SPOON BREAD

1 cup coarsely ground cornmeal
1 teaspoon salt
½ teaspoon dry mustard
dash cayenne or Nepal pepper

3 cups scalded milk
3 large eggs
1 cup grated Cheddar or Jack
  cheese
1 teaspoon baking powder

Combine the cornmeal, salt, dry mustard, and cayenne or Nepal pepper. Gradually stir into the scalded milk, stirring to avoid lumps. Cook, over medium heat, stirring constantly, until mixture starts to thicken. Remove from heat. In a separate bowl, beat the eggs with a fork until whites and yolks are just blended. Stir a little of the hot mixture into the eggs and blend well. Now stir the cheese, and the eggs, into the hot cornmeal batter. Stir the baking powder through the batter last. Pour into a but-tered 8- by 12-inch pan and bake in a 350° oven for 30 to 35 minutes, or until firm. Serve immediately.

SPOON BREAD WITH BACON

¼ cup butter
1 large egg
1 tablespoon sugar
½ teaspoon salt
½ teaspoon soda
¾ cup coarsely ground cornmeal

¼ cup flour
½ cup sour cream
8 slices bacon, cooked until
  crisp and then crumbled
½ cup sweet milk

Melt the butter in a 2-quart casserole. Combine the egg, sugar, salt, soda, cornmeal, flour and sour cream. Stir until thoroughly blended. Stir in the crumbled bacon. Pour into the casserole over the melted butter. Gently pour the sweet milk over the batter. Do *not* stir. Bake in a 375° oven for 30 minutes.

HOMINY STICKS

1 cup flour, sifted	½ cup hot boiled hominy
1⅓ cups cornmeal	⅓ cup melted butter
4 teaspoons baking powder	1 cup milk
1 teaspoon salt	2 large eggs

Combine the dry ingredients and the hominy. Make a well in the mixture and stir in the butter, milk, and eggs. Mix lightly but thoroughly. Pour into well-greased cornstick pans and bake in a 350° oven for 25 minutes.

WHOLE-KERNEL CORNBREAD

1 cup flour, sifted	2½ cups scraped sweet corn
1 tablespoon sugar	kernels
1 teaspoon salt	1 large egg, beaten
3 teaspoons baking powder	¼ cup butter, melted

Combine the dry ingredients and sift over the corn. Mix thoroughly. Stir in the egg alternately with the melted butter. Turn into a well-greased 8-inch square pan. Bake in a 425° oven for 30 to 35 minutes. Serve hot.

NORTHERN SWEET CORNBREAD

¾ cup butter	2 cups flour
¾ cup sugar	3 teaspoons baking powder
3 large eggs	½ teaspoon salt
1½ cups coarsely ground corn-	2 cups milk
meal	

Cream butter and sugar until fluffy. Add the eggs and beat until blended. Stir in the cornmeal. Sift the flour, baking powder, and salt. Stir the sifted dry ingredients into the creamed mixture alternately with the milk. Turn into a buttered 9- or 10-inch square pan. Bake in a 375° oven for 40 to 50 minutes, or until the cornbread is browned and tests done with a toothpick.

APPLE CORNBREAD. Make batter as in preceding recipe. Stir into the batter 1 to 1½ cups peeled and diced apple. Bake as in preceding recipe.

BLUEBERRY CORNBREAD. Using the recipe for Northern Sweet Cornbread, increase the sugar to 1 cup, and add 1 cup of cleaned blueberries. Very good.

BACON CORN PONE

A crisp and delicious accompaniment to soup, salad, or just any time with coffee.

2 cups coarsely ground corn- meal	½ pound bacon, fried crisp and crumbled
1 cup boiling water	½ teaspoon salt

Scald the cornmeal with the boiling water. Combine all ingredients. Shape with the hands into flat cakes. Place on a buttered cookie sheet and bake in a 425° oven until a golden brown. These may also be fried, which is traditional.

GRITS BREAD

An old bread, one that your grandmother probably made. Serve it as bread, or as a substitute for potatoes.

4 cups water	⅓ cup butter
1 teaspoon salt	3 large eggs
1 cup hominy grits	⅓ cup cream

Bring the water to a boil and add the salt. Stir in the hominy grits and cook over low heat for 45 minutes, stirring often to keep from burning. Add the butter. Beat a little of the hot mixture into the eggs, and then add them to the remaining hot mixture, along with the cream. Pour into a buttered 2-quart casserole and bake in a 350° oven for 1 hour, or until the crust is thick and brown.

WHEAT-GERM CORNBREAD

A deliciously different and very nutritious cornbread.

1 cup flour	1 cup cornmeal
1 teaspoon salt	3 large eggs
⅓ cup sugar	1½ cups milk
5 teaspoons baking powder	⅓ cup melted butter
1 cup wheat germ	

Sift the flour, salt, sugar, and baking powder. Add the wheat germ and cornmeal and blend. Beat the eggs into the milk and add the melted butter. Stir into flour mixture just to moisten. Turn the batter into a well-buttered loaf pan and bake in a 400° oven for 40 to 45 minutes, or until loaf is browned and done.

BREAKFAST BREAD WITH SAUSAGE

1 recipe Wheat-Germ Cornbread	1 can whole cranberry sauce
1 pound, or more, sausage links, fried until crisp and done	

Make the batter as for Wheat-Germ Cornbread. Arrange the cooked sausage links in a buttered 8- by 12-inch shallow pan, and spoon the cranberry sauce over them. Carefully spoon the cornbread batter over the cranberry sauce. Bake in a 400° oven for 25 minutes, or until cornbread is done.

HOT BREAD

A combination of flours is always delicious. If desired, use a cup of buckwheat or rye flour in place of as much graham flour. This bread makes good cream-cheese sandwiches.

½ cup cornmeal	3 tablespoons melted butter
2 cups graham flour	½ cup maple syrup
1 teaspoon soda	2 cups buttermilk
1 teaspoon salt	

Combine the dry ingredients, then the liquid ingredients. Stir the liquid ingredients into dry ingredients quickly but lightly. Pour into a buttered loaf pan, or 2 8-inch square pans. Bake in a 350° oven about 45 minutes for the loaf pan, and 20 to 25 minutes for the square pans. Always test before you remove from oven.

VARIATIONS. You could add raisins, nuts, chopped dates or prunes. If you do not have buttermilk you may use sweet milk omitting the soda and adding 1 tablespoon baking powder.

CHEESE WINE BREAD

For a luncheon, or light dinner, serve this bread with a tossed salad and creamed crabmeat or chicken or a light soup.

2 cups biscuit mix	¼ cup any dry white wine
1 tablespoon sugar	2 large eggs
1 tablespoon minced onion	¼ cup milk
½ teaspoon crushed dried herb	2 or 3 tablespoons grated Par-
of your choice	mesan, Romano, or Cheddar
¼ cup melted butter	cheese

Combine biscuit mix, sugar, onion, and herb. Add the liquid ingredients all at once. Beat until smooth and turn into a well-buttered round cake pan. Sprinkle with the desired cheese and bake in a 400° oven for 20 to 25 minutes, or until browned and done. Serve hot.

CARAWAY-SEED BREAD

A quick bread that is very good with ham or chicken.

1½ cups flour	⅓ cup butter
1 tablespoon baking powder	2 teaspoons caraway seed
¼ teaspoon salt	2 eggs
¼ cup sugar	½ cup milk

Sift into a bowl the flour, baking powder, salt, and sugar. Cut in the butter, add caraway seed, and blend well. Beat the eggs and add to the milk. Stir into dry ingredients, blending just to moisten ingredients. Spread in a buttered 9-inch pie pan. Bake in a 350° oven for 30 minutes, or until browned. Cut into wedges and serve hot.

IRISH SODA BREAD

This is the traditional bread of Ireland. It should be broken, not cut, and is usually served hot with tea, but is good, hot or cold, with anything.

4 cups flour	1⅓ to 1½ cups buttermilk
1 teaspoon salt	1 tablespoon caraway seed
1 teaspoon sugar	(optional)
1 teaspoon soda	

Sift the dry ingredients into a bowl. Make a hollow in the center and pour in 1 cup of the buttermilk. Mix with your hands and add enough more buttermilk to make a firm but not dry dough. Turn onto a floured board and knead lightly. Shape into a round loaf and cut across the top so that it will not crack. Sprinkle with caraway seed if desired. Place in a buttered skillet and bake at 350° for 40 to 45 minutes.

BRAN BROWN BREAD

This bread is wonderful with a pot of home-baked beans.

1 cup seeded raisins	1¾ cups flour, sifted
1½ cups water	2 teaspoons soda
3 tablespoons butter	½ teaspoon baking powder
½ teaspoon salt	1 cup bran flakes
1 cup sugar	½ teaspoon vanilla extract
1 egg	

Combine the raisins, water, butter, and salt in a sauce pan. Bring to boil and then cook for 2 minutes. Cool and drain, reserving the liquid. Beat the sugar and egg until fluffy. Sift the flour, soda and baking powder and add to the sugar mixture alternately with the reserved liquid. Add the raisin mixture, bran flakes, and vanilla extract. Combine thoroughly and turn into three well-buttered No. 2 cans. Bake in a 350° oven for 50 to 60 minutes. Cool in the cans for 10 minutes before turning out. Let stand for 24 hours before cutting.

STEAMED MOLASSES BREAD

½ cup soft breadcrumbs	1 teaspoon salt
1¾ cups buttermilk	1 teaspoon soda
1 cup cornmeal	⅔ cup light molasses
⅔ cup rye flour	½ cup dark raisins
¾ cup whole-wheat flour	

Soak the breadcrumbs in the buttermilk for 15 minutes. Press through a sieve and set aside. Sift the dry ingredients into a large bowl and stir in the crumb mixture, the molasses, and the raisins. Blend thoroughly. Fill three 1-pound cans two-thirds full; cover with foil and tie it in place. Place cans on a rack in a kettle and pour in boiling water to half cover the molds. Cover the kettle and boil gently for 3 hours. Remove the bread from the molds and serve hot, or cool completely, wrap the loaves in foil, and store in the refrigerator, reheating before serving.

BARBECUE BREAD

This one uses biscuit mix and can be whipped up in just a few minutes.

1 egg, well beaten	½ cup grated Cheddar cheese
½ cup milk	2 tablespoons grated Parmesan
1 package dried onion-soup	cheese
mix	1 tablespoon sesame seed
1½ cups biscuit mix	3 tablespoons melted butter

Combine the egg and milk. Add the onion-soup mix and the egg and milk mixture to the biscuit mix. Stir in the Cheddar cheese. Spread the dough in a well-greased 8-inch pie pan. Sprinkle the top with the Parmesan cheese and sesame seed and drizzle with the butter. Bake in a 400° oven for 25 minutes. Serve hot in pie-shaped wedges.

My clothes is all ragged as my language is rough,
My bread is corn dodgers, both solid and tough;
But yet I am happy and live at my ease,
On sorghum molasses, bacon, and cheese.

—OLD COWBOY CHORUS

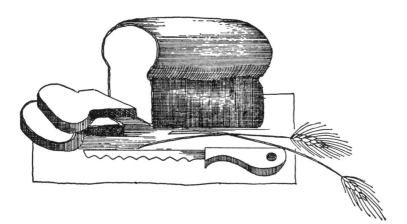

4. *Loaf Breads*

Breads from all over the world have been enthusiastically adopted by the American people, and are made or bought throughout the nation. No longer is French Bread the sole property of the Frenchman; no longer are Beaten Biscuits to be found only in the South, or the unleavened Knakke only among Minnesota's Norwegian population. Many of us have eaten Scandinavian Limpé, Mexican Tortillas, heavy, hearty German Pumpernickel. And now even more wonderful foreign breads are becoming popularly known and used—the excellent Portuguese Bread, the bun-like Arabic Bread, the chewy Cuban Bread.

Some breads have enjoyed a brief span of popularity and then been forgotten. It has been many years since I ate Pain Mollet des Ardennes anywhere but in my own home. And not many women make a yeast-raised Sally Lunn any more. Both are excellent breads and recipes for both are included in this book.

Thoreau wrote of bread (again I quote from *Walden*): "I made a study of the ancient and indispensable art of bread-making, consulting such authorities as offered, going back to the primitive days and first invention of the unleavened kind, when from the wildness of nuts and meats men first reached the mildness and refinement of this diet, and traveling gradually down in my studies through that accidental souring of the dough which, it is supposed, taught the leavening process, and through the various fermentations thereafter, till I came to 'good, sweet, wholesome bread,' the staff of life. Leaven, which some deem the soul of bread, the *spiritus* which fills its cellular tissue, which is religiously preserved like the vestal fire . . . some precious bottleful, I suppose, first brought over in the Mayflower, did the business for America, and its influence is still rising, swelling, spreading, in cerealian billows over the land."

Certainly home-baked bread provides a pleasure that has been enjoyed by man since primitive times, and there is no reason for this pleasure to disappear. Home-baked bread lifts the simplest of meals to epicurean heights, and I can guarantee a very real, personal sense of satisfaction each time you bake with yeast. There is just something earthy about the feel of leavened dough.

A woman who makes bread is feeding both herself and her family something that is at once physical and spiritual—even holy, for there *is* something holy about "breaking bread."

I have made virtually all of our bread for fourteen years, and always with a feeling of satisfaction and accomplishment. For each of my recipes that met with enthusiastic approval by my growing family, I've discarded several that did not. Those which follow are our personal favorites.

SPREADS FOR BREADS

The wide popularity of barbecues in recent years has inspired a special type of cookery, including the use of pre-spread and heated bread, which enhances any informal meal. Use a crusty bread—French, Italian, or other of your choice. Cut thick slices nearly through the loaf but not through the bottom crust and put the desired spread between the slices. Wrap the loaf in aluminum foil and place it on the back of the grill (or heat 20 to 30 minutes in a 350° oven). Turn the loaf occasionally so that it will heat through.

BARBECUE BUTTER. Blend ½ pound soft butter with 2 crushed cloves garlic and ½ teaspoon each celery salt, Worcestershire sauce, and minced parsley.

PARSLEY BUTTER. Blend 1 pound soft butter with 1 cup minced fresh parsley, 1 tablespoon lemon juice, 1 crushed clove garlic, and several tablespoons minced chives.

BLUE-CHEESE SPREAD. Blend ¼ pound blue cheese, ¼ cup minced ripe olives, ½ pound soft butter, ¼ cup wine vinegar, and 2 slices crisp bacon, crumbled.

CHEESE BREAD. With a casserole and salad this makes a good summertime meal. Cut the crust off an unsliced loaf. Slice the loaf in half lengthwise, then slice 8 times crosswise. This will give you 16 slices or chunks of bread. Mix 2 5-ounce jars sharp Cheddar cheese spread (such as Old English) and ½ cup softened butter (not margarine). Blend well. Spread this mixture on each cut surface of the bread. Put bread back together as a loaf and wrap in foil. Heat at 400° for 20 minutes.

SESAME SPREAD. Make your usual garlic bread and add sesame seed to the softened butter and garlic. Delicious!

HERB SPREAD. Mash a clove of garlic with 1 cup softened butter. Add the juice of a medium or small lemon, ½ teaspoon Worcestershire sauce, and ½ teaspoon (or more if desired) of any desired herb—oregano and sweet basil are our favorites. If you use oregano, sprinkle the bread with grated Parmesan or Romano cheese.

CHEESE-ONION SPREAD. Blend 1 teaspoon Worcestershire and 1 tablespoon grated onion with 1½ cups coarsely grated sharp Cheddar. Soften with equal amounts of mayonnaise and cream.

COOKED BARBECUE BUTTER. Sauté ½ cup minced onions in ¼ cup butter until golden. Add a crushed clove of garlic, ¼ cup chili sauce, 1 teaspoon Worcestershire sauce, 1 tablespoon wine vinegar, 1 tablespoon brown sugar, and 1 teaspoon prepared mustard. Simmer until thick, about 20 minutes.

RELISH SPREAD. Chop 2 large, firm tomatoes very fine. Blend with 1 small onion, grated; 1 clove garlic, crushed; 1 or 2 tablespoons hot chili sauce, and salt and pepper to taste. Drain mixture well. Spread on *slices* of bread, or pile in scooped-out rolls. Top Relish Spread with grated cheese and place the bread, or rolls, on cookie sheets. Heat in the oven until cheese melts. Relish Spread will keep, refrigerated, for up to 1 week.

OTHER COMBINATIONS. Grated cheese blended with cooked and crumbled bacon, a little prepared mustard, and catsup to make spreadable; crabmeat blended with an equal quantity of mayonnaise, a little grated onion, and half as much grated cheese as crabmeat.

BEFORE-BAKING GLAZES

In general, brush the rolls or breads with glaze once before baking and again just after removing from the oven.

1. For bread or rolls on which you want a rich brown crust: 1 egg yolk beaten with 1 or 2 tablespoons water.

2. For French, Italian, or Vienna bread or rolls, the crusty kind: 1 egg white slightly beaten and added to 1 or 2 tablespoons water.

3. For regular bread or rolls: 1 whole egg beaten with 1 or 2 tablespoons milk or water.

4. For some sweet breads or rolls: 1 egg yolk beaten with 3 tablespoons milk or water and 2 tablespoons sugar.

COUNTY FAIR EGG BREAD

Simple and delicious, and because the dough is rich, many things may be done with it.

1½ cups scalded milk	2 cakes yeast
½ cup butter	¼ cup lukewarm water
2 teaspoons salt	2 beaten eggs
½ cup sugar	about 9 cups flour, sifted

Pour the scalded milk over the butter, salt, and sugar. Cool. Dissolve the yeast in the lukewarm water and let stand until it bubbles, about 5 minutes. Add the yeast and the beaten eggs to the cooled milk. Gradually add the flour, beating it in thoroughly. Do not add any more flour than is necessary to make an easily handled dough, as the bread should be light and tender. Turn out onto floured board and knead until smooth and elastic. Place in greased bowl, cover, and let rise until doubled in size, about 1½ hours. Punch down and turn out onto a lightly floured board. Shape into 3 loaves and place in greased 8-inch loaf pans. Cover and let rise until dough is just to the tops of the pans. Bake in a 425° oven for 10 minutes, then lower heat to 350° and bake 40 minutes longer, or until bread is done. Makes 3 loaves.

WHITE BREAD EXTRAORDINAIRE. Reduce sugar in the preceding recipe to ¼ cup, use water in place of milk, and add ⅓ cup wheat germ. Very good.

CINNAMON BREAD. Roll a portion of the dough for County Fair Egg Bread 1-inch thick. Spread with melted butter and sprinkle liberally with brown sugar and cinnamon. Chopped nuts or raisins may also be added. Roll as for jelly roll and place in a greased pan with the seam at the bottom. Let rise until doubled and bake as for County Fair Egg Bread.

FAT CAKE

This and the following recipe are English delicacies made from a bread-dough base. Children especially love them.

Take one-third of the dough for County Fair Egg Bread, after its first rising. Knead into it ¼ cup sugar, ¼ cup very soft butter, and ½ cup raisins or a combination of raisins and nuts. Knead in thoroughly. Shape into a round loaf and place in a buttered pie tin or round cake pan. Cover and let rise until doubled. Brush with beaten egg and sprinkle liberally with sugar. Bake as for County Fair Egg Bread, watching carefully, as it may be done sooner. In England they cut this into thick wedges and serve it with tea.

LARDY JACKS

Take one-third of the dough for County Fair Egg Bread, after the first rising, and knead in ½ cup soft butter, ½ cup sugar, and ¾ cup mixed raisins and nuts. Roll the dough to a thickness of ½ inch and cut it into triangular shapes. Brush with milk and sprinkle with sugar. Let rise until doubled, and then bake on a greased cookie sheet at 400° until done. The children love these with milk.

ENGLISH BREAD CAKE

Take one-third of the dough for County Fair Egg Bread and roll it out on a floured board. Spread the dough with softened (not melted) butter. Fold the dough in half and roll out again. This time spread the dough with granulated or brown sugar. Fold over again, and roll the dough out a third time, this time spreading it with raisins. Roll the dough as for a jelly roll and place in a buttered bread pan. Cover dough and let rise until doubled. Bake in a 425° oven for 10 minutes, reduce heat to 350°, and continue baking another 30 minutes, or until bread is done. Frost with a thin glaze. This is a very good and very simple coffee cake to make as an extra treat when you are bread-baking.

ENGLISH BUNS

Many English buns and rolls have intriguing names, such as Johnny Boys, Chudleighs, Huffkins, Pope Ladies, and Soul Cakes. The only difference between these is in the shape. Johnny Boys had the vague shape of a boy with arms outflung. Chudleighs were small, flattish buns, which were split open, filled with marmalade, and eaten hot. Huffkins had a hole in the center, like doughnuts. Pope Ladies, traditional for New

Year's, had an oblong, almost heart-shaped piece of dough for the body, with a little arm set on each side and a round ball of dough for the head. Currants made the eyes and nose for Pope Ladies and Johnny Boys. Soul Cakes incorporated 1 tablespoon of cinnamon in the dough, and were shaped into small buns. In Chelsea they added ½ cup currants or raisins and ¼ cup candied lemon peel and called the sweet buns Chelsea Buns. All were made with basically the same dough. I use the dough for County Fair Egg Bread, but you could use any rich bread or roll recipe. Bake the different rolls and buns as for any roll, adjusting the time to the size.

EASY BUTTERMILK BREAD

Be sure to brush the dough of this tender bread with butter or margarine before rising.

1 cup buttermilk	1 cup warm water
¼ cup sugar	1 cake yeast
2½ teaspoons salt	½ teaspoon soda
⅓ cup butter	6 cups flour, sifted

Heat the buttermilk until it is hot enough to melt the butter. Stir in the sugar, salt, and butter. Cool. Dissolve the yeast in the water and add to the cooled milk mixture. Combine the soda and half the flour. Add to yeast mixture and beat until smooth. Stir in the rest of the flour and turn out onto a floured board. Knead until smooth and elastic. Place in a greased bowl, cover, and let rise until doubled. Punch down and turn out onto the board once more. Shape into 2 loaves and place in buttered 8-inch loaf pans, brush tops with melted butter, and let rise again. Bake in a 400° oven about 50 minutes.

VARIATION. Roll out the dough and spread with melted butter, then sprinkle with 1½ cups chopped sautéed onions and 1½ cups grated sharp Cheddar cheese. Roll as for jelly roll, cut in half, and fit into greased loaf pans. Bake in a 400° oven about 50 minutes.

SOUR-CREAM BREAD

This bread is so tender that it is best not to cut the loaf until the next day.

2 cakes yeast	2 tablespoons sugar
⅓ cup warm water	1 teaspoon salt
½ cup milk, scalded	1½ tablespoons butter, melted
1 cup sour cream	4½ cups flour, sifted

Dissolve the yeast in the water. Add the milk to the sour cream, sugar, salt, and butter. Beat into the yeast mixture. Add the flour gradually, beating it in. Place dough in a buttered mixing bowl, cover and let rise until doubled. Turn out onto a floured board and knead until smooth, elastic, and no longer sticky. Put back in the buttered bowl, cover, and let rise again. Knead down, working in a little more flour if necessary, and shape. Place in a large loaf pan or in two small ones. Brush with butter and let rise again until doubled, then bake in a 400° oven for 30 to 35 minutes.

CARAWAY-SEED BREAD

A wonderful bread to serve with barbecues.

1 cake yeast	¼ cup melted butter
¼ cup warm water	2 large eggs
1 teaspoon salt	1 tablespoon celery seed
¼ cup honey	1 tablespoon caraway seed
1 cup scalded milk	4 cups flour or more

Dissolve the yeast in the warm water. Dissolve the salt and honey in the scalded milk. Stir in the yeast, butter, and eggs. Beat thoroughly. Add the seeds and 4 cups of the flour and blend well. Turn out onto a floured board and knead, using more flour if necessary. Place in a buttered bowl, cover, and let rise until doubled. Punch down and place in a buttered bread pan. Cover and let rise again. Bake 20 minutes in a 400° oven, then reduce heat to 350° and bake 20 minutes longer, or until bread is done.

VARIATION. Use 3½ cups flour and ½ cup wheat germ instead of 4 cups flour.

JEWISH BRAIDS

Jewish cookery is a blend of that of many countries. From each country the best has been taken over and improvements added. This bread is one of the best.

2 cakes yeast	7 cups flour
1¾ cups warm water	4 large eggs, beaten
1 tablespoon salt	sesame seed or poppy seed
½ cup sugar	
¼ cup melted butter	

Dissolve the yeast in the water. When it bubbles (about 5 minutes), add the salt, sugar, and butter. Blend in 3 cups of the flour and the eggs. Beat thoroughly. Now add the rest of the flour and mix it in with your hands. Turn out onto a floured board and knead until smooth and elastic. Place in a buttered bowl, cover, and let rise until doubled. Punch the dough down and turn it out again onto a floured breadboard. Divide it in half. Cut one half into 3 equal pieces and roll into strips about 18 inches long. Braid these strips and place on a buttered cookie sheet. Divide two-thirds of the remaining dough into 3 equal pieces and braid. Place on top of the first braid. Form the remaining dough into a braid, or just twist the strip. Lay the braid or strip over the first two braids. Now brush the loaf with melted butter. (Don't brush the braids separately, or the upper braids will slide off during the baking.) Cover and let rise until doubled. Brush again with melted butter. Sprinkle heavily with sesame seed or poppy seed. Bake in a 350° oven for approximately 1 hour. Makes 1 large braid, or 2 small ones.

QUICK LOAF BREAD

This recipe makes one of the most delicious breads I have ever tasted. I often use 1 cup each of rice polish and wheat germ in place of 2 cups of the flour. The family never knows that they are being fed important vitamins and minerals with their delicious homemade bread.

3 cups warm water	9 or 10 cups flour
3 cakes yeast	5 teaspoons salt
¼ cup sugar or honey	5 tablespoons oil

Combine the water, yeast, and sugar or honey. Stir until yeast dissolves. Add half of the flour and the salt. Beat hard with a spoon until batter is smooth. Add the remaining flour and blend well. Pour the oil over the dough and knead, in the bowl, for just a few minutes, no more than 2 or 3. The dough will absorb most or all of the oil. Cover the bowl and let the dough rise until doubled, about 45 minutes. Punch down and turn out onto lightly floured board and knead slightly. Shape into 2 loaves and place in buttered loaf pans. Cover and let rise again until doubled, about 30 minutes. Bake in a 400° oven for 30 minutes, or until done.

NOTE. The small loaf pans that come with a child's cooking set are wonderful for this bread. The recipe will make about 15 individual loaves. Bake for 20 minutes, or until done.

VARIATIONS

WHEAT-GERM QUICK LOAF BREAD. Replace ½ to 1 cup of the flour with the same amount of wheat germ. No other substitutions needed.

HERB QUICK LOAF BREAD. Add to dough ½ teaspoon each savory and marjoram, ¼ teaspoon thyme or sage, and 1 teaspoon fresh minced parsley.

COCOA QUICK LOAF BREAD. Add ½ cup cocoa, 2 large eggs, beaten, ¼ cup soft butter, and ½ cup sugar. Follow recipe. Frost the top after baking.

MUFFIN-MIX BREAD. For a delicious whole-grain bread use ½ cup wheat germ and 3½ cups muffin mix in place of 4 cups of the flour.

FISHERMEN'S BREAD. Men who make their living from the sea, and who, too often, give their lives to it, are often of a deeply religious nature. The typical Fishermen's Bread is baked in loaves with a cross cut into the top of each loaf. Bake in a 400° oven, with a pan of boiling water on the oven floor, 30 minutes or until done.

FRENCH BREAD

This is about as authentic a French bread as you can make in a home oven. To make real French bread, you need unbleached, hard-wheat flour (available in health food stores), and an oven with the heat coming from top, bottom, and both sides. If you place a pan of boiling water on the oven floor, and sprinkle the cookie sheets with cornmeal after buttering them, you can approximate the commercial product.

1 cake yeast	1 tablespoon sugar
1½ cups lukewarm water	2 teaspoons salt
4 cups sifted flour	

Dissolve the yeast in the water. Sift the dry ingredients, stir them into the yeast mixture, and work the dough with your hands until it will absorb no more flour. Knead the dough on a slightly floured board until it is no longer sticky. Place the dough in a buttered bowl, cover, and let rise until doubled. Then punch it down and turn it out onto a floured board. Divide into 2 parts. Shape each piece into a long narrow loaf. Place the loaves on a greased cookie sheet that has been sprinkled with cornmeal, cover, and let rise again. Brush tops with egg-white glaze and bake in a 400° oven for 35 to 40 minutes. Brush again with glaze about 5 minutes before loaves are done. Makes 2 small loaves or 1 large one.

ONION FRENCH BREAD. Add 1 package onion-soup mix to the dry ingredients and blend thoroughly. If you like an onion flavor in bread, you may occasionally add a package of onion-soup mix to any plain bread dough with delightful results.

ARABIC BREAD

For practical purposes, there is no difference between Arabic Bread, and the Armenian Peda or Lavash. Peda is rolled into oblong pieces and placed on buttered cookie sheets. Some Armenians let the dough rise until almost doubled in bulk; others bake it immediately as with Arabic Bread. Lavash uses more flour and is sometimes called cracker bread. It is rolled to make a circle approximately 12 inches in diameter and, after a rest of 10 minutes, is baked on the floor of the oven as is Arabic Bread. For Peda you may use this recipe as is, although some Armenians would use milk in place of water and add 2 tablespoons soft butter. However, since it is the shape and method of baking that makes this bread different, you could also use any favorite white bread recipe, or a hot-roll mix.

My grandmother has made dozens of these round puffy loaves every week for more than fifty-five years. When I was a child, we used to spread them, hot from the oven, with butter and roll the loaves, taco style, to dunk in cold milk.

8 cups flour	1 cake yeast
1 tablespoon salt	2½ cups warm water
2 tablespoons sugar	

Sift the dry ingredients. Soften the yeast in the water. When it is bubbly, stir the yeast mixture into the flour mixture. Mix thoroughly with clean hands. Knead in a bowl, adding more flour or water as necessary. The dough should be smooth and firm, but not stiff. Brush the top of the dough with soft butter and cover the bowl. Let the dough rise until doubled in bulk, then punch the dough down and turn it out onto a floured board. Divide into 12 pieces. If you have a kitchen scale, you will find that the pieces weigh out at 5 ounces each. Shape the pieces into balls and let rest, covered, for 10 minutes. Remove the racks from the oven and heat it to 450°. When oven is hot, take 1 or 2 balls at a time and roll or pat to a thickness of about ¼ inch. Make certain that there are no creases in the dough, or it will not rise properly in the oven. Now, with a floured wooden peel, or your hands, slide the shaped loaves directly onto the floor of the oven. Bake for about 10 minutes, or until tops are browned and puffy. Repeat for the remaining balls of dough. Best served warm, although the loaves keep well and are easily reheated. Makes 12 small loaves.

If the loaves tend to burn on the bottom before the tops are browned, bake only until done, then brown under the broiler.

NOTE. You might like to split these open and use with hamburgers. Or, if you are of Middle Eastern descent as I am, you'll fill the loaves with a *kibbé* or *kufté* mixture.

One of the favorite spreads for Arabic Bread is Lebanie, a cheese made by draining homemade yogurt or leban. The Cheese Filling for Beureks, in another section of this book, is also excellent. In either case, just spread the filling on the loaves and roll up, taco style.

CUBAN WATER BREAD

Note the similarity of this to Arabic Bread and French Bread. The difference lies in the method of baking. This one is deliciously crisp. If you prefer Whole-Wheat or Graham Water Bread, replace half the flour with whole-wheat or graham flour, and use 2 tablespoons brown sugar in place of 1 tablespoon granulated sugar.

1 cake yeast	1 tablespoon sugar
2 cups warm water	1 tablespoon salt
or warm potato water	about 8 cups flour

Dissolve the yeast in the water. Add the sugar and salt. Stir in 7 cups of the flour and mix thoroughly. Turn out onto a lightly floured board and knead in about 1 more cup of flour. Knead until smooth and elastic, about 7 minutes. Place in a greased bowl, cover, and let rise until doubled in bulk, about 1½ hours. Turn out onto a floured board and divide in half. Form into 2 long or round loaves. Place on buttered cookie sheets which have been sprinkled with cornmeal. Slash the tops with a sharp knife, cover and let rise again until almost, but not quite, doubled. Brush with cold water. Sprinkle with sesame seed if desired. Place in a *cold* oven. This is important. Set the oven at 400° and bake until bread is nicely browned, about 45 minutes. During the baking, brush loaves twice with cold water. The dough can be shaped into 1 large loaf if preferred.

VIENNA BREAD

This is the real thing, and worth every bit of the time and trouble it takes.

2 cakes yeast	1 cup scalded milk
1 tablespoon sugar	1 tablespoon salt
¼ cup warm water	8 cups flour
1 cup cold water	

Dissolve the yeast and sugar in the warm water. When dissolved, add the cold water to the scalded milk and stir into the yeast mixture. Sift the salt with the flour and gradually stir this into the milk-yeast mixture. Knead well on a lightly floured board for about 10 minutes, or until smooth and elastic. Place in a buttered bowl, cover, and let rise until doubled, about 1½ hours. Punch down and turn out again onto a lightly floured board. Knead again for 5 minutes. Now shape the dough into 2 long or round loaves and place them on buttered cookie sheet that has been sprinkled with cornmeal. Make gashes in the top with a sharp knife, as for French Bread. Cover and let rise again until doubled. Brush with egg-white glaze and bake in a 450° oven for 10 minutes, lower heat to 350° and bake for 50 minutes longer. Remove from oven, brush again with glaze, and return to oven for another 30 minutes. It is this long, long baking that gives the bread its distinctive flavor and crisp crust.

DANISH FRANSKBROD

The Danes, who seem to have an aversion to giving the name Danish to anything—good, bad or indifferent—call this "French bread."

2 cakes yeast	3 tablespoons sugar
1 cup scalded milk, cooled	2 teaspoons salt
2 eggs	5 cups flour, sifted

Dissolve the yeast in the scalded, cooled milk. Add the eggs and sugar and beat thoroughly. Sift in 4 cups of the flour and the salt and blend thoroughly. Use the other cup of flour as needed. Turn out onto a floured board and knead until smooth and elastic. Place in a buttered bowl, cover, and let rise until doubled. This will take just about 45 minutes. Then punch the dough down and carefully press all the air out. Turn the dough out onto a floured board and shape into 2 long loaves. Place on buttered cookie sheet and brush with beaten egg. Cover and let rise until doubled, about 30 minutes. Bake in a 400° oven until done, about 20 to 25 minutes.

MY GOOD FATHER'S SHEPHERD'S BREAD

This recipe makes an excellent snowy white round loaf. I bake mine on an earthenware bread plate, but a regular baking sheet will do.

SPONGE

1 cake or package yeast
2 cups lukewarm water
4 cups flour (use a blend of flours if preferred)

2 tablespoons malt or honey

Dissolve the yeast in the water slowly, and thoroughly blend in the flour and malt or honey. Cover with a clean towel and let rise in a warm place for approximately 4 hours.

DOUGH

1 cake or package yeast
1 cup lukewarm water
1 tablespoon salt

2 tablespoons malt or honey
2 cups flour

Dissolve the yeast in the water. Blend in the salt, malt or honey, and flour. Blend well. Thoroughly incorporate with the sponge until pliable and smooth—dough will pull away from bowl. Turn out on a lightly floured board and knead for 3 to 5 minutes, then let rest for 10 minutes. Shape into one long or round loaf, cut a cross in the center, and place on a cornmeal-sprinkled baking tin. Cover and let rise until *almost* doubled. Then place a pan of boiling water on the floor of the oven, place bread in oven, set temperature for 400°, and bake the bread for 45 minutes, or until it is golden brown and done. Brush with egg-white glaze before and after baking.

PAIN MOLLET DES ARDENNES
(Soft Ardennes Bread)

This recipe made the rounds a few years ago, with just about everyone I knew making and proudly serving it, but I haven't seen or heard of it lately, and it is too good to be relegated to the limbo of forgotten recipes.

3 eggs	¼ teaspoon mace, optional
3 tablespoons sugar	2 cakes yeast
½ cup softened butter	3 tablespoons milk or cream,
2 cups sifted flour	scalded and cooled
½ teaspoon salt	

Beat the eggs with the sugar until light. Add the softened butter. Sift the flour with the salt and the mace. Add. Dissolve the yeast in the scalded, cooled milk or cream. Add to batter and beat hard for about 3 minutes, or until batter is smooth. Place in a well-buttered loaf pan or small tube pan. Cover and let rise until doubled, about 1½ hours. Bake in a 450° oven for 20 minutes, or until done. Serve hot and pull apart with forks. Makes 1 loaf.

PORTUGUESE BREAD

Portuguese foods are virtually the same as Spanish, and the breads, like the Spanish breads, are uniformly excellent.

3 cups water	11 cups flour, sifted
1 tablespoon salt	2 cakes or 2 packages yeast
2 tablespoons sugar	⅓ cup warm water
⅓ cup butter	1 cup water

In a saucepan combine the first 4 ingredients. Bring to a boil and then cool. Sift the flour into a large bowl. Dissolve the yeast in the ⅓ cup warm water. When dissolved, stir the yeast mixture and the 1 cup water into the flour. Now add the cooled water-sugar mixture. Mix well, with the hands, using a punching technique, until the dough no longer sticks to the hands. This will take about 10 minutes and eliminates any kneading. At this point the Portuguese sprinkle the dough lightly with more flour, and make the sign of the cross on the dough with the side of the hand. I've found it best to rub the dough with softened butter. Cover with a clean towel and let rise until doubled, about 1¼ hours.

When the dough has doubled, punch it down and divide into three parts. Butter 3 9-inch layer-cake pans, and place the dough in the pans. Cover and let rise again until doubled, about 1 hour. When ready to bake, cut into the top of each loaf lightly with a sharp knife, to make the sign of the cross. Bake at 450° for 10 minutes, then lower the heat to 350°, and continue baking until browned and done, about another 35 to 45 minutes.

SALLY LUNN
(Yeast)

This is the yeast version of this famous English bread which has been popular for several hundred years. (See page 34 for the baking-powder version.) Serve the bread for tea or afternoon coffee, with bowls of fresh fruit, or at breakfast with butter and plenty of homemade jam.

⅓ cup sugar	1 cake yeast
½ cup butter	¼ cup lukewarm water
1½ teaspoons salt	3 eggs, beaten
1 cup scalded and cooled rich milk	4 cups flour, sifted

Cream the butter, sugar, and salt. Add the cooled milk. Dissolve the yeast in the water and add to the creamed mixture along with the beaten eggs. Add the flour a little at a time, beating thoroughly between additions. Cover and let rise until doubled. Then punch down and pour into a well-greased loaf pan or small tube pan. Cover and let rise again. Bake in a 350° oven for about 40 minutes, or until loaf is golden brown and tests done.

NOTE. To bake as buns pour the batter into well-greased muffin pans, cover and let rise. Brush with beaten egg and bake in a 400° oven for 20 minutes, or until done.

RAISED CORNMEAL BREAD

A bread with a pleasingly gritty texture, from the way in which the corn-meal is incorporated into the dough. Very good with chili con carne and a green salad.

1 cake yeast	2 teaspoons salt
1 cup lukewarm water	2½ cups flour or more, sifted
2 tablespoons melted butter	⅓ cup skim-milk powder
2 tablespoons honey	½ cup cornmeal

Dissolve the yeast in the water. When thoroughly dissolved, stir in the melted butter, honey, and salt. Stir until dissolved. Beat in 2 cups of the sifted flour and the skim-milk powder. Beat until smooth. Cover the bowl and let the dough rise until doubled. Then punch down. Add the corn-meal and enough additional flour to make a stiff dough that may be kneaded. Knead for 5 minutes, place in a buttered bowl, cover, and let rise until doubled. Punch down again and turn out onto a floured board. Shape into a loaf and place in a buttered 8-inch loaf pan. Cover and let rise again until doubled. Bake in a 350° oven for 45 minutes, or until done.

YEAST CORNBREAD

This recipe is probably close to a hundred years old and well worth pre-serving.

6 cups medium or coarsely ground cornmeal	4 cups boiling water
10 cups flour, sifted	2 cups mashed sweet potatoes
3 cups warm water	1 tablespoon salt
3 cakes or 3 packages yeast	½ cup butter, melted

Combine 2 cups of the cornmeal, 2 cups of the sifted flour, 3 cups warm water, and the yeast. Stir together to blend well. Cover with a clean cloth and let rise until light and bubbly—approximately 1 hour, though in cool weather it may take longer.

When the sponge is very light, stir it down with a wooden spoon and set it aside. Now pour the boiling water over the remaining 4 cups cornmeal and stir until mixture is thick and cooled. Stir this into the sponge. Add 6 cups of the sifted flour, and the mashed sweet potatoes, salt, and butter. Knead these ingredients in with your hands, working the dough well. Add the remaining 2 cups of flour as needed. Brush the dough with softened, or melted, butter, cover, and let rise until doubled. This will take about 2 hours. When dough has doubled in bulk, punch it down and turn it out onto a lightly floured board. Divide dough into 4 parts. Let set for 10 minutes and then shape it, with the hands, into loaves. Place in buttered loaf pans, cover, and let rise again. Bake in 350° to 375° oven until browned and done, about 45 minutes.

ANADAMA BREAD

1 cup scalded milk	2 teaspoons salt
1 cup boiling water	2 cakes yeast
1 cup yellow cornmeal	½ cup warm water
¼ cup butter	6 cups flour, sifted
½ cup molasses	

Combine the hot milk and water; slowly add the cornmeal. Add the butter, molasses, and salt. Let stand until lukewarm. Sprinkle the yeast into the warm water and let stand until it bubbles, about 5 minutes. Stir into the cornmeal mixture. Beat in the flour. Turn out onto a lightly floured board and knead until smooth and elastic, about 8 minutes. Place the dough in a buttered bowl, cover, and let rise until doubled, about 1½ hours. Knead again and divide into 2 loaves. Place in 2 buttered loaf pans, cover, and let rise until doubled again. Bake in a 375° oven for 40 to 50 minutes. Remove from pans immediately and cool on racks.

NOTE. Bacon fat makes a delicious shortening for any quick cornbread or yeast-raised cornbread.

The kitchen is a country in which there are always discoveries to be made.

—LA REYNIÈRE

COTTAGE-CHEESE ONION BREAD

The combination of cottage cheese and onion-soup mix makes for a most delicious bread.

3 cakes or 3 packages yeast, dissolved in ¾ cup warm water
3 tablespoons sugar
3 cups cottage cheese
1 teaspoon salt

¾ teaspoon soda
⅓ cup soft butter
3 large eggs
1 or 2 packages onion-soup mix
8 to 9 cups flour

Add the sugar to the yeast and warm water, and stir until dissolved. Combine the cheese, salt, soda, butter, eggs, and soup mix. (The amount of soup mix used depends entirely on how strong an onion flavor you want.) Stir to blend. Add the yeast mixture, and then stir in 4 cups of the flour. Blend well. Now stir in enough of the remaining flour to make a stiff dough. Turn out onto a lightly floured breadboard and knead thoroughly. Place in bowl, brush with softened or melted butter, cover, and let rise until doubled. Turn out onto a lightly floured board again and knead lightly. Divide dough into 2 pieces, cover, and let rest for 10 minutes. Then shape into 2 loaves. Place in buttered loaf pans. Cover and let rise until doubled and then bake in a 350° oven until browned and done, approximately 40 to 45 minutes. Makes 2 large loaves.

CRUSTY CHEESE BREAD

This is the French cheese bread called Gannat. Makes excellent tea sandwiches when sliced very thin and buttered. It is also very good toasted. It may be baked in two shallow 9- or 10-inch square baking pans if desired.

2 cakes yeast
½ cup warm water
6 cups flour
1 tablespoon sugar
1 teaspoon salt
⅔ cup butter

2 cups shredded Gruyère cheese
1¼ cups warm or cold mashed potatoes
4 large eggs
½ cup scalded milk

Dissolve the yeast in the water. Sift the flour, sugar, and salt together. Combine the butter, cheese, mashed potatoes, eggs, and milk. Beat until blended. Add the yeast mixture and the dry ingredients. Mix thoroughly. Turn onto a floured board and knead for 5 minutes. Place in a buttered bowl, cover, and let rise. Punch down and knead again for about 2 minutes. Shape into 2 loaves, or 2 20-inch rolls. Place in well-buttered loaf pans or 9-inch ring molds. If you are making the rolls, pinch the edges to seal. Cover and let rise until doubled. Bake in a 375° oven for 25 to 45 minutes.

NOTE. A pleasing addition to any cheese bread is 1 or 2 teaspoons coarsely ground black pepper, sifted with the other dry ingredients. Freshly ground pepper is best, but if you don't own a pepper mill, coarsely ground pepper can be bought at grocery stores.

PARMESAN BUBBLE LOAF

This light fragrant loaf makes a delicious company bread. Just pull off the buttery rounds of bread—they're good either as is or split and spread with still more butter.

1 cup grated Romano or Parmesan cheese	⅓ cup lukewarm water
3 tablespoons sugar	3 large eggs
⅓ cup soft butter	½ cup skim-milk powder
2 teaspoons salt	10 cups flour, approximately
3 cups hot water	2 medium or large cloves garlic, pounded or crushed
2 cakes or packages yeast	½ cup butter

Combine in a bowl the grated cheese, sugar, soft butter, salt, and hot water. Stir until the butter melts, and then set aside to cool. Dissolve the yeast in the lukewarm water. Stir into the cooled cheese mixture, add the eggs, and beat to blend thoroughly. Sift the flour, and blend with the skim-milk powder. Take approximately 7 cups of the flour mixture and stir into the batter. Mix with a wooden spoon until batter is fairly smooth. Add enough more of the flour mixture to make a medium stiff dough. Turn the dough out onto a lightly floured board and knead for 5 minutes. Place the dough in a buttered bowl, cover with a clean towel, and let rise until doubled, about 1 hour. Punch dough down, turn it out again onto a lightly floured board, and divide it into 3 pieces. Divide each piece into 14 pieces, shape into balls, and let rest for 10 minutes.

While the balls of dough are resting, melt the ½ cup of butter with the crushed or pounded garlic. Butter 3 loaf pans very lightly. Roll each ball of dough in the melted-butter-garlic mixture. Place in loaf pans. Make 2 layers in each loaf pan, using 14 balls of dough for each loaf. Set the loaves aside to rise until doubled, about 45 minutes. Bake in a 400° oven for 30 to 35 minutes, or until browned and done. Makes 3 loaves.

VARIATION. If desired, the balls of dough may be rolled first in the butter-garlic mixture and then in sesame seed before they are placed in the pans.

ONION BREAD

For years I searched for a good recipe for the kind of onion bread or rolls that we used to buy in a Jewish delicatessen in New York City. I searched Jewish cookbooks, German cookbooks, and articles in all the magazines. Finally, after a bit of experimenting, I came up with this recipe which I think you will like as much as I do.

1¾ cups scalded milk	2 cakes yeast
4 tablespoons butter	½ cup warm water
2 tablespoons sugar	6½ cups flour, sifted
1 teaspoon salt	1 teaspoon celery salt
2 cups minced onions	½ teaspoon sage

Pour the scalded milk over 2 tablespoons of the butter, the sugar, and the salt. Stir until butter is dissolved. Sauté the onions in the rest of the butter until golden, about 10 minutes over low heat. Dissolve the yeast in the water. Add to the cooled milk mixture. Add the herbs to 2 cups of the flour and mix well. Add to the milk-yeast mixture and mix well, then add the onions and the remaining flour and mix thoroughly. Turn out on a floured board and knead until elastic. Place in a buttered bowl, cover and let rise until doubled. Punch down and let rise again for 30 minutes. Shape into loaves and place in buttered loaf pans. Let rise again until doubled and bake in a 400° oven for 10 minutes, then bake at 350° until browned and done, about 30 to 35 minutes more.

NOTE. Makes excellent rolls or bread sticks.

ONION ZEMMEL. Cut the dough into pieces the size of an apple. Knead each piece and shape them into flat cakes 1 inch thick and 3 inches in diameter. Place on cookie sheets and press a crease in the center of each with the side of your hand. Cover and let rise. Brush with egg and water, sprinkle with poppy seed, and bake at 400° for 20 minutes.

WHOLE-WHEAT EGG BREAD

A fine loaf that rises very high. If desired, raisins and/or walnuts may be added. With raisins, this makes especially delicious toast.

2 cups milk, scalded
½ cup butter
1 teaspoon salt
½ cup honey or brown sugar
1 cake yeast
1 teaspoon honey

¼ cup warm water
3 cups whole-wheat or graham flour
4 large eggs, separated
½ teaspoon soda

Pour the scalded milk over the butter, salt, and the ½ cup honey or brown sugar. Let cool to lukewarm. Dissolve the yeast and the 1 teaspoon honey in the ¼ cup warm water. Stir into the milk mixture. Stir the flour and the egg yolks into the liquid mixture just until thoroughly moistened. Beat the egg whites until very stiff, sprinkle the soda over the beaten whites, and gently fold into the batter. Cover and let rise until doubled. Stir down and let rise again until doubled. This is necessary to obtain a light loaf. Turn into 2 buttered, 7-inch loaf pans, and let rise again until doubled. Bake in a 350° oven for 30 to 40 minutes, or until browned and done.

GRAHAM BREAD

This is an excellent whole-grain bread. Remember that graham flour and whole-wheat flour are always interchangeable.

½ cup mild molasses
½ cup melted butter
1 tablespoon salt
2 cakes yeast dissolved in ⅓ cup warm water

3 cups milk, scalded and cooled
5 cups graham flour
4 cups white flour

Stir the molasses, butter, salt, and dissolved yeast into the scalded and cooled milk. Stir in the graham flour and beat well. Cover and let the sponge rise until light. Then stir it down and add the white flour. The dough should be almost soft, but not sticky. Let rise until doubled again. Then stir down again and shape into 2 loaves, or into 3 smaller loaves. Place in buttered bread pans, cover, and let rise again until doubled. Bake in a 375° oven for 35 to 40 minutes, or until done.

BUTTER-BRAN BREAD

This is a delicious dark bread utilizing almost any dark flour that you wish.

1½ cups boiling water	1 cup warm water
2 teaspoons salt	2 or 3 cups bran flakes, buck-
⅓ cup butter	wheat flour, graham flour,
⅓ cup brown sugar	whole-wheat flour, or soy
2 tablespoons molasses	flour
2 cakes yeast	5 or 6 cups white flour

Combine the boiling water, salt, butter, brown sugar, and molasses in a large bowl. Let cool until it is only warm. Dissolve the yeast in the warm water. Stir the yeast and the bran flakes or dark flour into the hot water mixture. Stir in half of the white flour and beat until smooth. Add enough of the remaining white flour to make a medium-stiff dough. Place in a buttered bowl, cover, and let rise until doubled. Then turn out onto a floured breadboard and divide dough into 2 parts. Shape into loaves and place in 2 buttered bread pans. Cover and let rise until doubled, then bake in a 325° oven for 1 hour, or until done. Brush the finished bread with softened or melted butter.

CRACKED-GRAIN BREAD

I especially enjoy breads made with the various kinds of cracked grains. These, like whole-grain flours, should be bought from a health food store, or from a local miller, as those commonly available in markets are likely to be flavorless and full of preservatives.

½ cup each rye grits and cracked wheat
2 teaspoons salt
2 tablespoons soft butter
¼ cup honey
1¾ cups hot water

1 cake or 1 package yeast
⅓ cup warm water
1 teaspoon sugar
1 cup whole-wheat or graham flour
2 cups white flour

Combine the cracked grains, salt, soft butter, honey, and hot water in a bowl. Let cool to lukewarm. Dissolve the yeast in the ⅓ cup warm water with the sugar. Add to the softened grains. Now stir in the flours and blend thoroughly. The dough should be firm but not stiff. Brush the dough with softened or melted butter, cover, and let rise until doubled, about 1½ to 2 hours. Turn the dough out onto a floured board and knead it down. Shape into a loaf and place in a buttered loaf pan. Cover and let rise again until doubled, which will take about 45 minutes this time. Bake in a 350° oven for 25 minutes, then reduce heat to 325° and bake for 30 minutes longer.

WHOLE-WHEAT SPICED BREAD

A deliciously different whole-wheat bread. The faintly spicy taste comes from the cumin seed.

2 cups scalded milk
¼ cup brown sugar
1 teaspoon salt
¼ cup honey
⅓ cup soft butter
⅓ cup orange juice

2 cakes yeast
¼ cup warm water
1 large egg
2½ cups white flour
4 cups whole-wheat flour
½ teaspoon cumin seed

Pour the scalded milk over the brown sugar, salt, honey, and butter. Cool until lukewarm, then add the orange juice. Dissolve the yeast in the water and let set until bubbly, about 5 minutes. Add to the milk mixture along with the egg, and blend well. Sift in the white flour and beat until smooth. Add the whole-wheat flour and cumin seed and blend in. Turn the dough out onto a floured board and knead until smooth and elastic. Place in a buttered bowl, cover, and let rise until doubled. Punch down and knead for 1 minute. Cover and let rise for 30 minutes. Turn out onto floured board again and shape into 2 loaves. Place in buttered 9-inch loaf pans, cover, and let rise again until doubled. Then bake at 425° for 10 minutes, then at 350° for 25 to 30 minutes longer. Brush the tops of the hot loaves with softened or melted butter.

OATMEAL BREAD

When I make this absolutely delicious bread I frequently substitute brown sugar for the molasses and make part of the dough into rolls, on which I make faces, using raisins for eyes, nose, and mouth, then brush the rolls with melted butter and bake at 400°.

1 cake yeast	¼ cup butter
¼ cup lukewarm water	½ cup molasses
4 cups boiling skim milk	1 tablespoon salt
2 cups rolled oats	10 to 11 cups flour, sifted

Dissolve the yeast in the warm water. Add the skim milk to the rolled oats and butter and let stand for 30 minutes. Add the molasses, salt, and the dissolved yeast. Add enough of the flour to make a soft dough. Put dough into a buttered bowl, cover, and let rise until doubled. Turn out onto floured board and knead until elastic, about 10 minutes. Divide into 3 loaves and place in buttered 9-inch loaf pans and let rise again. Brush the tops with melted butter and bake in a 400° oven for 40 to 50 minutes.

VARIATION. To the preceding recipe add ½ cup sugar, 1 cup raisins, and 1 cup chopped nuts before adding the flour.

CRACKED-WHEAT BREAD

I developed this recipe in trying to approximate a commercial bread that I particularly like. The cracked wheat may be bought at a health food store.

2 cups boiling water	2 cakes yeast
1¼ cups cracked wheat	⅔ cup warm water
½ cup brown sugar	1 tablespoon granulated sugar
1 teaspoon salt	3¾ cups flour, sifted
2 tablespoons butter	

Pour the boiling water over cracked wheat. Add the brown sugar, salt, and butter. Cool. Dissolve the yeast in the warm water and add the granulated sugar. Combine with the cooled cracked-wheat mixture. Add the flour and mix thoroughly. Turn out on a floured board and knead until smooth. Place in a buttered bowl, cover, and let rise for 1 hour. Punch down and let rise again for 30 minutes. Punch down and turn out onto a floured board. Shape into 2 loaves. Place in buttered loaf pans and let rise until the dough reaches the tops of the pans. Bake in a 350° oven for 1 hour and 15 minutes.

GARLIC POTATO BREAD

This is a highly unusual but delicious bread. It's best served at barbecues, or with a hearty meal. I always serve it with barbecued spareribs.

1 large potato, boiled, cooled, and grated (enough to make 1½ cups grated potato)	1 cup warm potato water
	1 cake yeast
	2 teaspoons sugar
1 large clove garlic put through a garlic press	2 cups flour
	softened butter
1 teaspoon salt	

Combine the potato, garlic (use more garlic if desired), salt, potato water, yeast, and sugar. Stir until the yeast is dissolved and then add the flour. You will have to finish mixing this dough with your hands. When it is thoroughly blended, brush the top of the dough with soft butter, cover, and let rise until doubled. Punch the dough down and turn it into a well-buttered 8- or 9-inch skillet. Brush the top of the dough with soft butter again and let rise again. Bake in a 425° oven until well browned and done, approximately 25 to 30 minutes.

REFRIGERATOR POTATO BREAD

A very handy and very good recipe to have on hand and use often. The dough makes good pizza when rolled out onto oiled pans. Or use it for Fried Bread, or as loaf bread, or—and this is our favorite—braid the dough and make 1 great, big, beautiful loaf of bread, glazed and liberally sprinkled with poppy seed.

1 large potato	3 large eggs
1 teaspoon salt	2 cakes yeast
1 cup water	¼ cup warm water
½ cup butter	1 teaspoon sugar
½ cup sugar	5 to 5½ cups flour
½ cup skim-milk powder	

Peel and dice the potato. Add the salt and the cup of water and boil until tender. Remove from heat and stir in the butter and ½ cup sugar. Beat with electric mixer until potato is mashed. Now add the milk powder and eggs and beat until well blended. Dissolve the yeast in the warm water with the 1 teaspoon sugar. Add to potato mixture and stir in the flour, using enough to make a soft dough. Knead until smooth and elastic. Place in a buttered bowl, cover, and let rise until doubled. Knead down and store in refrigerator. The dough will keep as long as a week or 10 days. When ready to use let the dough rise at room temperature for 2 hours Shape into rolls, loaf bread, braided breads, or what have you. Put into pans, cover and let rise again until doubled. Bake rolls in a 400° oven. Bake loaves or braids at 425° for 10 minutes, then reduce heat to 350° and bake until done, about 30 to 45 minutes, depending on size.

CHOCOLATE NUT BREAD. To Refrigerator Potato Bread recipe add ¼ cup sugar, ¼ cup cocoa, and ½ cup chopped nuts. Bake in 2 medium loaves and glaze with a thin chocolate or powdered-sugar glaze.

FLOWERPOT BREAD. Refrigerator Potato Bread lends itself well to baking in flowerpots. If you have never tried this you have a real treat in store. Use new flowerpots of any desired size, except the great big ones. Grease the pots thoroughly, line with waxed paper, and grease the paper. Fill the pots no more than two-thirds full and let dough rise as usual. Bake at temperatures approximately 25° lower than for regular loaves, as the clay pots hold the heat. Set the pots on the lowest shelf of the oven. Cool the baked breads in the pots, laying the pots on their sides and loosening the bread a little so that air can circulate. Any of the heavier breads are especially delicious baked in this way. Batter breads or the lighter breads will fall.

TRIPLE-RICH POTATO BREAD. Add ½ cup soy flour and ¼ cup wheat germ to the recipe for Refrigerator Potato Bread.

WHOLE-WHEAT POTATO BREAD. In the recipe for Refrigerator Potato Bread, use honey in place of sugar and 2 or 3 cups whole-wheat flour in place of that amount of white flour.

RICE BREAD

A delicate bread with an unusual texture and a transparent look.

¼ cup scalded milk	3 cups cooked rice
3 tablespoons butter	1 cake yeast
3 tablespoons sugar	¼ cup scalded milk, cooled
1 teaspoon salt	4 cups flour, sifted

Pour the scalded milk over the butter, sugar, and salt. Add to the cooked rice. Dissolve the yeast in the cooled scalded milk and stir into rice. Work in the flour to make a firm dough. Turn out onto a floured board and knead until smooth and elastic. Place in a greased bowl, cover, and let rise until doubled. Punch the dough down and turn it onto the board again. Knead for 2 or 3 minutes, and then shape into 2 loaves. Place in well-buttered loaf pans, cover, and let rise until doubled. Brush the top with melted butter and bake in a 375° oven for 45 to 50 minutes, or until golden brown and done. Makes 2 small loaves.

SWEDISH LIMPÉ

One of the best of the many excellent Swedish breads.

4 cups water	2 teaspoons grated orange rind
1 cup brown sugar	1 cake yeast
1½ tablespoons caraway seed	6 cups white flour, sifted
2 teaspoons fennel seed	4 cups rye flour
2 tablespoons butter	2 teaspoons salt

Boil the water, sugar, caraway and fennel seeds, butter, and orange rind for 3 minutes. Cool mixture until lukewarm. Add the yeast. Stir thoroughly. Add enough white flour to make a soft dough. Place the dough in a buttered bowl, cover, and let rise until doubled, about 1½ hours.

Then punch the dough down and work in the rye flour and salt, making a stiff dough. Let rise again until doubled, about 2 hours. Knead down and shape into 2 large loaves. Place in greased loaf pans and let rise for 45 minutes. Bake in a 350° oven for 1 hour, or until done.

SWEDISH RYE BREAD

All the Scandinavian countries make rye breads, and several other European countries also. Germany's rye is heavy and dark, as is the Russian rye. The Swedish make several kinds of rye bread, usually flavored with beer, orange, and fennel. The Norwegians prefer a good, light rye, with or without seeds. This recipe makes a typical Swedish rye, though without the seasonings, and is our particular favorite.

1 cup scalded milk	1 cake yeast
2½ teaspoons salt	3½ cups white flour, sifted
2 tablespoons molasses	1 tablespoon caraway seed
2 tablespoons butter	2 cups rye flour
1 cup water	

Pour the milk over the salt, molasses, and butter. Add the water. When cooled to lukewarm add the yeast and the white flour and beat until smooth. Stir in the caraway seed. Gradually add the rye flour and mix to make a medium-stiff dough. The dough will be sticky. Turn it out onto a floured board and knead until smooth, about 10 minutes. Place in a buttered bowl, cover, and let rise until doubled, about 2 hours. Punch down and let rise again. Turn out and shape into 2 oblong loaves. Place on buttered cookie sheets that have been sprinkled with cornmeal. Let rise until doubled. Bake in a 375° oven for 30 to 40 minutes.

ONION RYE BREAD

You can easily tell that I like an onion flavor in breads. You'll like this one too.

1 cup milk, scalded
3 tablespoons sugar
1 teaspoon salt
3 tablespoons butter
1 cake or 1 package yeast

½ cup warm water
3 cups white flour, sifted
2 tablespoons caraway seed
⅓ cup minced onion
about 1½ cups rye flour

Pour the scalded milk over the sugar, salt, and butter, and let cool to lukewarm. Dissolve the yeast in the warm water and add to the milk mixture. Stir in the sifted white flour, and blend until smooth. Now stir in the caraway seed, onion, and enough rye flour (about 1½ cups) to make a firm dough. Turn out onto a lightly floured board and knead until elastic. Place in a buttered bowl, cover, and let rise until doubled. Turn out again onto a board sprinkled with rye flour and shape into a large loaf. Place the loaf in a buttered loaf pan. If desired you may shape the dough into an oval and place it on a buttered cookie sheet that has been sprinkled with cornmeal. Cover and let rise until doubled. Bake in a 350° oven for 45 to 50 minutes, or until browned and done. When done, brush the hot loaf with soft butter.

NORWEGIAN RYE BREAD

In Norway they combine rye and wheat flours with buttermilk for another very good rye bread.

2 cakes or 2 packages yeast
⅓ cup warm water
2 cups buttermilk
1½ teaspoons salt
⅔ cup light molasses
2 tablespoons caraway seed

⅓ cup butter, melted
2 cups white flour, sifted
2 cups rye flour
2 cups whole-wheat or graham
    flour

Dissolve the yeast in the warm water. Heat the buttermilk in a saucepan, over a low to medium flame, until just warm. To the buttermilk, add the salt, light molasses, caraway seed, melted butter, and the dissolved yeast. Blend these ingredients, and then gradually stir in the flours. With clean hands, work the flours into the dough until it is fairly stiff. Now turn the dough out onto a floured board and knead until smooth and elastic. Place in a buttered bowl, cover, and let rise until doubled, about

1¼ hours. When dough is doubled, punch it down and turn it out onto a floured board again. Divide dough into 2 parts, and shape each part into a loaf. Place in buttered 8-inch glass loaf pans. Cover and let rise again until doubled, about 1¼ hours. Brush the top of loaf with softened or melted butter, and bake in a 325° oven for 45 minutes, or until browned and done.

SWEDISH BEER RYE BREAD

An excellent light bread. The beer gives it a tangy flavor which makes it especially good with cheese spreads.

1¾ cups beer	2 teaspoons salt
½ cup warmed molasses	3 cups rye meal or flour
2 cakes yeast, dissolved in ¼	3 cups white flour
cup warm water	1 tablespoon caraway seed
⅓ cup butter	

Combine the beer and molasses and add the dissolved yeast. Beat in the rest of the ingredients and blend well. Brush the top of the dough with softened or melted butter, cover, and let rise until doubled. Then punch the dough down, turn it out onto a floured board, and knead thoroughly, about 7 to 8 minutes, using as much more white flour as is necessary to keep the dough from sticking. Shape into 2 loaves and place in buttered 8- by 4-inch loaf pans, or shape into 2 oval loaves and place on buttered cookie sheets. Cover and let rise until doubled. Bake in a 350° oven for 35 to 45 minutes, or until done.

PUMPERNICKEL

This dark, moist German bread was named after the baker who developed it, one Pumper Nickel. It makes excellent cheese sandwiches.

3 packages active dry yeast	2 tablespoons soft shortening
1½ cups warm water	2 cups unsifted coarse rye
4 teaspoons salt	meal, or 2¾ cups sifted
½ cup molasses	rye flour
1 to 3 tablespoons caraway	3½ to 4 cups sifted white flour
seed	

Dissolve the yeast in the water in a large mixing bowl. Stir in the salt, molasses, and caraway seed. Add the shortening. Mix and remix the flours in a large bowl until perfectly blended. Add half the flour mixture to the liquids, mix with large spoon, and add the rest of the flour mixture. Blend with the hands. Turn onto a lightly floured board. Knead until satiny smooth. Turn dough into a greased bowl and round it up completely. Cover with a damp cloth. Set in a warm place and let rise until doubled in bulk—nearly 2 hours. Punch dough down; cut into 2 parts. Round into smooth balls. Place on a floured cookie sheet or pan sprinkled with cornmeal or poppy seed. Cover with a damp cloth again and let rise for 30 to 40 minutes. Brush tops of loaves with cold water or butter. Bake in a 450° oven for 10 minutes; reduce heat to 350° and bake nearly 30 minutes longer.

NOTE. In place of the rye meal or flour, you could use a blend of dark flours—bran, graham, whole-wheat, rye, stone-ground or white cornmeal. Equal parts of rye and buckwheat flours are a good combination.

OLD WORLD RYE BREAD

This bread is moist and dark with lots of flavor. In Germany during the Second World War people were so hungry for good bread that they used to beg the soldiers for what they called "soldiers' bread"—dark, heavy, and full of flavor. I can only think that that bread was very similar to this one. The recipe doubles easily, and if desired, you may add ½ cup brown sugar and 1 cup each of raisins and walnuts.

2 cups rye flour	2 teaspoons salt
¼ cup cocoa	2 tablespoons caraway seed
2 cakes yeast	2 tablespoons butter
1½ cups warm water	2½ cups white or whole-wheat
½ cup light molasses	flour

Combine the rye flour and cocoa. Do not sift. Dissolve the yeast in ½ cup warm water. Combine the molasses, the remaining 1 cup warm water, the salt and caraway seed in a large bowl. Add the rye flour and cocoa, the yeast mixture, the butter and 1 cup white or whole-wheat flour. Beat until dough is smooth. Spread the remaining flour on a breadboard and knead it into the dough. Add more flour if necessary to make a firm dough that is smooth and elastic. Place in a buttered bowl, cover, and let rise. It will double in about 2 hours. Punch dough down, shape into a round loaf, and place on a buttered cookie sheet that has been sprinkled with cornmeal. Let rise about 50 minutes. Bake in a 375° oven 35 to 40 minutes.

CORN-RYE BREAD

I have great fun experimenting with different flours in breads. With know-how it is possible to get a tremendous amount of extra nutrition into your family's food without their ever being aware that they are being fed "health foods" and the best way to do this is with homemade breads. For example, I substitute 1 cup of rice polish for the same amount of flour in all the white breads I make. It adds a tremendous amount of important vitamins and minerals, without affecting the flavor or texture of the bread. I use wheat germ in all breads, with or without the rice polish. In all dark breads you may substitute ½ cup, or more, of wheat germ for the same amount of flour, without anyone but the cook's being the wiser for it.

1 cake yeast	¼ cup butter
⅓ cup lukewarm water	2 cups rye flour
⅓ cup brown sugar	1½ cups white flour
1 cup very hot water	½ cup cornmeal
1 teaspoon salt	2 tablespoons caraway seed

Dissolve the yeast in the warm water. Combine the brown sugar, hot water, salt, and butter and stir until butter is dissolved. Add the yeast mixture, the flours, and the cornmeal. Stir with a spoon and then knead until smooth. Cover and let rise until doubled. Punch the dough down and turn it into a greased loaf pan. Cover and let rise again until doubled. Sprinkle with caraway seed. Bake in a 325° oven for 1 hour, or until done.

WHEAT-GERM BREAD

A bread as good as it is nutritious. If desired you may use 2 cups of whole-wheat or graham flour in place of the same amount of white flour.

2 cups milk or potato water, scalded and cooled
¼ cup butter, melted
2 tablespoons brown sugar
1 tablespoon mild molasses
2 teaspoons salt

1 large egg
1 cake yeast dissolved in ½ cup warm water
4½ cups flour
2 cups wheat germ

Combine the milk or potato water with the butter, brown sugar, molasses, salt, and egg. Stir in the dissolved yeast. Add 3 cups of the flour and beat thoroughly. When batter is smooth stir in the rest of the flour and then the wheat germ. Turn out onto a floured breadboard and knead thoroughly. Place in a buttered bowl, cover, and let rise until doubled. Punch down and shape into 2 loaves. Place in buttered loaf pans, cover, and let rise again until doubled. Bake in a 400° oven for 40 to 45 minutes, or until browned and done.

CORNELL BREADS

Experiments at Cornell University and other nutrition laboratories showed that, by adding certain ingredients, bread could be so improved that life could be sustained, healthily, on bread and butter alone. In contrast, animals fed on ordinary commercial bread did not grow normally and died early deaths. The popularity of Cornell Bread (also called Triple-Rich Bread) has grown increasingly over the last decade. You can make any bread, cake, or cookie "triple rich" by simply adding 1 tablespoon soy flour, 1 tablespoon skim-milk powder, and 1 teaspoon wheat germ to the bottom of the cup before measuring each cup of flour. Certainly no book of bread recipes would be complete without these healthful and revolutionary recipes.

CORNELL TRIPLE-RICH BREAD

3 cups warm water
2 cakes yeast
2 tablespoons sugar or honey
7 cups flour or more
3 tablespoons wheat germ

½ cup full-fat soy flour
¾ cup skim-milk powder
4 teaspoons salt
2 tablespoons salad oil

Combine the water, yeast, and sugar or honey. Let stand for 5 minutes. Measure and sift the flour, wheat germ, soy flour, and skim-milk powder. Stir the yeast mixture and while stirring add the salt and 3 cups of the flour mixture. Beat 75 strokes by hand or 2 minutes with an electric mixer. Add the salad oil and 3 more cups flour mixture. Blend and then turn out onto a floured board, adding 1 cup or more additional flour as needed. Knead thoroughly, about 5 minutes or until dough is smooth and elastic. Place in a greased bowl, brush the top with soft butter or oil, cover, and let rise until doubled. Punch dough down, fold over the edges, and turn dough upside down. Let it rise another 20 minutes. Turn onto a board, shape into 2 loaves, place in buttered bread pans, cover, and let rise until doubled. Bake in a 350° oven for 50 to 60 minutes. If loaves begin to brown too soon, say in 15 or 20 minutes, reduce heat to 325°.

FIFTY-FIFTY WHOLE-WHEAT BREAD. Follow the preceding recipe, substituting 3 cups whole-wheat flour for 3 cups of the white flour. The loaves won't be quite as large. This makes excellent rolls.

CORNELL OATMEAL BREAD

½ cup warm water
2 cakes yeast
⅓ cup brown sugar
2 cups uncooked oatmeal
2½ cups boiling water
3 tablespoons oil

4 teaspoons salt
6 cups flour or more
2 tablespoons wheat germ
½ cup full-fat soy flour
¾ cup skim-milk powder

Place the ½ cup warm water, the yeast, and the brown sugar in a small bowl and let stand for 5 minutes. Combine the oatmeal, boiling water, oil, and salt. Let cool till only warm. Measure and sift the flour, wheat germ, soy flour, and skim-milk powder together. Stir the yeast mixture into the oatmeal mixture. Add 2½ cups of the flour mixture and beat 75 strokes by hand or for 2 minutes with an electric mixer. Blend in another 2½ cups flour mixture and turn dough onto a floured board, kneading in the remaining flour mixture as needed. Knead for 5 minutes, or until dough is smooth and elastic. Place in a buttered bowl, cover, and let rise until doubled. Turn the dough out and shape it into 2 loaves, or make slightly smaller loaves and make a pan of rolls also. Let rise until doubled. Bake the loaves in a 350° oven 50 to 60 minutes.

CORNELL WHOLE-WHEAT BREAD

2 cups warm water
2 cakes yeast
¼ cup molasses (or honey)
¼ cup brown sugar
1 egg
6 cups whole-wheat flour

½ cup soy flour
¾ cup skim-milk powder
3 tablespoons wheat germ
2 tablespoons brewer's yeast
2 teaspoons salt

Place the warm water, yeast, molasses, and brown sugar in a bowl and let stand for 5 minutes. Into the yeast mixture beat the egg, and 3½ cups whole-wheat flour. Beat for 100 strokes by hand, or 3 minutes with an electric mixer. Let this mixture stand while you combine the remaining flour and the rest of the ingredients. Work the dry ingredients into the batter, adding as much as is needed to make a soft dough. Cover the bowl and let the dough rise for 45 minutes. Then mix the dough again, cover, and let rest for 10 minutes. Divide dough into 2 portions. Turn out onto a lightly floured breadboard and shape into 2 loaves. Place in buttered glass loaf pans. Cover and let rise until dough reaches the tops of the pans. Bake in a 350° oven for 50 to 60 minutes, or until bread is browned and done.

NOTE. If this recipe makes too compact a loaf, the wheat germ and/or brewer's yeast may be omitted. I found that I obtained a lighter loaf by cutting the water to 1½ cups and using 3 large eggs.

WHOLE-WHEAT SWEET BREAD. Add nuts, raisins, dates or candied fruit peel to Cornell Oatmeal Bread, or Cornell Whole-Wheat Bread, if desired, for a very tasty sweet bread. Glaze tops when done.

Alexis Soyer, "father of modern cookery," stated that those who earn their bread "by the sweat of their brow" should eat only whole-grain breads. He also said, "It is only the effeminate and delicate that should partake of fine flour."

5. *Rolls*

When you are pressed for time, bread baked in roll form is easier than that baked in loaf form. The rising time as well as the baking time is shorter. Any bread recipe (except batter breads) may be baked as rolls; it is the method of shaping the rolls that creates the difference in flavor between the loaf and the roll. Pan rolls, baked close together and with little crust, will be softer and fluffier than the same rolls baked on a buttered and cornmeal-sprinkled cookie sheet. The latter will have more crust and a firmer crust—a feature preferred by many people.

As with other types of bread, it is fun to experiment with various shapes. For ease and expediency the pan rolls can't be beat. But balls of dough can be baked in buttered muffin pans; shamrocks can be made by placing three equal-sized pieces of dough into buttered muffin pans. Crescents and fan-tans are always interesting, as are spirals, baked either in muffin pans or on a cookie sheet. Balls of dough can be rolled around a square of cheese, or a piece of frankfurter, or a Vienna sausage, before rising and baking.

Various seeds—sesame, poppy, celery, or caraway—add interest as well as flavor to bread, and are especially desirable on rolls. Brush the rolls with beaten egg white or whole egg before sprinkling them with the seeds. In this way the seeds will stay on after baking.

Unless otherwise specified, all rolls should be baked in a 400° oven for 15 to 25 minutes, depending on size.

FILLINGS FOR HOT ROLLS

Filled hard French or Italian rolls make good lunches or after-school or midnight snacks. For picnics, keep the rolls wrapped in foil; they will stay hot for about an hour. The following recipes will fill approximately 12 rolls, depending on size. For all the recipes, cut off the tops of the rolls and scoop out a little of the center. Save the tops. Mix the filling ingredients thoroughly and put some of the filling in each roll. Cover with the tops and wrap the rolls in aluminum foil. Bake in a 325° oven for 30 to 45 minutes. To keep them hot in the oven lower the heat to about 250°.

1. 1 pound grated Cheddar; ½ teaspoon chili powder; 1 very small onion, minced; 1 small can sliced olives, drained; 1 tablespoon melted butter; 3 hard-cooked eggs, chopped.

2. 1 pound Tillamook cheese, grated; 5 green onions (scallions), minced; 12 stuffed ripe olives, minced; ¼ cup melted butter. Mix the ingredients and thin with tomato soup.

3. 1 pound bologna; ½ pound Cheddar; 2 tablespoons prepared mustard; 3 green onions; 1 or 2 sweet pickles. Grind all ingredients.

4. ½ pound crabmeat, lobster meat, or chicken; ¼ cup minced parsley; 1 tablespoon prepared mustard; ¼ cup mayonnaise; salt and pepper. When the rolls are filled, top each with grated Cheddar before putting on the roll tops.

5. 8 hard-cooked eggs, chopped; ¼ cup oil (preferably olive oil); ¼ cup catsup or chili sauce; 1 small green pepper, minced; 1 small can sliced olives, drained. When the rolls are filled, top each with grated Cheddar before putting on the roll tops.

6. Combine ground ham with grated sharp cheese, chopped hard-cooked eggs, pickle relish, and prepared mustard. Thin the mixture with mayonnaise and a little melted butter, or with tomato soup or tomato sauce.

PEACEMAKERS.   These are so called because tardy husbands in New Orleans and San Francisco used to bring them home to their wives.

Use oval, or largish, hard-crusted rolls. Cut the tops off and scoop out the insides. Brush the insides with melted butter and fill with fried oysters or clams. Brush the tops with more melted butter, wrap rolls in foil and place the rolls in a 350° oven to heat through.

BAGELS

Bagels are unique, and uniquely Jewish, hard-crusted rolls. They are traditionally served with cream cheese and lox (smoked salmon) and have been a favorite bread of mine since I was a child in New York. We used to make regular Sunday afternoon trips from Staten Island to the city, where I was permitted to choose the movie or stage show to be seen, and also to choose a place to eat. I always chose a Jewish delicatessen and always ordered the same "meal"—bagels with cream cheese and lox, and that wonderful New York cheesecake. Year after year I untiringly ate the same Sunday dinner and didn't lose my taste for either treat. Then we moved to California and I didn't get a good bagel or cheesecake until I learned to make my own. Don't try to cut the dough with a doughnut cutter, as it just isn't the same. Always cut the dough into strips and pinch the edges together.

3 cups flour plus ¼ cup for the breadboard	⅔ cup warm potato water
1 teaspoon salt	3 tablespoons salad oil
4 tablespoons sugar	2 eggs
1 cake yeast	4 quarts boiling water

Sift the flour, salt, and 2 tablespoons of the sugar into a mixing bowl. Dissolve the yeast in ⅓ cup of the warm potato water and add yeast to the flour mixture. Add the oil to the remaining potato water and stir into the flour mixture. Then add the eggs and stir until dough forms a ball. Turn out onto a floured board and knead thoroughly for at least 5 minutes. Place the dough in a buttered bowl, cover, and let rise until doubled. Then punch the dough down and let it rise again. Punch down again, turn out onto a floured board, and knead again, until the dough is smooth and elastic. Divide the dough into 12 to 15 portions and form each portion into a strip about 6 inches long and ¾ inch thick. Pinch the ends together to form rings. Add the remaining 2 tablespoons sugar to the boiling water. Drop the bagels into the water one at a time, cooking 4 or 5 at once, depending on the size of the pot. Simmer the bagels for 5 to 6 minutes from the time they rise to the surface of the water. Then lift them out of water with a long-handled fork and place them on a very lightly greased cookie sheet. Let them cool for about 5 minutes. Then place them in a 375° oven, and bake for 25 to 35 minutes, or until the crust is golden brown and crisp.

VARIATIONS.   You may sprinkle the bagels with poppy seed or sesame seed before baking. Or blend some finely minced, sautéed onion into the dough before kneading and sprinkle more finely minced, sautéed onion on the tops of the rolls before baking.

BRIOCHE

Brioche is typically French. Some authorities believe that it was named for the town of Brie, where it supposedly originated, and that originally it was always made with Brie cheese. It is a rich basic dough with many uses. This recipe, my favorite, is based on the one given in Catherine Owen's *Culture and Cooking, or Art in the Kitchen* (1881 edition), which she said was from the Paris Jockey Club.

1 or 2 cakes or packages yeast	4 cups flour
¼ cup warm milk or water	1½ cups soft butter
3 tablespoons sugar	2 teaspoons salt
7 eggs, or 6 egg yolks	1 egg yolk mixed with 1 table-
and 4 whole eggs	spoon cream

If dry yeast is used dissolve it in the warm milk or water along with the sugar. If fresh yeast is used, cream it with the sugar and add the milk or water. Add the 7 whole eggs, or the egg yolks and eggs, and stir well to blend. Add 2 cups flour, the salt, and the butter and beat thoroughly. Add the remaining flour, blend, and beat well. Beating Brioche dough is very important, as it is too soft to knead. Either beat it in a heavy-duty mixer, or else pick up the dough in your hands and slap it down on a breadboard. (This will become frustratingly sticky, which is why I beat the dough in a mixer, very thoroughly, before and after adding the last 2 cups of flour.) When the dough has been well beaten, brush the top with melted butter, cover the bowl, and let it rise until doubled. Then punch it down, cover the bowl again, and place in the refrigerator to chill thoroughly. This will take at least 12 hours, so it is best to make Brioche dough the day before it is needed. It will keep in the refrigerator for several days. When needed, remove from refrigerator. Handle it quickly, as it soon becomes too soft to use. Brioche dough can be shaped in various ways. You might braid small pieces of dough and place the braids in small, buttered loaf tins. Or pinch off small, equal-sized pieces and place in buttered Brioche tins (these are fluted tins available in specialty shops). Or make small loaves, or regular-sized loaves, or buns to be baked in buttered muffin tins. In any case, let the shaped dough rise until doubled. Glaze with egg yolk and cream. Bake rolls or buns at 400° for 20 minutes; large loaves at 375° for 45 to 50 minutes.

NOTE.   If desired add another ½ cup flour to the dough. Shape it into a crown or large round loaf and place on a buttered cookie sheet. Let rise until doubled and bake in a 375° oven until browned and done.

BRIOCHE AU FROMAGE.   To the dough add 2 cups of grated or finely diced cheese. Gruyère is traditional, but I have used a good Cheddar. Shape and bake as desired.

BRIOCHE GOUBAND.   Line a buttered baking pan with sides with a thin layer of Brioche dough. Take small pieces of Brioche dough and wrap each piece around some dried or preserved fruit that has been soaked in cognac, rum, or any liqueur you prefer. Place pieces of fruit-filled dough all over the top of the dough in the pan. Let rise until doubled and bake in a 350° oven 35 to 40 minutes or until golden brown and done. Brush top with hot apricot jam.

BRIOCHE MOUSSELINE.   Butter a 2-quart coffee can. Tie a piece of aluminum foil, also buttered, around the coffee can so that the foil extends about 2 inches above the top of the can. Place the dough in the buttered can, filling it two-thirds full. Let rise until doubled and bake in a 375° oven for 1 hour, or until bread tests done when you insert a cake tester in the center. Lay the can on its side on a rack for 10 to 15 minutes, before turning out carefully. I very often bake Brioche au Fromage this way. Children love the round slices.

BUCKWHEAT ROLLS

1 cake yeast	¼ cup mild molasses
warm water	1½ cups buckwheat flour
⅓ cup melted butter	3½ cups white flour
⅔ cup milk, scalded	1 teaspoon salt

Soften the yeast in ¼ cup warm water. Combine the butter, ⅔ cup warm water, the scalded milk, and the molasses. Cool to lukewarm and then stir in the yeast. Sift the flours with the salt and stir gradually into the liquid mixture. Blend well and then turn out onto a floured board and knead until dough is smooth and satiny. Place in a buttered bowl, cover, and let rise until doubled. Punch down and let rise again until doubled. After the second rising, punch the dough down and then shape it into small rolls, about 1½ inches in diameter. Roll them in melted butter and arrange them, close together, on buttered cookie sheets. Cover and again let rise until doubled. Bake in a 400° oven for 20 to 25 minutes. These are best served warm.

BUTTERMILK HERB ROLLS

2 cups buttermilk	2 tablespoons brown sugar
or sour milk	1 tablespoon dried rosemary,
¼ cup butter	basil, or oregano
1 cake yeast	1 teaspoon salt
½ teaspoon soda	5 to 6 cups flour

Scald the buttermilk or sour milk and pour it over the butter. When cooled to lukewarm stir in the yeast and stir until it is dissolved. Add the next 4 ingredients and 3 cups of the flour. Stir thoroughly. Add the rest of the flour and turn the dough out onto a floured board. Knead thoroughly and then place in a buttered bowl, cover, and let rise until doubled. Punch dough down and turn it out onto the board. Roll the dough to a thickness of slightly more than ½ inch. Cut into rounds with a biscuit cutter. Place the rounds in a buttered jelly-roll pan or sheet cake pan, far enough apart so that they don't touch. Cover and let rise again until doubled. Brush with melted butter. Bake in a 400° oven for 15 to 20 minutes, or until browned and done.

CREAM ROLLS

Wonderful light rolls. With the heavy cream, no shortening is required.

1 cake or 1 package yeast	1 teaspoon salt
¼ cup warm water	approximately 6 cups flour
2 large eggs	
2 cups heavy cream, unwhipped	

Dissolve the yeast in the warm water. Combine the eggs and heavy cream, and beat just until blended. Do not whip. Add the yeast mixture, the salt, and enough flour (about 6 cups) to make a medium-stiff dough. Turn out onto a lightly floured breadboard and shape into rolls. (No first rising is necessary.) Place the rolls on buttered cookie sheets, cover, and let rise until doubled, about 2 hours. Brush the tops with more cream, or with beaten egg, and bake in a 400° oven for 15 to 20 minutes, or until browned and done.

DINNER SEED ROLLS

⅓ cup sugar	3 large eggs, beaten
1 tablespoon salt	6 cups flour
⅓ cup butter	poppy seed, sesame seed, or
1 cup boiling water	celery seed
1 cup cold water	melted butter
2 cakes yeast	

Combine the sugar, salt, butter, and boiling water. Stir to melt the butter. Add the cold water and cool to lukewarm. Add the yeast and let it dissolve. Beat in the eggs and half the flour. Add the rest of the flour and beat until the ball of dough leaves the sides of the bowl. Turn out onto a lightly floured board and knead for 3 minutes. Place in a buttered bowl, cover, and let rise until doubled. Punch down and turn out onto the board again. Knead lightly and then roll out to a thickness of ½ to ¾ inch. Cut into rolls and place them on buttered cookie sheets. Let rise again until doubled. Before baking brush them with melted butter and sprinkle with seeds. Bake at 400° for 20 minutes.

CROISSANTS

Croissants are a time-consuming but delicious pastry. The homemade kind are so far superior to the store variety that they are well worth the time involved, even if you only make them a few times a year.

1 cake yeast	1 tablespoon butter
1 tablespoon sugar	2½ cups flour
1 teaspoon salt	1 cup butter
1 cup milk, scalded	1 egg yolk blended with 1 or 2
and cooled to barely	tablespoons heavy cream or
lukewarm	evaporated milk

Cream the yeast with the sugar and salt until mixture is syrupy. Put the flour in a large mixing bowl and make a well in the center. Into this well put the milk, yeast, and the 1 tablespoon butter. Blend well and knead just until dough is barely smooth—too much kneading will make the Croissants compact instead of flaky. Put the dough back in the mixing bowl and chill on the bottom shelf of the refrigerator for 15 minutes. Do not let the dough rise yet. Remove the dough from the refrigerator and roll it out on a floured board in a rectangle. In the center of the rectangle spread half of the cup of butter. Fold one end of the dough over the butter. On this spread the rest of the butter. Fold the other end of the dough over the butter and press the edges together to seal in the butter. With a rolling pin, roll out the dough to make another long rectangle. Fold as before. Wrap the envelope of dough in waxed paper and chill for 1 hour. Then remove the dough from the waxed paper, place it again on a floured board, and roll out again into a rectangle. Fold as before, wrap in waxed paper again, and chill for 2 hours. Unwrap the dough and place again on a floured board. Roll it out to a thickness of no more than ⅛ inch. Cut the dough into 6-inch squares and then cut the squares into triangles. Roll the triangles, beginning with the wide end. Shape into crescents and place on buttered cookie sheets. Place in the refrigerator to chill for at least 30 minutes. Brush with the egg yolk blended with heavy cream or evaporated milk. Bake in a 475° oven for 5 minutes, then reduce heat to 400° and bake until the Croissants are a golden brown, approximately 8 or 9 minutes longer. Makes about 2 dozen.

CRUSTY FRENCH DINNER ROLLS

2 egg whites
¾ cup hot water
1 tablespoon sugar
1 teaspoon salt
2 tablespoons butter

1 cake yeast dissolved in ¼
  cup lukewarm water
4 cups flour
cornmeal

Beat the egg whites until stiff. In another bowl combine the water, sugar, salt, and butter. Stir until the butter melts. Add the blended yeast and 2 cups of the flour. Beat 3 minutes with an electric mixer to make a soft but elastic dough. Fold in the beaten whites and the remaining flour. Turn onto a floured breadboard and knead until smooth and elastic. Cover and let rise for 2 hours. Punch down and let rise for 1 hour. Turn the dough onto a floured board again and knead lightly. Divide into 18 to 24 pieces and let rest for 10 minutes. Shape the pieces into rolls and place them on a buttered cookie sheet that has been sprinkled with cornmeal. Cover and let rise for 45 minutes. Bake in a 425° oven for 15 to 20 minutes. If you wish a crustier roll place a pan of hot or boiling water on the lowest rack of the oven.

HONEY ROLLS

Delicious hot or cold; good keeping qualities because of the honey.

1 cup milk, scalded
¼ cup butter
⅓ cup honey
1 cake yeast

¼ cup warm water
1 teaspoon salt
5 cups flour
2 large eggs

Stir the butter and honey into the hot scalded milk and stir until the butter melts. Cool until only lukewarm. Dissolve the yeast in the warm water and add to the cooled milk mixture along with the salt and 2 cups of the flour. Blend in the eggs and the rest of the flour to make a soft dough. Knead lightly until smooth. Place in a buttered bowl, cover, and let rise until doubled. Shape into rolls and place on a buttered cookie sheet or in a jelly-roll pan. Cover and let rise again, bake in a 400° oven for 20 minutes, or until done.

HOMEMADE READY-TO-SERVE ROLLS

These delicious and convenient rolls may be stored in the refrigerator for up to 2 weeks. The secret is in the baking, so that almost any roll dough could be used as a brown-and-serve roll. The rolls are baked so that they are completely baked inside, but not browned. Then at serving time you just brown them.

1 cake yeast	1 teaspoon salt
½ cup warm water	1 tablespoon sugar
½ cup scalded and cooled milk	4 cups flour, or more
2 tablespoons butter	

Dissolve the yeast in the water. Add the butter, salt, and sugar to the milk. Cool to barely lukewarm. Add the yeast mixture and 2 cups of the flour. Beat until smooth. Cover and let rise until doubled. Punch the dough down and add the other 2 cups flour. Turn out onto a floured board and knead thoroughly, kneading in more flour as necessary to make a stiff dough. Cover the dough and let it rest for 10 minutes. Shape into rolls and place them in buttered square or oblong pans. Cover and let the rolls rise until not quite doubled. If they rise too high they will fall during the long baking. Bake the rolls in a 275° oven for 30 minutes. Remove from oven and set the pans on a rack to cool. Do not remove from pans until the rolls have cooled for 15 minutes. Turn them out of the pans and continue cooling the rolls on the rack. When they are completely cooled, wrap them in plastic wrap or waxed-paper. They may be kept in the refrigerator for up to 2 weeks, or at room temperature for no longer than 1 week. When ready to serve, place the rolls on cookie sheets and put in a 450° oven for just long enough to brown them—5 to 7 minutes.

NOTE. To use your favorite roll recipe for ready-to-serve rolls, simply add a little more flour to make the dough stiff. After shaping, let the rolls rise but not double. Bake for 30 minutes in a 275° oven, cool, and store as directed, and brown at 450°.

RICH BRAN ROLLS

These good rolls, with the addition of chopped nuts and golden raisins, make very tasty sweet rolls. The dough may be stored in the refrigerator overnight or for several days. Or you can make the dough the day before, or when convenient, spoon it into buttered muffin tins, brush the tops with melted butter, and refrigerate. In this case let the dough rise at room temperature until doubled, about 2 hours, before baking.

2 cakes yeast	2 cups bran flakes
1 cup warm water	1 teaspoon salt
1 cup boiling water	3 large eggs
1 cup butter	5 to 5½ cups flour
⅔ cup sugar	

Dissolve the yeast in the warm water. Pour the boiling water over the butter, sugar, bran flakes, and salt. Stir until the butter melts and the mixture has cooled. Add the yeast mixture. Beat in the eggs. Blend in the flour 1 cup at a time until liquid is absorbed. Don't knead; this dough is so rich it doesn't require kneading. Brush with melted butter, cover the bowl, and let the dough rise until doubled. Punch down and spoon into buttered muffin tins, filling them only half to two-thirds full. Cover and let rise again until almost but not quite doubled. Bake in a 375° oven until done —15 to 20 minutes. These are very light and tender, wonderful for breakfast.

ITALIAN ROLLS

These are Italian Guastelle as made by a friend of mine who sells them in her Italian market. The variations are my own, and although they may be made using any roll dough or bread dough, they seem to be extra good when made with this recipe.

2 cups water	⅓ cup warm water
½ cup oil (*not* butter)	2 cakes yeast
¼ cup sugar	2 large eggs
1 tablespoon salt	6 cups flour

Heat the 2 cups water to boiling. Pour over the oil, sugar, and salt. Cool until only lukewarm. Dissolve the yeast in ⅓ cup warm water. Add to cooled mixture along with the eggs and half the flour. Stir until smooth. Add the rest of the flour and blend in. Turn out onto a lightly floured breadboard and knead lightly. Shape into rolls and place them on buttered cookie sheets. Let rise until doubled. Bake in a 375° to 400° oven until golden brown—15 to 20 minutes.

NOTE. If desired, crease the rolls in the middle with the back of a knife, brush with an egg-white glaze, and sprinkle with sesame seed or poppy seed. Any kind of roll is good cut in half, spread with melted butter, and dipped in grated Parmesan or Cheddar cheese (combined with sesame seed if desired), and heated in a 350° oven.

ONION TURNOVERS. Cook 1 cup (or less if desired) sesame seed and the same amount of finely minced onion, in 2 tablespoons butter until onion is golden and seeds are lightly browned. Roll some of the dough to a thickness of no more than ⅛ inch and cut into circles. Place some of the filling in the center of each circle. Fold over and seal the edges. Let rise and bake as usual, checking the baking time so that they do not overcook. I sometimes cut the dough into saucer-sized circles, but more often I use a biscuit cutter.

CHEESE TURNOVERS. Combine grated Cheddar cheese, poppy seed as desired, and a little soft butter. Roll the dough as for Onion Turnovers, cut into circles, and place some filling in center of each circle. Fold and seal edges. Let rise and bake as usual.

FRANKFURTER ROLLS. Roll and cut dough as for Onion Turnovers. Spread the center of each circle of dough with a small amount of prepared mustard and/or frankfurter relish. Place a frankfurter on each circle, using the cocktail-size wieners for small circles and regular-size frankfurters for larger circles. Roll the dough around the frank and seal the edges. Place on buttered cookie sheets, let rise just a short time, and bake in a 400° oven until browned and done—10 to 20 minutes.

They that have no other meat,
Bread and butter are glad to eat.

—OLD ENGLISH PROVERB

GRISSINI (Bread Sticks)

We love these crispy, salty sticks. Stuck in a tall container and served with almost anything Italian or French, they add much to a meal.

1 cake yeast	2 tablespoons salt
¼ cup warm water	2 tablespoons melted butter
1 cup milk, scalded and cooled	¾ cup warm water
2 tablespoons sugar	6 cups flour

Dissolve the yeast in the ¼ cup warm water. Pour the milk into a large bowl and add the sugar, salt, butter and ¾ cup warm water. Cool until only lukewarm and add the yeast mixture. Slowly stir in half the flour, beat until smooth, and then add the rest of the flour. Turn out onto a lightly floured board and knead until smooth and elastic. Shape into a ball, place in a buttered bowl, cover, and let rise until doubled. Punch down dough, turn out onto a floured board again, and roll to a thickness of approximately ½ inch. Cut into long strips and roll so that each will be long and pencil-like. Place on oiled cookie sheets, cover, and let rise again until doubled. Brush with egg-white glaze and sprinkle with poppy seed, sesame seed, or coarse salt. Bake in a 425° oven for 15 minutes, or until browned and done.

REFRIGERATOR ROLLS

Refrigerator rolls are especially handy, since you can mix the dough when convenient, and have fresh dough for 3 days to a week.

2 cakes yeast	2 cups mashed potatoes
1 cup warm water	2 cups hot potato water
1⅓ cups soft butter	3 large eggs
1½ cups sugar	about 9 cups flour
1 tablespoon salt	

Dissolve the yeast in the warm water. Add the butter, sugar, salt, and mashed potatoes to the hot potato water. When cooled stir in the yeast and the eggs. Add enough flour to make a stiff dough, approximately 9 cups. Turn out onto a lightly floured board and knead well. Put into a buttered bowl, cover well, and place in refrigerator. The dough will keep about a week. Punch the dough down as it rises in the refrigerator, or it will sour. When ready to use, remove the amount needed from refrigerator and let it warm to room temperature. Shape into rolls and place them on buttered cookie sheets. Cover and let rise until doubled. Bake in a 400° oven until browned and done—about 20 minutes.

These can be shaped, before baking, into any shape desired: Parker House, cloverleaf, snails, braids, twists, or bowknots.

C O R N   R O L L S.   Substitute 2 to 3 cups of coarsely ground cornmeal for the same amount of flour. Stir the cornmeal into the hot potato water before adding the flour. These are delicious.

B R A N   R O L L S.   Substitute 2 cups of bran flakes for same amount of flour. Follow recipe.

C H E E S E   R O L L S.   Add along with the flour 2 cups, or more, of grated cheese—sharp Cheddar or Tillamook is good.

H E R B   R O L L S.   Add 2 teaspoons, or more if desired, of any favorite dried herb to recipe. Before baking, sprinkle rolls with beaten egg and grated hard cheese, such as Parmesan.

C O C O N U T   R O L L S.   Into half of the dough blend 1 cup of moist coconut and 2 teaspoons vanilla extract. Bake in buttered muffin tins. Frost with powdered-sugar glaze and sprinkle with more coconut.

WHOLE-WHEAT REFRIGERATOR ROLLS

A wonderfully delicious, nutritious, and dependable recipe. The method of shaping could be used with any favorite roll recipe.

2 cakes yeast	2½ cups white flour
1½ cups milk, scalded	½ cup wheat germ
and cooled	4 cups whole-wheat flour
½ cup sugar	4 large eggs
2 teaspoons salt	⅓ cup melted butter
½ teaspoon soda	

Dissolve the yeast in the scalded and cooled milk. Add the sugar and salt. Blend well. Sift the soda and white flour and add to the wheat germ and the whole-wheat flour. Add to the milk mixture along with the eggs and the melted butter. Beat well. Put the dough in a buttered bowl, cover, and refrigerate. (It will keep 1 week.) When ready to bake, knead the dough very lightly, adding just a little more flour if necessary. Roll the dough out until no thicker than ⅛ inch. Cut into rounds with a biscuit cutter. Brush both sides of each round with melted butter and stack the rounds one above the other, 3 deep. Place 2 inches apart in a pan with sides. Cover and let rise until doubled. Then bake in a 400° oven for 20 minutes, or until browned and done.

SQUASH, CARROT, OR PUMPKIN ROLLS

A use for extra or leftover vegetables. The results are very good, with pleasing color and flavor. A teaspoon of grated orange rind or lemon rind adds much to the flavor.

⅔ cup scalded, cooled milk
1 cup cooked and mashed squash, carrots, or pumpkin, or a 12-ounce package of frozen cooked squash or pumpkin (thawed)

⅓ cup brown sugar
½ teaspoon salt
⅓ cup butter
1 cake yeast dissolved in ¼ cup warm water
4 to 5 cups flour

Combine the milk, vegetable, sugar, salt, and butter. Blend well. Add the dissolved yeast to the mixture, along with 2 cups of the flour. Beat well with a spoon. Then gradually stir in more flour until the dough is stiff enough to knead. Turn out onto a lightly floured board and knead well. Place in a buttered bowl, cover, and let rise until doubled. Punch down and turn out onto a floured board again. Shape as desired into twists, Parker House Rolls, cloverleaf rolls, or plain bun shapes. Place on buttered cookie sheets, or in buttered muffin tins, cover and let rise until doubled. Bake in a 400° oven for 20 minutes. Brush with soft butter while hot.

SHREDDED-WHEAT OR GRAPE-NUTS ROLLS

These delicious rolls can be made with either Shredded Wheat or Grape-Nuts. If you prefer baking this as a loaf bread, the recipe makes 1 large loaf, or 2 small ones.

2 large Shredded Wheat biscuits, or 1 cup Grape-Nuts	¼ cup butter
	1 cake yeast
2 cups boiling water	1 teaspoon salt
¼ cup sugar	4 cups flour

Combine crumbled Shredded Wheat Biscuits or the Grape-Nuts with the boiling water, sugar, and butter. Cool until only lukewarm. Stir in the yeast and stir until it is dissolved. Blend in the salt and flour, then cover the dough and let rise until doubled. Punch dough down and turn it out onto a floured board. Knead the dough, kneading in more flour if necessary to make a firm dough that can easily be shaped. Shape the dough into rolls, or into a loaf or 2 small loaves. Place in buttered pans, cover, and let rise again until doubled. Bake rolls in a 400° oven for 20 minutes, or until done. Bake loaves in a 350° oven, the large loaf for 45 minutes, the small ones for about 30 minutes.

6. *Fried Breads*

Except for "baking" flattened cakes of meal and water on hot stones in the sun, frying is the oldest form of bread cookery. In some parts of the world today fried bread is a staple part of the diet, with baked breads, if used at all, reserved for holidays or special occasions.

Among the western American Indians, fried bread is a staple food. It is usually made of flour and salt, with just enough water added to make a dough that can be rolled very thin. Cut into squares or circles, it is deep-fried. More modern Indians add baking powder and use milk, or milk powder, added to the water. The Mexicans have several fried breads that are very popular, of which the well-known tortilla is only one. And in India, puris, chappaties, and parathas are all fried rather than baked.

One European cookbook that I know calls fried bread an "unusual American dish," and gives instructions for cutting and deep-frying a plain bread dough. Certainly fried breads were very popular in early America, being the most easily made child-pleaser in those busy days. Most house-wives made them out of a plain bread dough with pieces of dough either cut or pinched off and deep-fried. But a few early American cookbooks suggested working more butter, and a little sugar, into a "light bread dough," and then rolling the dough out and cutting it into circles or squares. These were left to rise a little and then carefully dropped into lard "an inch deep," and served for breakfast with molasses or butter.

Biscuits were very often patted to the size of a pancake and fried in a small amount of lard or shortening. They were served somewhat like pancakes. We tried them and they were surprisingly good.

Early America called its fried breads by an intriguing variety of names, among them Baptist cakes, wonders, wonderfuls, doughgods, fried saucers, doughboys, jollyboys, and flyaways.

An Italian friend recalls that her mother used to pull off chunks of bread dough, flatten the chunks between the palms of her hands, and then fry the flattened dough in lard. Eaten hot with plenty of butter, the fried chunks of bread remain as one of her fondest memories.

According to many authorities, doughnuts, as such, originated with the Dutch, and the Dutch *Oliekuchen* or *Olie ballen* is the great-granddaddy of all doughnuts. Most countries have a fried sweet bread of their own, but very often the only difference is a touch of spice or the addition of currants or preserved fruits. Thus the German drop-doughnut and the Italian *sfinge* are virtually the same except that the German uses cardamom while the Italian uses nutmeg or mace. The French and the Hungarians use quantities of eggs, and the Scandinavian countries as well as many other European countries have sweet crullers so similar that I have used only one, the Czech *Milosti*.

In many instances it is extremely difficult to distinguish clearly between a fried bread, a cruller, a doughnut, and a pancake. Thus the Danish *Aebleskiver* is considered a doughnut by many Danes, and a pancake by others. Some people regard baking-powder doughnuts as crullers, while others say that a cruller has no leavening at all and is always rolled very thin. Still others say that whether you use yeast, baking powder, or no leavening at all, if the dough is twisted before it is deep-fried, it is a cruller. Scones and Bannocks could certainly be considered fried breads, but I have included them in another section of this book. And pancakes and waffles, while most certainly fried breads, require a chapter of their own.

The appeal of fried breads seems to be in their method of preparation, so a hot-roll mix, or a commercial frozen bread dough, could be used. The most important thing to remember is that the dough must always be ready to bake—in other words, it should have risen once or twice at least before it is fried. Most fried breads, except crullers and doughnuts, can, if desired, be fried in a shallow amount of lard, shortening, or oil. But, regardless of instructions given in old cookbooks, the fat should be at least 2 or 3 inches deep.

BUNUELOS

There must be as many recipes for Bunuelos as there are Mexican cooks, for I've seen no two the same. The following is our favorite, and has been an after-school treat for many years. In Mexico this crisp fritter-type sweet bread is made only at Christmas time. Some cooks pat the dough rounds over a napkin-covered knee to attain the thinness of dough required for the best Bunuelos; some roll the dough with a rolling pin or work the rounds between floured hands until they are thin enough. This last method is my favorite, as I do not like to use the extra flour required when rolling the dough. I replace 2 tablespoons of the flour in the recipe with the same amount of wheat germ or rice polish.

4 cups sifted flour	1 teaspoon salt
2 tablespoons sugar (Vanilla Sugar or Lemon Sugar if desired, but this is not traditional)	4 large eggs
	½ cup milk
	¼ cup butter, melted

Sift the dry ingredients into a bowl; beat the eggs, milk, and melted butter together, and add to the dry ingredients. Blend thoroughly. Turn dough out onto a lightly floured board and knead very lightly. Divide dough into approximately 18 pieces, shape into rounds, cover with a clean towel and let stand for 15 minutes. Now roll or pat the rounds out, one at a time, into large circles about the size of tortillas. Let the rounds stand another 5 minutes, and then fry in deep hot fat until browned. If you are using a frying pan with hot fat about 1 inch deep, turn the Bunuelos over to brown on the other side. They may be served with butter, or sugar, or crumbled into a bowl and served with a syrup.

BUNUELO PUFFS

These are slightly different and also excellent. We prefer them sprinkled with sugar, but they could be served with a syrup, or glazed. In Mexico these are a holiday tradition. They puff up almost like doughnuts.

4 large eggs, separated   1 tablespoon sugar
4 cups flour   1 cup milk
2 teaspoons baking powder

Beat the egg yolks and egg whites separately and then fold the beaten whites and yolks together. Blend the flour, baking powder, and sugar. Fold this into the egg mixture alternately with the milk. Drop spoonfuls of the batter into deep hot fat. Fry until well browned and then turn to brown the other side. Drain and turn into a bowl.

To make a syrup to serve with Bunuelos, boil 1 cup sugar and ¾ cup water together for 10 minutes (or until syrup has thickened). If desired flavor with a cinnamon stick, or use lemon sugar.

FRIED BREAD

In the nineteenth century, this basic recipe, a simple biscuit-type dough, without shortening, was called "Wonderfuls." Dunked in a molasses sauce, these were considered a delicacy among the after-school set. When cut into saucer shapes they were known as fried saucers. My children love these, without the molasses sauce, as a between-meal snack, or as a breakfast bread, served with plenty of butter and jam.

5 cups flour   ⅓ cup wheat germ
1 teaspoon salt   enough warm water to make a
5 teaspoons baking powder   soft dough, about 2 cups
½ cup nonfat skim-milk
    powder

Combine the dry ingredients in a bowl. Add enough warm water to make a soft dough. A little more or less water may be needed. Oil or butter your hands well and knead the dough. Now, keeping your hands oiled or buttered, so that the dough doesn't stick, pinch off pieces of dough about the size of an egg, and flatten them with your hands until the dough is very thin, and about 5 inches in diameter. If desired you may roll the dough with a rolling pin and cut into shapes, but to do this you will need more flour. Have a large frying pan ready, with hot fat about 2 inches deep. Drop in 2 or 3 rounds of dough at a time, and fry until browned on one side, then, using a cooking fork, turn them over and fry until browned on the other side. Drain well and serve stacked in a bowl, with butter and jam.

FRIED BREAKFAST TWISTS

The dough may be twisted, cut into diamond shapes, or braided, as desired.

3 cups flour	2 tablespoons butter
2 teaspoons baking powder	2 large eggs
1 teaspoon salt	1½ cups buttermilk

Sift the dry ingredients together. Cut in the butter as for pastry. Stir in the eggs and buttermilk. The dough should be soft, but workable. Roll it out on a floured board and cut it into strips. Fry in hot fat until golden brown. Serve with butter and jam, or a syrup.

FRENCH FRIED BREAD

You can make Fried Bread with almost any plain bread or roll dough, but this one is especially delicious. I add wheat germ to the recipe, substituting it for the same amount of flour.

½ cup boiling water	½ cup evaporated milk
2 tablespoons butter	or cream
¼ cup sugar	1 cake yeast
½ teaspoon salt	3 large eggs
	3½ cups flour

Pour the boiling water over the butter, sugar, and salt. Add evaporated milk or cream, and cool until lukewarm. When cooled, stir in the yeast and then the eggs and flour. Beat thoroughly, adding a little more flour if necessary. The dough should be soft but not sticky. Now, with floured hands, pull off pieces of dough and flatten. Fry in hot fat, drain on paper towels, and serve hot.

MILOSTI

Milosti is a Czechoslovakian delicacy, the name of which, according to one authority, translates as "celestial crusts." Virtually the same cruller is found throughout Europe as far north as Scandinavia, the only differences being the addition of brandy, or the same cruller in a different shape.

½ cup egg yolks
½ cup cream, or ½ cup rich
   milk and 1 tablespoon
   melted butter
½ cup sugar

dash of salt
dash of mace
¼ teaspoon grated lemon rind
2½ to 3 cups flour

Beat the egg yolks, cream or milk, and sugar together. Add the rest of the ingredients, adding 1 tablespoon melted butter if milk is used instead of cream. The mixture should be stiff enough to roll out as for pie crust. If not, add enough more flour to make the dough stiff enough to roll out. Roll to a thickness of no more than ⅛ inch and cut into squares. Prick the squares several times with a fork, and then drop them into hot deep fat and fry until golden brown. If desired sprinkle the squares with sugar.

PURIS

In India they use all whole-wheat flour in this delicious bread, but if desired you could use half white flour. One delicious Puris recipe calls for equal parts of whole-wheat flour and mashed potatoes with just a pinch of salt. The dough is rolled very thin and fried on each side in a buttered skillet. The following recipe is a little more complicated but well worth trying.

4 cups whole-wheat flour
1 teaspoon salt

¼ to ½ cup butter
2 cups yogurt or leban

Combine ingredients and knead thoroughly. Then cover the bowl containing the dough and let stand at room temperature for 30 minutes. Roll the dough out very thin and cut into saucer-sized pancakes. Fry in hot deep fat, or in a skillet in enough hot fat to make the Puris float. Fry until lightly browned on both sides, drain on paper towels, and serve immediately.

CHAPPATIES

An excellent Indian pancake-type bread that is a must with curries. You may use half white flour if desired.

2 cups whole-wheat flour	2 tablespoons melted butter
½ teaspoon salt	¾ cup to 1 cup cold water

Combine all ingredients, adding just enough water to make a stiff but workable dough. Knead the dough very well and then let stand at room temperature for several hours, covered with a damp towel. When ready to use, pinch off pieces of the dough and roll into very thin rounds. Bake on a lightly buttered griddle, turning several times to brown the dough evenly. Serve hot, with or without butter.

PARATHAS

Use the recipe for Chappaties, substituting 2 tablespoons of cold milk for the same amount of cold water. Knead the dough very well and then let stand at room temperature for several hours, covered with a damp towel. Pinch off pieces of the dough and roll them out into thin rounds. Rub a little melted butter on the top of each round. Fold the round in half and rub with more melted butter, then fold in half again, making a triangular shape. Roll the Parathas out, keeping the triangular shape. Fry on a buttered griddle, turning just once.

LEFSE

This recipe comes from a Norwegian community in South Dakota, by way of a friend. The dough should be rolled with a Lefse rolling pin, which has lengthwise grooves, but an ordinary rolling pin may be used. My friend turns the Lefse with a long thin stick that was once part of a son's bow and arrow set, but lacking this a long thin spatula may be used. Some Norwegian cooks use part or all rye flour, but we prefer the white flour. Traditionally Lefse is served with *lutfisk,* a lye-prepared fish (available in Scandinavian stores), and is folded into quarters and buttered. But we find that it is good just as a between-meal snack.

5 large potatoes	3 tablespoons butter
½ cup sweet cream	approximately 2½ cups flour
1 teaspoon salt	

Boil the potatoes and mash them, while hot, with the cream, salt, and butter. While the potatoes are still warm, stir in as much flour as is necessary to make a smooth paste. This is usually ½ cup per potato, but a lot depends on the size of the potatoes. Cool the dough. When ready to use, turn out portions of the dough onto a floured breadboard and roll into thin circles. Bake on a hot griddle, turning the circles of dough several times during the baking. Do not grease the griddle, as these breads bake rather than fry. The oftener you turn the Lefse the crisper they will be. We prefer a softer Lefse and so turn them as little as possible. Some cooks spread the Lefse with equal parts of sour cream and butter, whipped together.

HUSH PUPPIES

Tradition says that the Hush Puppy originated around fishermen's campfires in the South, when, to quiet hungry, barking dogs, spoonfuls of batter were fried in the hot fat and then tossed to the dogs with the admonition, "Hush, puppy." Whatever its origin, it is an excellent bread, made more or less so by the grade of cornmeal used. Some cooks use only white cornmeal; we prefer the yellow. For camping trips the ingredients may be mixed in advance, using nonfat milk powder and dried onion flakes. Then water is the only thing added, and the Hush Puppies may be enjoyed at their delicious best, which is when they are fried in fat that has first been used to fry fish. Traditionally, the batter is dropped by spoonfuls into deep fat, but shallow fat may be used, and we love them made into ¼-inch-thick cakes and fried in butter.

2 cups coarsely ground cornmeal
1 teaspoon salt
2 teaspoons baking powder

1 medium onion, minced
1 to 1½ cups milk
1 or 2 large eggs (optional)

Blend the ingredients in the order given, using just enough milk to make a fairly thick batter. This will take about 1½ cups milk, but if desired (and I think this is an improvement), you may use 1 cup or 1¼ cups milk and add 1 or 2 large eggs. Drop the batter by spoonfuls into hot fat, or shallow fry as suggested above.

VARIATION. Buttermilk or sour milk may be used. With either, use only 1 teaspoon baking powder and add ½ teaspoon soda. The onion may be omitted.

TORTILLAS

Tortillas are the bread of Mexico, and a well-made Tortilla can be very good. There is a blend called Masa Harina on the market, which, if you follow directions and add 1 or 2 tablespoons lard, will make very good Tortillas.

For Cornmeal Tortillas stir 1 cup of boiling water into 1 cup cornmeal. Add 1 teaspoon salt and 1 tablespoon lard to the mixture. Shape into thin, flat cakes and bake on a hot ungreased griddle. If you make many Tortillas a tortilla press is a good investment.

To make Flour Tortillas, which are preferred by many people, take 2 cups flour and blend it with ⅓ cup milk or water, ½ teaspoon salt and ⅓ cup lard or butter. Knead mixture thoroughly and then make small balls of the dough. Roll these small balls out until they are very thin. Bake them on a hot ungreased griddle.

The traditional way of shaping Flour Tortillas is to toss the rounds, stretching them as they are tossed, in much the same way that an Italian chef stretches and shapes the dough for Pizza, but since this takes practice, rolling the balls of dough will do.

DOUGHNUTS

Although any sweet roll dough may be cut into rounds or squares, and fried as doughnuts, there is a secret to truly superior doughnuts. Doughnuts should include egg yolks for richness, and whole eggs for lightness; the ideal flour is a combination of half bread flour and half pastry or cake flour. Lacking this, all-purpose flour will do. Since the dough for doughnuts should be soft, it will help greatly to chill the dough before cutting. Roll and cut the doughnuts as you are ready to deep-fry them, so that the extra dough will not have a chance to warm up. The best temperature for deep-frying doughnuts is 375°. A lower temperature will allow the dough to take in too much grease before it cooks through; a higher temperature will make a hard crust, and the outside will burn before the inside is done. To prevent doughnuts, especially cake doughnuts, from cracking, turn them frequently while frying.

Fried doughnuts may be eaten as is, or they may be shaken in a bag with some powdered or granulated sugar. Any regular frosting may be spread on the tops of doughnuts, and then if desired they may be dipped in chopped nuts, coconut, or chocolate shot.

The following glaze is excellent, and if desired the flavoring may be changed to suit.

GLAZE FOR DOUGHNUTS

Some cooks use 3 cups granulated sugar in this recipe.

2 cups granulated sugar	1 teaspoon vanilla extract, or
2 cups water	grated lemon rind, cinnamon, or spice of your choice

Combine the sugar and water. Bring to a boil and boil for 4 minutes, or to the thread stage. Remove from heat and cool for 10 minutes. Then stir in the flavoring or spice you prefer. Dip the doughnuts into the syrup and drain on waxed paper.

BUTTERMILK DOUGHNUTS

½ cup each buttermilk and   1 teaspoon vanilla extract
  sour cream, or 1 cup sour   4½ cups flour
  cream   2 teaspoons baking powder
1 cup sugar   ½ teaspoon soda
2 egg yolks   ½ teaspoon salt
1 whole egg

Combine the buttermilk, sour cream, sugar, egg yolks, whole egg, and vanilla extract. Beat until smooth. Sift the dry ingredients, and stir into the buttermilk mixture. Chill dough 1 hour, or longer if desired. Divide dough into 2 parts. Roll out 1 part at a time on a floured board and cut with a doughnut cutter. (Dough should be rolled no thicker than ½ inch.) Fry at 375°, turning once.

VARIATION. If desired, add 1 teaspoon grated lemon rind, or ½ teaspoon nutmeg, mace, or cinnamon, to the dough.

BAKING-POWDER NUT DOUGHNUTS

4 cups flour   ¾ cup chopped walnuts, or
4 teaspoons baking powder   slivered almonds, or sliced
½ teaspoon salt   Brazil nuts
¼ teaspoon nutmeg and   2 whole eggs
¼ teaspoon cinnamon, or 1   2 egg yolks
  teaspoon grated lemon rind   2 cups sugar
  or orange rind   ¼ cup melted butter
                                   1 cup milk

Sift the flour, baking powder, salt, and spices, if used. Stir the nuts into the dry mixture. Beat the whole eggs, egg yolks, and sugar until blended, then stir in the melted butter. To this mixture, add the dry mixture, stirring in alternately with the milk. Stir gently to blend. Turn out onto a floured board and roll dough to a thickness of ½ to ¾ inch. Cut with a floured doughnut cutter and fry in deep fat at 375°, turning once.

BROWN-SUGAR DOUGHNUTS

¾ cup milk, scalded
¼ cup butter
½ cup egg yolks
1 cup brown sugar
½ teaspoon cinnamon

½ teaspoon nutmeg
4 cups flour
½ teaspoon salt
4 teaspoons baking powder

Scald the milk and pour over the butter. Cool. Beat the egg yolks with the sugar and spices. Stir the milk into the egg-sugar mixture, blending well. Sift the flour with the salt and baking powder and fold into the liquid blend. Blend lightly but thoroughly. Chill dough for 1 hour and then roll out on a floured board to a thickness of about ½ inch. Cut with a floured doughnut cutter and fry in deep fat at 375°.

VARIATION.   Omit the cinnamon and nutmeg and add 1 teaspoon each vanilla extract and grated lemon rind. Use white sugar in place of the brown sugar.

GERMAN DROP DOUGHNUTS

¼ cup soft butter
1 cup sugar
2 egg yolks
1 whole egg
4 cups flour
2 teaspoons baking powder

½ teaspoon soda
½ teaspoon crushed cardamon
  seed, or ¼ teaspoon nutmeg
  or mace
¾ cup buttermilk

Cream the butter and sugar. Stir in the egg yolks and whole egg. Sift the dry ingredients and add to the creamed mixture alternately with the buttermilk. Stir to blend ingredients well. Do not chill. Drop spoonfuls of dough into 375° deep fat. Turn to brown on both sides. Sprinkle with powdered sugar.

ORANGE DOUGHNUTS

2 tablespoons butter
1 cup granulated sugar
2 large eggs
1 tablespoon grated orange
 rind
4 cups flour
½ teaspoon salt

2 teaspoons baking powder
¾ teaspoon soda
¾ cup orange juice
1 cup powdered sugar
1 tablespoon grated orange
 rind

Cream the butter and sugar. Blend in the eggs and grated orange rind. Sift the dry ingredients. Add to the egg mixture alternately with the orange juice. Chill dough for 3 hours, or overnight. Roll ½ to ¾ inch thick and cut with a floured doughnut cutter. Let the doughnuts stand while the fat heats. Fry at 375° to 385°. Turn once. Shake in a bag with 1 cup powdered sugar and 1 tablespoon grated orange rind.

SWEET-POTATO DOUGHNUTS

These doughnuts have, over the years, become a Halloween tradition at our house.

5 cups flour
7 teaspoons baking powder
1½ cups warm mashed
 sweet potatoes
1 teaspoon salt

3 large eggs
2 cups sugar
2 tablespoons melted butter
1 teaspoon nutmeg
1 cup milk

Sift the flour and baking powder. Whip the potatoes, gradually add the salt, eggs, sugar, melted butter, nutmeg, and milk, and blend thoroughly. Stir in the flour and mix until well blended into a soft dough, as for biscuits. Chill well for at least 1 hour. Turn a portion of the dough onto a floured board and roll or pat to a thickness of ½ inch. The dough should be soft but firm enough so that it doesn't stick to the board. Cut with a floured doughnut cutter and drop into 375° fat. Turn doughnuts as they brown. Drain and sprinkle with powdered sugar. Best served hot.

VARIATION. If desired the nutmeg may be omitted and 1 table-spoon grated orange rind used instead. Frost these doughnuts with a light orange glaze.

CALÁS

Calás are really sweet rice fritters, made famous in New Orleans. They were made and sold by the Negro women of an earlier time, who used to carry baskets of the hot Calás on their heads, and wind their way through the streets of New Orleans, singing, *"Calás, Calás, Calás tout chaud."* Some recipes use yeast, but this one, which is our favorite, uses baking powder. Sprinkle the Calás while hot with powdered sugar, and serve as you would any hot doughnuts.

2 egg yolks	2 cups flour
1 cup cold boiled rice	2 teaspoons baking powder
1 cup sugar	2 egg whites, stiffly beaten
½ teaspoon cinnamon or nut-meg, or 1 teaspoon grated lemon rind	

Beat together the egg yolks, rice, and sugar. Stir in the spice or lemon rind, flour, and baking powder until well blended. Then fold the stiffly beaten egg whites through the mixture. Drop by spoonfuls into hot deep fat.

OLD-FASHIONED CAKE DOUGHNUTS

4 cups flour	pinch of ginger
4 teaspoons baking powder	½ cup egg yolks
¼ teaspoon soda	½ cup buttermilk
½ teaspoon salt	1 cup light cream
1 teaspoon nutmeg	1 cup sugar

Sift the first 6 ingredients. Beat the egg yolks with the buttermilk and light cream and add the sugar to the cream mixture. Stir into the flour mixture until smooth. Chill the dough for 1 hour and then, taking a small piece at a time, pat it out on a floured board to a thickness of ½ inch. Cut with a floured doughnut cutter and fry in deep hot fat. Turn frequently.

CHOCOLATE CAKE DOUGHNUTS. Add 2 tablespoons cocoa (preferably Dutch cocoa) to the dry ingredients in the preceding recipe.

BROWN-SUGAR YEAST DOUGHNUTS

2 cups milk, scalded	4 eggs
1 cup brown sugar	1 teaspoon salt
⅔ cup butter	4½ to 5 cups flour
1 cake yeast	

Pour the scalded milk over the brown sugar and butter. Cool until luke-warm, then stir in the yeast. Beat in the eggs and salt. Add flour gradually to make the dough soft, but not quite sticky. Let dough rise once until doubled. The dough may now be rolled and cut, or stored in the refrigerator for several days to be used as needed. If it is to be stored in the refrigerator, punch the dough down as it rises. Roll the dough on a floured board to a thickness of ½ inch. Cut with a floured cutter and let rise until doubled. Carefully lift the doughnuts off the board and drop into deep hot fat (375°). Fry until browned, turning several times.

FRENCH DOUGHNUTS

Many people have the mistaken notion that any yeast-raised doughnut is a French Doughnut. The real French Doughnut is made with chou paste; it has been known for several centuries. The Spanish Churros and the Portuguese Sonhos are the same mixture, with a slight difference in flavoring, but are always dropped from a spoon into the hot fat.

2 cups milk	1 teaspoon vanilla extract, or
¾ cup butter	2 teaspoons grated lemon
⅓ cup water	rind or orange-flower water
2½ cups flour	¼ cup sugar
1 teaspoon salt	7 large eggs

Combine the milk, butter, and water in a saucepan. Bring to a boil and then add the flour all at once. Stir, cooking over medium heat, until the mixture leaves the sides of the pan and forms a ball. Remove the pan to a breadboard and add the salt, then vanilla extract or lemon rind or orange flower water, and the sugar. Add the eggs, one at a time, beating each in thoroughly. Put the dough in a pastry bag with a large tip—the kind used to make cream puffs and éclairs. Form the dough into 3-inch circles on individual pieces of waxed paper. Slip the doughnuts off the paper into hot fat. Cook until well browned and puffed. If desired you may fill the doughnuts with whipped cream, or else glaze them or sprinkle them with powdered sugar.

NOTE. If you do not have a pastry bag, the dough may be dropped into the hot fat from the tip of a spoon, dipping the spoon into the hot fat each time, so that the dough will slip off easily.

FASTNACHT KRAPFEN

In Germany, Shrove Tuesday is an important holiday. Either as a last gastronomic splurge before the forty days of Lenten fasting, or to use up the butters and fats that weren't allowed during Lent, the making of these delicious rich doughnuts was, and in some places still is, a tradition among German people.

1 cup hot mashed potatoes	1 cup warm water or scalded
2 cups sugar	and cooled milk
1 cake yeast	¾ cup melted butter
1 cup warm water	3 large eggs
or potato water	1 teaspoon salt
7 cups flour	

Combine the hot mashed potatoes, 1 cup of the sugar, the yeast, warm water or potato water, and 1 cup of the flour. Beat until smooth and let rise until dough is light and full of bubbles. Then stir the mixture down and add the remaining 1 cup sugar, the warm water or scalded and cooled milk, melted butter, eggs, salt, and the remaining 6 cups flour. Beat together, adding more flour if necessary to make a firm dough. Brush with butter, cover, and let rise until doubled. Punch the dough down and turn out onto a floured board. Knead lightly. Roll out and cut with a doughnut cutter, or cut with a knife into the traditional diamond shapes. Let set for about 20 minutes. Fry in deep fat at 375° until browned. Roll in powdered sugar when done. This recipe makes from 5 to 6 dozen doughnuts but is easily halved. If desired the dough may be kept in the refrigerator for several days to be used as needed.

HUNGARIAN DOUGHNUTS

The Hungarians have a reputation for delicious pastries and doughnuts. While I would never argue about the pastries, loving them one and all, I had never tasted a good Hungarian doughnut until a friend made these.

1 cake yeast	2 tablespoons sugar
½ cup milk, scalded and cooled	3 egg yolks
	grated rind of 1 lemon
½ cup sour cream, scalded	½ teaspoon salt
2 tablespoons butter	2½ to 3 cups flour

Dissolve the yeast in the scalded and cooled milk. Stir the scalded sour cream into the butter and sugar. Cool. Combine the two liquid mixtures and add the egg yolks. Beat to blend. Stir in the rest of the ingredients, using enough flour to make a soft but workable dough. Refrigerate, punching the dough down as it rises, or if desired let the dough rise at room temperature. Punch the dough down, roll out, and cut into shapes. Let the doughnuts rise again. Deep-fry at 375°. Sprinkle with powdered sugar and serve hot if possible.

PORTUGUESE MALSADAS

These doughnuts may just be sprinkled with powdered sugar, but the traditional way is to dip them in a glaze and let them drip dry.

1 cake yeast	⅓ cup sugar
1 teaspoon sugar	⅓ cup melted butter
¼ cup warm water	1 cup evaporated milk
6 large eggs	1 cup water
6 cups flour	½ teaspoon salt

Dissolve the yeast and the 1 teaspoon sugar in the ¼ cup warm water. Beat the eggs until thick. Put the flour in a large bowl and make a well in the center. Put the dissolved yeast, beaten eggs, and all the remaining ingredients into this well and beat together to make a dough that is soft and smooth. Cover and let rise until doubled. Then stir the dough with a spoon and let it rise again. Now take spoonfuls of the dough, working carefully from the top so that the dough is not disturbed, and drop the spoonfuls into hot deep fat. Fry, turning often. Drain. Glaze or sprinkle with powdered sugar as desired. Best served hot.

DANISH AEBLESKIVER

Aebleskiver translates as "apple slices," and these light doughnuts are so called because the traditional way of serving them is to split them in half and serve with applesauce. There is a special pan for cooking them but lacking this the dough may be dropped from a tablespoon into hot butter and fried as for pancakes, which is just what many Danes insist they are.

3½ cups flour	1 cake yeast
5 large eggs, separated	grated rind of 1 lemon, or 1 tea-
¼ cup sugar	spoon vanilla extract
2 cups milk, scalded and	½ teaspoon salt
cooled	crushed cardamom seed (op-
½ to ⅔ cup butter, melted	tional)

Put the flour in a large bowl. Make a well in the center and into this put the egg yolks, sugar, 1¾ cups of the scalded and cooled milk, and the melted butter. Work together with a spoon. Dissolve the yeast in the remaining ¼ cup milk, and add along with the flavoring and the salt. Beat until smooth. Now beat the egg whites until stiff and fold into the mixture. Set aside to rise until doubled. If you have an Aebleskiver pan, put a little butter into each indentation, spoon some of the batter into each and cook until browned on one side. Then turn with a cooking fork and brown on the other side. Otherwise use a large frying pan and fry spoonfuls of the dough in butter. Serve hot, with powdered sugar, jam, or applesauce.

SNOWBALLEN. This Dutch recipe is very similar, except that it is made with 1 tablespoon baking powder instead of yeast, omits any flavoring ingredient, and adds currants, or raisins. With no flavoring ingredient added, real butter is a must. The traditional Snowballen are deep fried, but we prefer them fried in butter.

FRENCH PUFFS

These are the French Croquignolles, crunchy brown on the outside, snowy white on the inside. The French use equal amounts of sugar and flour, but we find this much too sweet. They also bake the Croquignolles, first cutting the dough in doughnut shapes. We prefer small rounds, deep-fried. Eaten hot, these need no embellishment, but once they cool, a glaze or a sprinkle of powdered sugar is nice.

1 cup sugar	1 teaspoon vanilla extract
5 large egg whites	¼ teaspoon grated lemon rind
3 cups flour	(optional)
1 teaspoon baking powder	

Combine all ingredients and blend well first with a wooden spoon, and then with clean hands. Turn dough out on a lightly floured breadboard and knead until mixture is a mass of dough. Roll or pat to a thickness of approximately ¼ inch Cut into small rounds with a 1½-inch biscuit cutter. Deep-fry the rounds, watching constantly, as they cook very quickly. Turn once or twice. Drain and serve hot.

7. *Pancakes and Waffles*

PANCAKES

Whether you call them slapjacks, flapjacks, wheats, flannel cakes, griddle cakes, batter cakes, hotcakes, stack o' cakes, pancakes, or crêpes, the chances are that the familiar pancake has been a family favorite as far back as you can remember. Probably the most universally popular "bread" in history, the pancake has achieved the distinction of having restaurant chains center their complete menus around various pancakes served with assorted syrups.

In England, Shrove Tuesday is known as "pancake day," and since the fifteenth century the town of Olney has celebrated Shrove Tuesday with a pancake race, during which only women over the age of eighteen can participate. Each woman must toss, and catch, a pancake at least three times during the race. In America, the town of Liberal, Kansas, has a pancake race, in sisterly competition with Olney.

In recent years pancakes have earned the right to appear at other meals besides breakfast, and in ways other than with syrup and link sausages. They can be rolled, enchilada style, with a cheese or meat filling inside and served with a sauce. Or they may be stacked in a round casserole with the filling between layers and a light sauce on top. This combination, baked and cut into wedges to serve, makes a delicious and filling main dish.

I must admit that my favorite desserts are based on crêpes, wafer-thin or puffy. Light or puffy crêpes, whatever the recipe, may be layered with a filling, sprinkled with powdered sugar, and glazed in the oven or under the broiler. One of our favorite dessert fillings consists of apricot preserves and whipped cream; another is cottage cheese and any sliced fresh fruit in season. With either of these a sour-cream sauce is very good.

The Hungarians make a famous dessert of thin crêpes, stacked, with grated German's sweet chocolate between layers. The top layer is spread with meringue, and the whole thing is put into the oven to brown the meringue. Cut into wedges, this is both delicious and impressive.

Pancakes have many uses, not all as dramatic, but often more practical. Leftover pancakes can be used as the basis for any layered and filled main dish. And children love leftover pancakes rolled around jam, or preserves, or peanut butter.

There are so many pancake recipes, all so very good, that a book could be written entirely about pancakes and the different ways of serving them.

Pancake batter is best when it stands for several hours before baking. This is convenient, as the batter may be then stored in the refrigerator for several days. In any pancake recipe, the eggs may be separated and beaten into the batter separately, making lighter, fluffier pancakes. If you store the batter, or let it stand for several hours, add the stiffly beaten egg whites at the last.

PANCAKE AND WAFFLE TOPPINGS

The toppings for pancakes and waffles are almost too numerous to list. You can use brown-sugar syrup, molasses, corn syrup, sorghum, maple syrup, melted butter, jelly, jam, preserves, crushed fresh fruit in season, or any number of vegetable, seafood, poultry and meat mixtures. Any of the flavored or whipped butters listed on page 189 may be used; these are in fact preferred by many people. Naturally not every topping goes with every pancake or waffle. Lemon Butter would be as ridiculous on Buckwheat Cakes as would a Cheddar cheese sauce on Cottage-Cheese Pancakes. Most of the toppings listed here are for dessert or breakfast pancakes; dinner sauces may be found in any basic cookbook.

HONEY SPREAD FOR WAFFLES, PANCAKES, OR FRENCH TOAST. Combine equal amounts of honey and heavy sweet or sour cream. Beat with an electric mixer until thoroughly blended and fluffy. Store in a refrigerator and use as needed.

BROWN-SUGAR SYRUP. Combine 1 pound brown sugar with 2 cups water. Boil for 3 minutes and then add ½ cup butter.

ORANGE-HONEY SYRUP. Combine 1 cup honey, 1 cup hot orange juice, ⅓ cup butter, and 1 tablespoon lemon juice. Heat thoroughly.

OUR FAVORITE PANCAKE SYRUP. A very simple mixture of equal parts of maple syrup and butter heated together. I occasionally add a tablespoon or more of brandy or rum.

HONEY FRUIT SYRUP. Equal parts of honey (or maple syrup) and fruit syrup, heated together, makes another excellent topping.

SOUR-CREAM TOPPING

1 cup commercial sour cream	1 tablespoon grated orange rind
1 teaspoon vanilla extract	2 tablespoons sugar

Mix ingredients until well blended. The character of this delicious sauce can be changed with the flavoring. A teaspoon of cinnamon or nutmeg could be added, or used in place of the vanilla extract or the orange rind. Brown sugar could be used instead of white, or lemon rind instead of orange rind. This is a variable and very good basic sauce.

LEMON BUTTER

An excellent recipe that has been in use for several centuries. Old cookbooks call it Lemon Cheese. It can also be used as a cake filling or as a filling for tarts. We like it on toast or rolls, and as a filling for dessert crêpes, rolled and served with spoonfuls of sour cream.

½ cup butter	1½ cups sugar
grated rind of 2 lemons	pinch of salt
½ cup fresh lemon juice	4 large eggs

Melt the butter in the top of a double boiler. Stir in the lemon rind and juice, the sugar, and a pinch of salt. Beat the eggs and blend into the sugar mixture. Cook over boiling water, stirring continuously, until thick —approximately 20 minutes. Cool and store in the refrigerator. This butter will keep for several weeks.

CRANBERRY SAUCE

In the Scandinavian countries lingonberries are used, but we prefer fresh cranberries. Very thinly sliced apples are sometimes added.

4 cups fresh cranberries	2½ cups sugar
1 cup water or orange juice	1 lemon, sliced very thin

Combine all ingredients in a saucepan. Bring to a boil and then reduce heat. Let the sauce simmer until thickened, stirring constantly. This will keep, refrigerated, for several weeks.

FRUIT SYRUP FOR PANCAKES

3½ cups chopped fresh apricots, peaches, cherries, or strawberries, or other berries	1 package powdered pectin
	1 cup light corn syrup
	1 cup water
½ cup fresh lemon juice	1½ cups sugar

Using a blender, blend the fruit and the lemon juice until smooth. Put the mixture into a 3-quart saucepan and add the pectin. Stir well and set aside for 30 minutes, stirring occasionally. Add the corn syrup and water and mix well. Stir the sugar into the mixture gradually. Using a candy thermometer, heat the mixture to 100° or until sugar is dissolved. Cool. Pour into jars or plastic containers. Store in refrigerator.

FRUIT SAUCE FOR CRÊPES

1 No. 2½ can fruit (fruit cock-
tail, peaches, or Bing
cherries)
1 teaspoon cornstarch or
arrowroot

1 or 2 tablespoons brandy,
rum, cognac or Cherry
Heering

Drain the fruit, reserving the juice—there will be about 1 cup. Mix the cornstarch or arrowroot with a little cold juice. Cook the remaining juice until it has thickened slightly, then add the cornstarch or arrowroot mixture. Cook at a very slow boil, until the sauce is thick and clear. Add the fruit and liquor. Pour the sauce over rolled crêpes and heat them in the oven.

FRENCH CRÊPES

French Crêpes are among the lightest, and most versatile of all pancakes. We give a few variations; you will think of many more. Always let the batter stand at room temperature for several hours before cooking, except when the eggs are beaten in separately. In this case mix the batter as directed but do *not* add the egg whites. Let the batter stand. Fold the stiffly beaten whites in at the last minute.

2 cups flour
½ cup sugar
5 large eggs
¾ cup cream

2 cups milk
2 tablespoons brandy
3 tablespoons melted butter

Sift the flour and sugar into a large bowl. Beat the eggs until light and pour them in. Add the remaining ingredients and beat until smooth. Let the batter stand at room temperature for several hours before baking. Make thin cakes on a lightly buttered griddle. Or use a 5- or 6-inch skillet and melt 1 teaspoon butter in the bottom. Pour in about ¼ cup of batter, tilting the pan so that the batter covers the bottom of it. The batter is so thin that crêpes baked in a skillet don't need turning. Use with any of the following variations.

FILLINGS FOR CRÊPES

1. Fill the crêpes with orange marmalade, using 2 tablespoons rum or brandy to each cup of marmalade. Roll the crêpes and sprinkle them with powdered sugar. Glaze under the broiler, or heat in the oven.

2. Serve the crêpes with sweet butter and a sprinkling of sugar and lemon juice.

3. Put half a fried banana in the center of each crêpe. Roll them up and place, seam side down, in a baking dish. Sprinkle liberally with brown sugar and flame with cognac or rum.

4. Roll the crêpes and keep them hot. Serve with a sauce made by beating together brown sugar and sour cream.

5. Mash any desired fresh berries with sugar to taste and a small amount of melted sweet butter. Spread on crêpes and roll. Sprinkle with powdered sugar and serve.

6. Spread with a mixture of brown sugar, chopped nuts, and cinnamon. Roll and serve with sour cream.

7. Combine 1 cup apricot preserves and ½ cup heavy cream, whipped. Spread on crêpes and roll. Sprinkle with sugar and serve.

BLINTZES

Use the recipe for French Crêpes, omitting the sugar and liquor, to make excellent Jewish Blintzes. Fry on one side only. Spread any of the following fillings on the fried side and roll. Place them on a platter seam side down until ready to finish. This may be done hours ahead and the final frying done at serving time. When ready to serve, brown the rolled Blintzes in butter. Those with sweet fillings should be sprinkled with sugar and cinnamon and a little melted sweet butter. Serve with sour cream if desired.

FILLINGS FOR BLINTZES

1. Combine 1 pound cottage cheese, drained, with 1 egg, 2 tablespoons sugar, 1 tablespoon heavy cream, and 2 teaspoons lemon juice. Serve these with sour cream.

2. To the preceding cottage-cheese filling, add 1 cup or more sliced fresh strawberries.

3. As a filling use grated Cheddar cheese. Roll Blintzes, fry in butter, and serve with a cheese sauce.

4. For a luncheon dish, roll the Blintzes around any desired filling, brown, and serve with gravy or a sauce.

5. Roll the Blintzes without a filling, brown them, and serve with gravy or a cheese or mushroom sauce.

6. For hot appetizers, make smaller Blintzes and roll them around pieces of smoked salmon. Brown at the last minute.

7. Fill the Blintzes with a mixture of sliced fresh mushrooms and minced onion, sautéed in butter. Roll, brown, and serve with a light gravy.

DELICIOUS-NUTRITIOUS HOTCAKES

This is an excellent recipe to use if you make hotcakes often. You can make the batter when convenient and keep it in the refrigerator.

1¼ cups whole-wheat flour	3 large, or extra large, eggs
¾ cup skim-milk powder	3 tablespoons melted butter
1 teaspoon salt	¾ cup wheat germ
2½ teaspoons baking powder	
2 cups milk, sour milk, buttermilk, or yogurt	

Combine the flour, skim-milk powder, salt, and baking powder. Add the liquid, the eggs, and the melted butter, then stir in wheat germ last. Bake as usual on a hot, lightly buttered griddle.

NOTE. If desired, ½ to ¾ cup of rice polish, soy flour, or cornmeal may replace the same amount of flour. All of these are very good.

DELICIOUS CORNMEAL PANCAKES

A wonderful Sunday morning hotcake recipe. Besides being delicious, these are quickly made. If you prefer thinner pancakes, add another large egg to the batter.

2 cups sour cream or yogurt
½ cup flour
1 teaspoon sugar
2 large eggs

1 teaspoon soda
1 cup coarsely ground corn-meal

Combine ingredients in the order listed. Beat until thoroughly blended. Bake as usual.

PIONEER HOTCAKES

These delicious hotcakes have been a Sunday morning tradition in one family for over fifty years. They serve the hotcakes with melted butter and brown sugar. We serve them as a dessert by stacking them three deep, with brown sugar and crushed fresh fruit between the layers and on top. A hearty dessert for a light meal.

2 cups boiling water
1½ cups cornmeal
2 tablespoons molasses
2 cups buttermilk
5 large eggs

3 cups flour
2 tablespoons baking powder
1 tablespoon salt
½ teaspoon soda
⅓ cup melted butter

Pour the boiling water over the cornmeal and molasses and stir until cooled and thick. Beat in the buttermilk and eggs. Sift the dry ingredients and stir into the batter. Add the melted butter last. Bake on a hot, lightly buttered griddle. We usually use ¼ cup of batter for each cake; for giant hotcakes, use ½ cup of batter.

PEANUT-BUTTER HOTCAKES

Children love these. Make batter several hours before using.

⅓ cup melted butter	1 teaspoon sugar
⅓ cup peanut butter	1¼ cups milk
2 medium eggs	1¼ cups flour
¼ teaspoon salt	6 slices bacon, cooked until
1¼ teaspoon baking powder	crisp and crumbled

Beat the melted butter, peanut butter, and eggs thoroughly. Add the rest of ingredients, stirring in the bacon last. Bake as usual and serve with melted butter.

SPECIAL CORN CAKES

Delicious cakes made with a combination of flours.

2 cups flour	1 teaspoon soda
1 cup cornmeal	1 tablespoon baking powder
1 cup whole-wheat flour	3 large eggs
1 cup bran flakes	1 quart buttermilk
1 teaspoon salt	¼ cup melted butter

Combine the dry ingredients and stir in the eggs, buttermilk, and melted butter, beating thoroughly. If the batter is too thick, thin with a little sweet milk, or with another large egg. Bake on a lightly buttered griddle.

COTTAGE-CHEESE PANCAKES

This and the following recipe and the variations are for dessert pancakes. The variations of these basic recipes are practically endless; I've included our favorites.

1 cup cottage cheese ⅓ cup flour
6 large eggs ⅓ cup melted butter
pinch of salt

Put the cheese in a blender and blend until smooth. Add the rest of ingredients and beat thoroughly. Make small pancakes by dropping the batter
from a spoon onto a hot buttered griddle. Serve with jelly, jam, or applesauce.

V A R I A T I O N. The Norwegians make a very similar pancake, using
rye flour. Whole-wheat flour may also be used.

SOUR-CREAM PANCAKES

1 cup cottage cheese 1 cup flour
1 cup sour cream 1 tablespoon sugar
6 large eggs 1 teaspoon baking powder
pinch salt

Put the cottage cheese in a blender and blend until smooth. Add the rest
of the ingredients and beat thoroughly. Drop the batter from a spoon
onto a hot buttered griddle, making small cakes.

VARIATIONS

1. Omit the cottage cheese and baking powder. Separate the eggs, and
beat in the yolks and whites separately.

2. Use only ½ cup flour and omit the cottage cheese and baking powder. Separate the eggs and beat yolks and whites separately before adding.

3. Make the basic recipe, omitting the cottage cheese and baking powder and using 2 cups sour cream, ¼ cup sugar, and 5 large eggs, yolks
and whites beaten separately before adding.

NOTE. Serve any Sour-Cream Pancakes with powdered sugar and lemon
juice, or with powdered sugar and orange wedges to squeeze over the

cakes. Or serve with jelly, jam, preserves, applesauce, or with brown sugar beaten with more sour cream.

DINNER CHEESE PANCAKES

We love these as a light meal, when we serve them with a sauce made with 1 small can evaporated milk, half as much regular milk, 2 egg yolks, and ½ pound (or a little less) grated Cheddar cheese, mixed and simmered, stirring constantly, over medium heat until thickened.

4 large eggs, separated	¼ cup flour
¼ cup melted butter	5 tablespoons cream
¼ cup grated Parmesan or Romano cheese	pinch of salt

Combine the egg yolks and the melted butter. Add the cheese, flour, cream, salt, and stiffly beaten egg whites. Bake as for regular pancakes on a hot griddle. Roll and serve with Cheese Sauce.

DINNER CRÊPES

Similar to Danish Pandekager, these excellent crêpes have the tang of beer, and are especially good with a filling of grated cheese and sliced ripe olives. Roll the crêpes, and serve with a sprinkle of grated cheese on top, or with a cheese sauce.

2 cups flour	3 large eggs
1 cup beer	½ teaspoon salt
½ cup milk or water	

Combine ingredients in the order listed and beat until the batter is smooth. Let the batter stand for several hours before baking. The secret of these fine crêpes is to make them very thin.

FAVORITE BUTTERMILK HOTCAKES

Our favorite hotcakes, and some variations.

3½ cups flour	5 large eggs
1 teaspoon salt	1 quart buttermilk
2 teaspoons soda	¼ cup melted butter
2 tablespoons sugar	½ cup wheat germ

Mix the dry ingredients, add the eggs, buttermilk, and melted butter to the dry ingredients, and stir in the wheat germ last. Bake on a lightly buttered hot griddle.

BACON CAKES. Fry the desired amount of bacon until crisp. Drain. Put the bacon on the griddle and pour the batter over it. Use 2 or 3 slices of bacon in each cake.

BLUEBERRY CAKES. Just before using the batter, stir in 1 cup, or more, of fresh blueberries, or 1 can of blueberries well drained.

FRANKFURTER CAKES. Slice frankfurters thin and brown on a buttered griddle. Pour hotcake batter over slices and bake as usual.

FRUITED CAKES. To the batter add 1 cup finely chopped, or grated and drained, apple; or 1 cup chopped bananas; or 1 9-ounce can crushed pineapple, well drained. Or right before using, stir in a cup of sliced strawberries.

OATMEAL CAKES. Use 1 cup of cooked oatmeal or other cooked cereal in place of as much flour. This is a good use for leftover cereal as any cooked cereal may be used.

ONION CAKES. Sauté 1 cup or more minced onions in butter until done. Stir into batter. Bake as usual. Serve as a base for gravy or creamed dried beef.

OYSTER CAKES. Make half the recipe for Favorite Buttermilk Hotcakes, using the oyster liquor in place of an equal amount of buttermilk. Use 3 or 4 small oysters in each hotcake and make the cakes small. Bake as usual. These are very good as a side dish.

RYE CAKES. Use rye flour instead of half the white flour.

WHOLE-WHEAT CAKES. Use whole-wheat flour instead of half the white flour.

RYE CAKES

These used to be known as Jolly Boys and are very good.

2 cups rye flour (part may be rye meal)	⅔ cup brown sugar
1½ teaspoons baking powder	4 large eggs
1 teaspoon soda	¼ cup melted butter
1 teaspoon salt	2 cups buttermilk

Combine the dry ingredients and stir in the other ingredients. Thin with more buttermilk if necessary, but do not stir too much. Bake on a hot griddle and serve with syrup.

FINNISH WHOLE-GRAIN PANCAKES

In Sweden the same pancakes are made, using white flour instead of whole-grain, and increasing the sugar to ¼ cup.

3 cups milk	2 cups graham or whole-wheat flour, or a mixture of rye and white
1 cup water	
1 teaspoon salt	
2 tablespoons melted butter	2 large eggs
	2 teaspoons honey or sugar

Combine ingredients and beat thoroughly. Let batter stand at room temperature for several hours before baking. If served as a dessert, sprinkle the cakes with powdered sugar and serve with Cranberry Sauce.

APPLE PFANKUCHEN
(German Apple Pancake)

This is one of the easiest and at the same time one of the most delectable dishes that I've ever come upon. It takes no ingredients that are not likely to be found in the average household and is as light as a soufflé, but more durable. Traditionally it is served as a dessert, but we like it with a soup or salad lunch. If any is left over, it is good cold. To make 6 servings, I've doubled the recipe as it was given to me; if you halve the ingredients, use a 10-inch skillet and bake for 10 minutes.

½ cup plus 1 tablespoon flour	1 teaspoon vanilla extract
½ teaspoon baking powder	¼ cup lemon juice
¼ teaspoon salt	3 cups pared and finely diced
6 large eggs, separated	apple
1 cup sugar	¼ cup butter
½ cup, plus 1 tablespoon milk	1 teaspoon cinnamon

Sift the flour, baking powder, and salt. Beat the egg whites until foamy and gradually beat in ¾ cup of the sugar. Continue beating until whites are stiff. Beat the egg yolks until thickened and beat in the milk and vanilla extract. Pour the lemon juice over the apples. Beat the milk mixture into the flour, beating until smooth. Now fold in the egg whites and the apples. Melt the butter in a 12- or 14-inch skillet. Pour the pancake mixture in and sprinkle it with the rest of the sugar and the cinnamon. Bake in a 375° oven until set and lightly browned—about 15 minutes. Cut into 6 large wedges and serve with sugar and lemon juice to sprinkle over the wedges.

WHEAT-GERM PFANKUCHEN. This is very good in addition to being nutritious. To the batter add ⅓ cup wheat germ. The wheat germ adds a nutty flavor.

RICE HOTCAKES

Serve these as you would Potato Pancakes, for a side dish with a meal.

1 cup cold boiled rice	1 teaspoon baking powder
2 cups flour	¼ cup melted butter
1 teaspoon salt	1 cup milk
2 large eggs	

Combine the ingredients in the order listed and beat just until thoroughly blended. Bake on a hot griddle.

POTATO PANCAKES

There are many varieties of the Potato Pancake. Some recipes use grated raw potatoes, well drained and mixed with crumbled cooked bacon and perhaps some flour. Our favorite uses leftover mashed potatoes. All the varieties are called pancakes, but essentially they are ways of cooking potatoes, and as such they are served as a side dish with ham or pork, usually accompanied by applesauce.

2 cups leftover mashed potatoes	½ teaspoon salt
	¼ to ⅓ cup cream
2 egg yolks	¼ to ⅓ cup flour
2 tablespoons minced onion	

Combine the ingredients in the order listed. Start with the smaller amounts of cream and flour and add more if necessary. Shape into cakes and fry in bacon fat.

I'm come a-shaving—for a piece of pancake,
Or a piece of bacon, or a little truckle cheese
Of your own making. If you give me a little I'll ask you no more;
If you don't give me nothing, I'll rattle your door.

—OLD ENGLISH FOLK CHANT

DUTCH BABIES

These are also called Dutch Nannies, the nanny coming from banana. Their similarity to the German Pfankuchen illustrates the common cuisine.

¾ cup cream (milk may be
    used)
6 large eggs
2 tablespoons sugar
¾ cup flour
dash nutmeg, or 1 teaspoon
    vanilla extract

½ teaspoon salt
1 tablespoon sweet butter
powdered sugar
lemon juice
bananas, peaches or other fruit

Beat the cream (or milk) with the eggs. Add the sugar, flour, nutmeg or vanilla extract, and salt. Beat until smooth. Melt the sweet butter in the bottom of a 10-inch skillet. Pour in the batter and fry over direct heat until bottom is browned, then place in a 400° oven until the top is browned and the pancake cooked through. If desired, the pancake may be baked in the oven entirely, at 425° for about 15 to 20 minutes. When the pancake is done, sprinkle it with powdered sugar and lemon juice, and spread with sliced bananas, peaches, or other fresh fruit. Roll up and cut into slices. Serve with more melted sweet butter and sugar.

NOTE. If desired, ⅓ cup of any chopped nuts may be added to the batter and the pancakes rolled around a filling of jam blended with more chopped nuts and 1 tablespoon brandy.

CHOCOLATE HOTCAKES

These are a dessert hotcake, best served sprinkled with powdered sugar and topped with whipped cream. Combine 3 cups flour with 1 tablespoon baking powder, 3 tablespoons sugar, 1 teaspoon salt, and ¼ cup cocoa. Beat in 4 large eggs, 1¾ cups milk, and ⅓ cup melted butter. Make small cakes and bake.

BREADCRUMB GRIDDLECAKES

The oldest American cookbooks all include recipes for this delicacy. Although some ingenious housewife must have invented it for strictly practical reasons, it is still a very good recipe, and worth a place in modern-day files.

1 cup soft breadcrumbs	1 or 2 large eggs
1 cup sour milk or buttermilk	1 tablespoon sugar
½ teaspoon soda	about ½ cup flour

Soak the breadcrumbs in the milk for several hours. Then stir in the rest of ingredients, using enough flour to make a batter thick enough to bake. Bake as usual and serve with any favorite syrup.

WAFFLES

Waffles must have originated in France, as they are known to have been very popular there as early as the twelfth century, when they were sold in the streets, as Sally Lunns and Bath Buns were later in England and Calás in New Orleans.

Waffle batter will keep in the refrigerator for up to a week. If it thickens too much to use, thin it with a little milk, or another egg. Any of the toppings used for Pancakes may be used with waffles, but the smoothness of ice cream, with the crispness of a waffle, makes a special treat.

For a crisp waffle, pour the batter onto the iron thinly; too much batter makes a thick, fluffy waffle. If desired the sugar may be omitted, or cut down, as too much sugar will also keep a waffle from getting crisp.

After you pour the batter onto the iron, and before closing the top, the waffle may be sprinkled with coconut, chopped nuts, or diced bacon, or bacon slices may be put on top.

As with pancakes, the eggs used may be separated and the yolks beaten in first; then the stiffly beaten whites folded into the batter just before using. Egg yolks only may be used in the batter, using 2 yolks for each whole egg called for.

BASIC WAFFLE RECIPE

2 cups flour
1 tablespoon baking powder
½ teaspoon soda
1 teaspoon salt

1½ cups buttermilk, sour milk, cream, milk, yogurt, or sour cream
3 large eggs
½ cup melted butter

Sift the dry ingredients and stir in the liquid ingredients, adding the butter last. Beat until smooth. If possible let batter stand for several hours before using.

BLUEBERRY WAFFLES. Just before using batter, fold in 1 cup of fresh blueberries and 2 tablespoons sugar.

FUDGE WAFFLES. Add ⅓ cup cocoa, 1 teaspoon vanilla extract, and ⅓ cup sugar. Delicious with ice cream.

NUT WAFFLES. Stir in ½ cup, or more, of any chopped nuts.

ORANGE WAFFLES. Use ½ cup orange juice in place of as much milk, and add 1 tablespoon grated orange rind. Slivered, blanched almonds may also be added.

WHOLE-GRAIN WAFFLES. Use ¾ cup cornmeal, rye meal, or whole-wheat or graham flour, in place of same amount of white flour. These are very good, especially the cornmeal variation.

YEAST WAFFLES. Omit the baking powder. Add ½ cake yeast and let the batter rise for several hours before using.

RICE WAFFLES

2 cups flour
½ teaspoon salt
1 tablespoon baking powder
1 tablespoon sugar
1 cup leftover cooked rice
  or cereal

3 large eggs, yolks and whites
  beaten separately
¼ cup melted butter
1¾ cups milk

Combine the dry ingredients with the rice. Stir in liquid ingredients, folding in the beaten egg whites last. Bake immediately.

SWEET-POTATO WAFFLES

2 cups pastry flour or cake flour
4 teaspoons baking powder
pinch of salt
1 tablespoon sugar

2 eggs, beaten separately
1 cup mashed sweet potatoes
1½ cups milk
½ cup melted butter

Combine dry ingredients. Beat in the egg yolks, sweet potatoes, milk, and butter. Beat until smooth. Fold in the stiffly beaten egg whites last. If desired, add ½ teaspoon cinnamon. These are delicious for luncheon or dinner.

8. Sourdough Breads, Biscuits, and Hotcakes

Sourdough breads were probably the first leavened breads known to man and thus are thousands of years old. In modern times, however, sourdough rightly belongs to the Far West. From Arizona to Alaska, the old-time mountain men, sheepherders, prospectors, and miners were so dependent on the pot or pail of sourdough which was always with their provisions that they were nicknamed "sourdoughs." Like the traditional French soup pot, the sourdough pail was self-perpetuating. Replenished regularly it provided its owner with a delicious variety of bread, biscuits, hotcakes, and even, in times of privation when other alcoholic beverages were unavailable, with a type of liquor called "hooch." This was the liquid that rises to the top of the sourdough. Poured off and drunk, it kept many a prospector happy during long winters.

At some time during the late nineteenth century sourdough breads lost their popularity with all but the old-time cooks, for most cookbooks written from that time until recently omitted any mention of what was evidently considered a "primitive" bread.

The best way to start your own sourdough pot is to borrow a starter from a friend who has a bubbly batch going. Lacking this, you may make your own starter by one of the following methods. There is also a commercial starter on the market which requires only water to activate it. For best results use a glass, pottery, or plastic container—never a metal container. Keep the starter in the refrigerator or some other cool place and use it weekly. If you do not use it at least once a week, freshen it every ten days to two weeks by pouring off half of the starter and then blending in equal amounts of milk and flour. Let mixture stand until it bubbles and then store in a cool place. The old sourdoughs warned against using the starter if it turned green but if it turned orange it was still all right. With modern refrigeration this warning is seldom necessary.

If you replenish the starter with equal amounts of milk and flour each time you use it, and either use it frequently or freshen it regularly, it may be kept going indefinitely, and in fact will become better with age.

My favorite starter, which has been in constant use in my home for several years, uses nothing but milk and flour. For those who prefer a yeast starter, a recipe is given.

MY FAVORITE STARTER

Put 1 or 2 cups of milk in a glass or pottery container, cover with cheesecloth, and let stand at room temperature for 24 hours. Then stir in an equal amount of flour and stir to blend well. Cover with cheesecloth again and set the jar outdoors in a protected place, for 12 to 24 hours. Now put the jar in a warm place—the back of the stove will be fine—until it starts to bubble and becomes full of bubbles. This will take from 2 to 5 days, depending on the weather and on the wild yeast cells in the air. Put the starter in a covered container, being careful to leave room enough in the container for the starter to rise if necessary without spilling over, and store it in the refrigerator. Each time it is used replenish the starter by stirring in equal amounts of milk and flour. My batch of starter is so good that I have on occasion used all but a few tablespoons of it and, upon stirring in 1 cup each of milk and flour, had it bubbling almost immediately. You have to learn by experience to gauge the amount of replenishing that the leftover starter will take. If I have quite a bit of starter left, and am planning to use a large amount very soon, I stir in several cups each of milk and flour. But if the starter has been pretty well used, and only a small amount is left, then ½ to 1 cup each of milk and flour is best to start with. Stir in more as the starter reaches the bubbling point.

YEAST STARTER

1 cake yeast	2 cups flour
2 cups warm water	1 tablespoon sugar (optional)

Combine ingredients and place in a glass or pottery container. Cover with cheesecloth and let stand at room temperature for 48 hours, stirring it down several times. If desired, potato water may be used in place of tap water.

Replenish Yeast Starter with equal amounts of water and flour.

NOTE. *Never* add leftover batter to any starter recipe. Whenever a recipe calls for a sponge to be made using the entire amount of starter, plus flour and liquid, be sure to reserve part of the sponge as starter *before* adding any other ingredients. The addition of any ingredients other than those used in a starter recipe (that is, flour, salt, sugar, yeast and liquid) will ruin the starter.

Many sourdough recipes call for blending the starter with an equal amount of flour and either milk or water the night before using, and letting it set at room temperature overnight. When ready to use, the amount needed is poured off and the rest returned to the refrigerator. This method may be followed with any starter recipe. However, if you use the starter often, and keep a large enough quantity of it, you only need to allow it to reach room temperature before using. Then pour off the amount needed, replenish the rest, and let it stand until it bubbles before refrigerating.

Almost every bit of information pertaining to sourdough recommends using soda to counteract the sourness of the sourdough. However, I have found that many recipes using sourdough are better with baking powder than with soda. The omission of soda from several of the recipes in this section is deliberate, not accidental. However, an older sourdough will sometimes need some soda. If the starter is quite sour, you should add ½ to ¾ teaspoon soda to a recipe using 2½ to 3 cups of flour. Experience is required to gauge the sourness, but as you use the starter more often you will learn exactly how to handle it. One final word of caution: never cap the starter jar tightly—they have been known to explode! I use a plastic container and top and have had no problems.

SOURDOUGH STEEL-CUT-OATS BREAD

This is a delicious, crunchy bread, one of our favorites. Steel-cut oats can be bought at health food stores.

2 cups boiling water	⅓ cup melted butter
2 cups steel-cut oats	⅓ cup brown sugar
¼ cup brown sugar	2 teaspoons salt
2 cups white flour	2 cups graham or whole-wheat
1½ cups starter	flour
1 cake yeast	3 cups white flour
½ cup warm water	

Pour the boiling water over the steel-cut oats and let stand until lukewarm. Stir in the ¼ cup brown sugar, 2 cups white flour and the starter. Blend thoroughly, cover the bowl, and let stand for several hours, or in cold weather overnight.

When the sponge is ready, dissolve the yeast in the warm water and add to the sponge along with the rest of the ingredients. Blend well and turn out onto a floured breadboard. Knead, adding more flour as necessary to make a firm, unsticky dough, until dough is smooth and elastic. Return to bowl, brush dough with melted butter, cover, and let the dough rise until doubled.

When dough has doubled, turn it out onto a floured board and knead it down. Then cut it into three pieces and shape into three loaves. Place in buttered loaf pans, cover, and let rise until doubled. Bake in a 350° oven for 45 to 55 minutes. Five minutes before loaves are done, brush them with butter. Turn out onto racks to cool. This bread makes wonderful toast.

SOURDOUGH CRACKED-WHEAT BREAD. Substitute cracked wheat for the steel-cut oats, and use honey or maple syrup in place of the brown sugar. Very good.

SOURDOUGH NUT BREAD. In either of the two preceding recipes, use 1 cup brown sugar and add 1 or 2 cups chopped walnuts.

SOURDOUGH GRAHAM BREAD

2 cups water	⅓ cup brown sugar
1 cup starter	1 cake yeast
6 cups white flour	2 teaspoons soda
1 cup scalded milk	½ cup wheat germ
¼ cup butter	4 cups graham flour
2 teaspoons salt	

Combine the water, starter, and 2 cups of the white flour. Let stand 1 or 2 hours, or overnight if weather is cold. Then pour scalded milk over the butter, salt, and sugar. Stir to melt the butter and then cool the mixture to lukewarm. When it is cooled, stir in the yeast, add to the sourdough batter, and blend well. Then stir in the rest of the white flour and the other ingredients, using enough flour to make a firm dough that is easily workable. Turn out onto a floured board and knead thoroughly. Return to the bowl, cover, and let rise until doubled. Shape into 3 loaves and place in buttered loaf pans. Cover pans and let dough rise until doubled. Then bake in a 400° oven for 15 minutes. Reduce heat to 325° and bake until bread is done, about another 30 minutes.

VARIATION. Replace 1 or 2 cups of the white flour with the same amount of rye flour, rye meal, or cornmeal. Quick oats or old-fashioned oats may also be used in any quantity up to 4 cups replacing an equal amount of flour.

SOURDOUGH FRENCH BREAD

This is probably the most famous of the sourdough breads. There are many recipes, each with a slight but seemingly important difference. This one is our favorite.

1 cup hot water

3 tablespoons sugar

2 tablespoons butter

1 cake yeast, dissolved in 2 tablespoons warm water

1½ cups starter

4 to 5 cups flour

2 teaspoons salt

Pour the hot water over the sugar and butter. Stir to melt the butter. Cool mixture to lukewarm, then add the yeast, starter, 2 cups of the flour, and the salt. Beat to blend ingredients. Now stir in the rest of the flour, using just enough to make a firm dough. Turn the dough out onto a floured breadboard and knead very thoroughly. Place in a buttered bowl, cover, and let rise until doubled. Punch dough down and let rise another 30 minutes. Now turn the dough out onto a floured board again and let it rest for 10 minutes before shaping. The dough may then be shaped into a large round loaf, an oval loaf, or a long, thin loaf, and placed on a cookie sheet. Or it may be put in a 10- by 5-inch loaf pan. Either the cookie sheet or the loaf pan should be well buttered and sprinkled with cornmeal. Let the bread rise until doubled and bake in a 400° oven for approximately 50 minutes. The dough is usually slashed in several places with a very sharp knife or razor blade just prior to baking. If a very sharp instrument is used, the bread will not fall. The best glaze for any hard-crusted bread is an egg white beaten just to blend with 1 tablespoon cold water. Brush this on the bread several times during the baking.

NOTE.   This recipe can also be used to make 12 delicious rolls. Shape the rolls after the first rising and place them on cookie sheets that have been buttered and sprinkled with cornmeal. Cover and let rise again until doubled. Bake in a 400° oven 20 minutes, or until browned and done.

SOURDOUGH ITALIAN BRAID

1¼ cups starter

1 teaspoon salt

1 cup lukewarm water

1½ cups flour

2 cakes or packages yeast

1⅓ cups lukewarm water

½ cup plus 1 teaspoon grated Romano or Parmesan cheese

½ teaspoon salt

½ teaspoon black pepper (preferably coarsely ground)

4 to 5 cups flour

1 teaspoon sesame seed

Early in the morning combine the starter, 1 teaspoon salt, 1 cup luke-warm water, and 1½ cups flour. Beat to blend thoroughly. Cover with a clean towel and set aside for approximately 5 hours. If the sponge has to set for a little longer or shorter period of time, it won't be hurt.

When ready to finish the dough, stir the sponge down. Dissolve the yeast in the lukewarm water and add to the sponge. Now stir in the next 4 ingredients in the order given, adding 4 cups of flour first, and then using the other cup of flour if needed. Turn the dough out onto a lightly floured breadboard and knead thoroughly, about 7 to 10 minutes. Then return the dough to a buttered bowl, cover with a clean towel, and set aside to rise until doubled, about 1 hour. When doubled, punch the dough down and set aside, covered, for another ½ hour.

Now turn the dough out onto a lightly floured board again, and divide into 6 pieces of dough. Roll and stretch each piece of dough into a long rope. Braid 3 of the ropes together for each loaf. Tuck the ends under, and lift each braid into a buttered glass loaf pan. Cover and set aside to rise until doubled again, about 1 hour. Brush loaves with melted butter and sprinkle each loaf with a mixture of 1 teaspoon each sesame seed and grated Romano or Parmesan cheese. Bake loaves in a 375° oven un-til browned and done, about 40 to 45 minutes.

SOURDOUGH CORNBREAD

Sounds unusual, but this is a very good cornbread.

2 cups coarsely ground corn-meal	½ cup butter
	2 cups starter
3 tablespoons brown sugar	2 large eggs
1 teaspoon salt	2 teaspoons baking powder
2 cups scalded milk	

Combine the cornmeal, brown sugar, salt, scalded milk, and butter. Stir to melt the butter and then let the mixture cool to lukewarm. When mix-ture has cooled, stir in the rest of the ingredients and beat well. Pour into a 9- by 13-inch or 8- by 12-inch well-buttered pan. Bake in a 425° oven until the cornbread is browned and done, about 35 to 45 min-utes.

SOURDOUGH BISCUITS

Each sourdough cook seems to have his or her own favorite way of making these biscuits. Some cooks add an egg to the dough; some use less starter. This particular version is our favorite and makes frequent appearances at our breakfast table.

2 cups flour (part whole-wheat)	½ teaspoon salt
1 tablespoon sugar	½ cup butter
2 teaspoons baking powder	2 cups starter

Sift the dry ingredients into a bowl. Cut in butter as for regular biscuits. Stir in the starter until well mixed. Turn the dough onto a lightly floured breadboard and knead very lightly. Roll dough ½ inch thick and cut into small rounds. Place them on a buttered cookie sheet and bake in a 425° oven for about 10 minutes. Watch these as they burn quickly.

SOURDOUGH HOTCAKES

Some good cooks separate the eggs and fold the beaten whites in separately. Almost any variation used with regular pancakes can be used with sourdoughs.

1 cup starter	⅓ cup milk, evaporated milk, cream, or half-and-half
2 cups lukewarm water	
2½ cups flour	2 tablespoons bacon fat
2 large eggs	1 teaspoon soda
2 tablespoons sugar	

Combine the starter, water, and flour. Let stand in the bowl for several hours or overnight. When ready to use the batter, stir in the rest of ingredients and beat thoroughly. Let the mixture stand for 10 minutes, then fry on a lightly greased griddle, using 2 tablespoons batter for each cake.

SOURDOUGH BUCKWHEAT HOTCAKES. Use up to 1½ cups buckwheat flour in place of same amount of white flour.

SOURDOUGH CORNMEAL HOTCAKES. These are delicious! I add ½ cup cornmeal to the batter. Or you can use 2 cups flour and 1 cup cornmeal.

SOURDOUGH POTATO HOTCAKES. Grate 3 or 4 medium-sized raw potatoes and add to batter. Fry as usual, and serve with applesauce and sausage, preferably Polish sausage.

SOURDOUGH WAFFLES. To the batter for Sourdough Hotcakes add another 2 tablespoons bacon fat. Make as usual. Very good.

SOURDOUGH MUFFINS

These are similar to English muffins. They are equally good served hot from the griddle or split and toasted. If desired, they can be made the day before, cut, placed on cookie sheets, covered with plastic wrap, and refrigerated for up to 24 hours before baking.

1 cup starter	3 tablespoons sugar
2 cups milk	1 teaspoon salt
1 cup cornmeal	1 teaspoon soda
3½ cups flour	1 large egg

Combine the starter, milk, cornmeal, and 1½ cups of the flour. Stir to blend ingredients, cover the bowl, and let the mixture stand overnight. When ready, stir mixture down and add the rest of the flour and all the other ingredients. Mix well, then turn out onto a floured breadboard and knead thoroughly. Roll the dough to a thickness of no more than ½ inch and cut with a large biscuit cutter. Cover the muffins. Let them rise at room temperature for 45 minutes. Bake on a lightly buttered griddle at 300° for 10 to 12 minutes on each side. Turn only once. If you are refrigerating the muffins, cut, and refrigerate. When you take them out of the refrigerator let them come to room temperature and then rise for 45 minutes before baking. Bake the same way.

9. Baking-Powder Tea Breads and Coffee Cakes

Baking powder, as a prepared mixture designed to make breads rise faster, was invented by a German, for German housewives. Before this, European breads, if not yeast-raised, were raised either with stiffly beaten egg whites, or with the gentle action of thickly beaten, slightly warmed whole eggs (as was the Mandel Kuchen), or else were intended to make a compact loaf (as was the French Pain d'Épices), which was then cut into very thin slices and served with either sweet butter or a berry jam.

American housewives had already, for many years, been raising "quick" breads with a combination of soda, called saleratus, and either alum or cream of tartar. Some old recipes called for "pearlash, the size of a hazle-nut." Many old griddle cake and corn cake recipes called for no leavening at all; these were expected to be compact and filling, rather than light and fluffy.

The vast assortment of baking-powder-raised sweet breads is uniquely American, brought about by a desire for something more substantial than cake, without the tedium of kneading, shaping, and leavening to rise. The method of mixing the breads is the same as that for mixing a muffin batter—that is, the liquid ingredients are stirred into the dry ingredients just until everything is moistened. The batter is never beaten unless a recipe specifically calls for it.

Because the flavoring ingredients in baking-powder breads are so flexible, the variations are literally endless. For example, in a marmalade nut bread, the marmalade used is usually orange, but a grapefruit or lime marmalade could be used, or a combination of marmalades, or a combination of orange marmalade and apricot preserves. Any of these would change the character of the bread. In a plain nut bread, maraschino cherries can be added, with the cherry juice substituting for part of the liquid called for; the bread is then quite different. Or any two compatible breads may be marbled, with delicious results. For example, a batch each of orange nut bread and banana nut bread, dropped by alternating spoonfuls into buttered loaf pans and baked, makes an intriguing and deliciously different loaf.

Many baking-powder bread desserts are based on a biscuit dough. A richer, slightly sweet biscuit dough is rolled into a rectangle, and spread with any desired filling: chopped apples, sugar, nuts, and cinnamon; blackberries and sugar; chopped, cooked sweet dried apricots; an orange filling, or chopped fresh peaches with cinnamon and sugar. Rolled jelly-roll fashion, the dough is placed, seam side down, on a buttered cookie sheet and baked in a 400° oven for about 25 to 30 minutes. These are called Roly Polys and are usually sliced and served with heavy cream. However, the dough can be sliced before baking, and the slices placed close together on buttered cookie sheets. Or the roll of dough can be placed in a buttered loaf pan. Frosted while warm, it makes an attractive loaf.

Quick breads freeze well and are so easily made that if you entertain often, or have a large family, it is a good idea to keep several varieties on hand. An assortment of baking-powder or yeast breads, sliced thin and served with whipped butter and whipped cream cheese and either Espresso or Turkish coffee, laced with cognac, makes a dessert acceptable to the most sophisticated tastes. The younger set prefers the thin slices buttered in advance and served with hot chocolate topped with marshmallows and stirred with a cinnamon stick.

All baking-powder breads are improved by being allowed to stand at room temperature for 20 minutes before being placed in the oven. This allows the batter to rise—very slightly, but enough to allow the bread to bake without having the top of the loaf crack open while baking.

Old-time cooks always added 1 tablespoon to ¼ cup of rum or brandy to sweet breads. The liquor makes the loaf somewhat lighter, and adds a pleasantly sophisticated flavor.

FRUIT AND NUT BREADS

APRICOT NUT BREAD

This basic recipe can be changed by using different fruit. Dried peaches, nectarines, or pears may be used, or a combination of these. Instead of slivered, blanched almonds, walnuts may be used. A teaspoon of grated orange rind is an excellent addition to any dried-fruit bread.

½ cup sugar	1 cup cooked dried apricots
2 tablespoons butter	2 cups flour
1 large egg	4 teaspoons baking powder
1 cup sour milk or sour cream	½ teaspoon soda
1 cup bran	½ teaspoon salt
½ cup slivered, blanched almonds	2 teaspoons grated orange rind

Cream the sugar and butter. Add the egg and the sour milk or sour cream. Stir in the bran, nuts, and the cooked, well-drained fruit. Sift the dry ingredients and stir into the mixture. Pour into a buttered 9-inch loaf pan and let stand at room temperature for 15 to 20 minutes. Bake in a 350° oven for about 1 hour. Cool overnight before cutting in thin slices.

VARIATION. Use 1 cup orange juice or apricot nectar as the liquid. Omit the soda and follow the directions in the preceding recipe.

AUSTRALIAN BRAN BREAD

This recipe comes from the editor of the *West Australian,* a Perth news-paper. The Golden Syrup called for is available in some large markets, but lacking it, honey is a most acceptable substitute. I happen to have two 7-inch cake pans, one 2 inches deep in which I put the batter, and one 1-inch deep with which I cover it. However, a loaf pan may be used with another loaf pan over it. This is a good breakfast bread and may be eaten hot or cold.

3 cups self-raising flour	1 tablespoon butter
1 cup bran flakes	1 cup boiling water
½ teaspoon salt	1 cup cold milk
4 teaspoons Golden Syrup or honey	golden raisins (optional)

Combine flour, bran flakes, and salt. Add the Golden Syrup or honey and the butter to the boiling water. Then stir in the cold milk, and immediately pour into the dry ingredients. If the raisins are used, stir them in ⅓ cup more flour until they are well coated. Stir this into the batter until well blended. Put the loaf into a 7-inch cake pan that has been well buttered. Cover with another pan, place in a 400° oven, and bake for 50 to 60 minutes. Remove the cover during the last 15 minutes, so that the bread will brown.

BANANA DATE LOAF

There are times when making even a quick bread from scratch is impossible. Then the mixes become a real blessing, especially when imagination is an added ingredient.

¾ cup mashed ripe bananas	1 package date muffin mix
⅓ cup water	

Combine the mashed bananas and water. Prepare the batter from the muffin mix according to package directions, using the banana-water mixture in place of water. Pour into a buttered 9- by 5- by 3-inch loaf pan. Bake in a 350° oven for 45 to 55 minutes, or until well done. Remove from pan and cool. The loaf will slice better the second day.

TEATIME SLICES

A quickie to make from a mix—and no one will ever guess.

1 package orange muffin mix   1 cup chopped walnuts
¾ cup canned whole-
    cranberry sauce

Prepare the batter from the muffin mix according to package directions. Fold in the cranberry sauce and nuts. Spoon into 6 greased 6-ounce frozen-juice-concentrate cans. Bake in a 375° oven 30 to 35 minutes. Cool 5 minutes, then immediately ease out of the cans with a spatula. For dainty, thin slices, wait until the second day to slice. This is good with cream cheese between the slices.

BASIC NUT BREAD

This is a gem of a recipe—a nut bread so simple that it can be whipped up in just minutes, and yet I've never tasted a better plain nut bread. Each of the variations is as simple as the basic recipe, and each makes a deliciously different bread.

1½ to 2 cups white sugar or   2 large eggs, beaten
    brown sugar   1 teaspoon salt
½ cup melted butter or very   5 cups flour
    soft butter   2 tablespoons baking powder
1¾ cups milk   2 cups chopped nuts

Combine the sugar, melted butter, milk, and eggs. Stir until well blended. Sift salt, flour, and baking powder. Add the nuts and stir them through the flour so that they are well coated. Stir the dry ingredients into the liquid ingredients until the dry ingredients are thoroughly moistened. Pour the batter into 2 well-buttered loaf pans and let stand for 20 minutes. Bake in a 350° oven until browned and done, about 1 hour. Be sure to test the loaves before removing from the oven. A toothpick or cake tester thrust into the center of the bread should come out clean.

APPLE-BUTTER NUT BREAD.   Substitute apple butter for the milk, and use 4 eggs. If desired, add 1 teaspoon cinnamon and use half brown sugar and half white.

APPLESAUCE NUT BREAD.   Use canned applesauce in place of the milk. If the batter is too thick, thin with another egg. Add 1 teaspoon cinnamon, and use half brown sugar and half white.

BUTTERMILK NUT BREAD.   Use 1½ cups buttermilk instead of the 1¾ cups milk. Use 3 eggs. Use 1 teaspoon soda and 4 teaspoons baking powder instead of 2 tablespoons baking powder.

CRANBERRY NUT BREAD.   Decrease baking powder to 1 tablespoon and add 1 teaspoon soda to dry ingredients. Substitute orange juice for milk. Last, fold in 3 to 4 cups chopped fresh cranberries blended with 2 tablespoons grated orange rind.

FILBERT BREAD.   Use brown sugar and buttermilk, and make the nuts chopped filberts or slivered Brazil nuts. Add 1 teaspoon soda, and decrease baking powder to 4 teaspoons.

FRUIT-NUT BREAD.   Omit the milk and use 1 cup each orange juice and mashed bananas. Use 1 cup of candied fruits in place of 1 cup nuts, if desired. This makes a good holiday bread.

HAWAIIAN NUT BREAD.   Use brown sugar. Omit the milk. Drain 2 cans mandarin orange slices (or mandarin orange slices and pineapple tidbits), and add water to the liquid to make 1½ cups. Combine the fruit and a 3½ ounce jar chopped macadamia nuts. Stir into the dry ingredients. Follow directions in Basic Nut Bread recipe, adding 1 tablespoon grated orange rind, if desired. Very good.

JAM OR MARMALADE NUT BREAD.   To basic recipe add ¾ cup of any stiff jam, preserve, or marmalade.

PEANUT-BUTTER BREAD.   In the basic recipe, replace the chopped nuts with 2 cups crunchy peanut butter. Use only 4½ cups flour.

PUMPKIN NUT BREAD. Omit milk and use 1¾ cups canned pumpkin. Use 3 eggs and add 1 teaspoon cinnamon, ½ teaspoon nutmeg, and the grated rind of 1 lemon.

SOUR-CREAM NUT BREAD. Substitute sour cream for milk. For leavening use 4 teaspoons baking powder and 1 teaspoon soda. Add 1 teaspoon each vanilla extract and grated lemon rind or orange rind. Bake 1¼ hours.

SWEET ORANGE SLICE. Add 1 tablespoon grated orange rind, and use 1 cup chopped candied orange slices in place of 1 cup of nuts.

WHOLE-GRAIN NUT BREAD. Use 1 or 2 cups whole-wheat or graham flour, in place of as much white. Or use 1 cup bran flakes in place of 1 cup of the white flour. When using whole-grain flour, use brown sugar as half or all the sugar. If desired 1 cup rye flour could be used. Any nuts or combinations of nuts may be used. Chopped papaya can be added to the basic recipe. And dates or raisins are delicious (about 1½ cups chopped dates or raisins to 1 cup chopped nuts). Any kind of fresh berries, in amounts up to 2 cups, could be used. One or 2 cups of fine dry breadcrumbs can replace the same amount of flour. If all brown sugar is used, you have a delicious Butterscotch Nut Bread. Candied fruit can replace part or all of the chopped nuts. For an Olive Bread, good with buffets, omit the sugar and add 2 cups sliced ripe olives. All of these ideas have been tried, and enjoyed.

BANANA NUT BREAD

A delicious bread that stays moist.

½ cup butter	½ teaspoon salt
1 cup white or brown sugar	½ teaspoon soda
2 large eggs	1½ cups mashed bananas
2 cups flour	½ cup chopped walnuts

Cream the butter and sugar. Add the eggs and beat well. Combine the dry ingredients and stir into creamed mixture alternately with the mashed bananas. Fold in the nuts last. Pour into a buttered loaf pan, let stand at room temperature for 20 minutes, and then bake in 350° oven 45 minutes to 1 hour.

BANANA-APRICOT NUT BREAD. To the recipe add 1 cup minced dried apricots.

BANANA BRAN NUT BREAD. A simple variation uses 1½ cups flour and 1 cup bran flakes. Add 1 teaspoon vanilla extract and 2 teaspoons baking powder.

BANANA PEANUT BREAD. Use only 1 cup mashed bananas and add ¾ cup crunchy peanut butter.

BLUEBERRY-ORANGE-NUT BREAD

Huckleberries, Juneberries, or raspberries could substitute for the blueberries in this delicious quick bread.

3 cups flour	1 cup chopped nuts
1 tablespoon baking powder	3 large eggs
¼ teaspoon soda	½ cup milk
½ cup sugar	½ cup butter, melted
1 teaspoon salt	1 tablespoon grated orange
1 cup fresh, frozen, or drained	rind
canned blueberries	⅓ cup orange juice

Combine the flour, baking powder, soda, sugar, salt, blueberries, and chopped nuts. Stir to blend thoroughly. Beat together the eggs, milk, melted butter, grated orange rind, and orange juice. Pour into the dry ingredients and stir until the flour is thoroughly moistened. Do not beat. Pour into a well-buttered loaf pan and set aside for 15 minutes. Bake in a 350° oven for 1 hour, or until loaf tests done.

And I go for the house where I can smell,
Hot dough of fresh baked bread.
—WILLIAM J. METER

BISHOP'S BREAD

6 large eggs, separated
⅔ cup sugar
1 cup flour
¾ cup blanched, slivered
   almonds

1 cup golden raisins
½ cup candied orange peel
6 ounces chocolate chips
1 tablespoon grated lemon rind

Beat the egg yolks with the sugar until light and creamy. Sift the flour and stir in, along with the almonds, raisins, orange peel, chocolate chips, and lemon rind. Beat the egg whites until stiff and fold in carefully. Pour into a buttered 9-inch loaf pan and bake in a 300° oven for 1 hour. Do not cut the bread until it is at least 24 hours old. Cut in very thin slices.

CURRANT BREAD

This spicy, heavily fruited bread will make a big hit with everyone. The Norwegians add 1 teaspoon crushed cardamom seed.

1 cup butter
1 cup sugar, white or brown
3 large eggs
3 cups flour
1 cup raisins
1 cup currants
1 cup chopped walnuts

1 teaspoon baking powder
½ teaspoon soda
½ teaspoon salt
1 teaspoon nutmeg
1 teaspoon cinnamon
1¼ cups buttermilk

Cream the butter and sugar. Beat in the eggs. Mix ¼ cup flour with the fruits and nuts. Sift the remaining flour with the other dry ingredients and add to the creamed mixture alternately with the buttermilk. Carefully fold in the floured fruits and nuts. Spread the batter in a well-buttered 9-inch loaf pan. Place in 350° oven and bake for approximately 1 hour.

   If desired, and this is very good, the bread may be sprinkled before baking with a Streussel made by combining ¼ cup each flour, brown sugar, and butter.

CARROT-RAISIN BREAD

A moist bread that is delicious with coffee, or as a nutritious lunch-box filler. It can also replace the traditional brown bread with baked beans.

2⅔ cups water	2 large eggs
2⅔ cups brown sugar	4 cups flour
2 cups shredded raw carrots	1 tablespoon soda
2 cups golden raisins	½ teaspoon salt
1 teaspoon cinnamon	1 cup chopped nuts
½ cup butter	

Combine the water, sugar, carrots, raisins, cinnamon, and butter in a saucepan. Bring to a boil, reduce heat and simmer for 20 minutes. Cool the mixture. When cooled beat in the eggs. Sift the flour, soda, and salt and add to mixture. Then fold in the chopped nuts. Turn into 2 buttered 8-inch loaf pans and bake at 350° for 45 minutes, or until done.

CARROT-NUT BREAD

1 cup graham flour	1 cup milk
1½ cups white flour	2 large eggs
1 teaspoon soda	¼ cup melted butter
1½ teaspoons baking powder	½ cup chopped walnuts
1 teaspoon salt	1 cup grated carrots
⅔ cup brown sugar	

Sift flours, soda, baking powder, and salt and stir in the brown sugar. Stir the milk, eggs, and melted butter into the dry ingredients as for muffins. Fold in the walnuts and the carrots. Pour into a buttered 8-inch loaf pan and bake in a 350° oven for about 1 hour.

DATE-NUT-ORANGE BREAD

In this delicious nut bread you can use walnuts, pecans, pistachios, almonds, or any combination of nuts.

1½ pound chopped dates	½ cup soft butter
2 cups chopped nuts	1½ cups brown sugar
2 cups boiling water	2 large eggs
2 cups white flour	2 teaspoons soda
1 teaspoon salt	⅔ cup orange juice
2 cups whole-wheat or graham flour	

In a large bowl combine the dates, nuts, and boiling water. Set aside. Sift the white flour with the salt. Add the whole-wheat or graham flour and stir to blend. Cream the butter, brown sugar, and eggs until light. Now stir the soda into the date-nut mixture. Add the blended flour and the date-nut mixture alternately to the creamed butter-sugar-egg mixture, beginning and ending with the dry ingredients. Blend the orange juice into the batter last. Pour into 2 well-buttered 8-inch loaf pans. Bake in a 350° oven for approximately 50 to 60 minutes, or until the bread tests done with a toothpick or cake tester.

BASIC DATE-NUT BREAD

In the Arab world, it is the date which is the "staff of life" to millions of people who require a concentrated food, rich in body requirements. The Arabs use not only the delicious fruit of the date palm, but all other parts: the trunk for timber and house building; the midribs of the leaves to supply material for furniture; the leaflets for basket weaving; the fruit stalks for rope and fuel; and the fiber for packing material. Even the pits are ground and used for stock feed. It is little wonder that the date palm has become almost a holy thing, with Mohammed himself putting the final stamp of approval on dates. During his years of poverty, he subsisted for days at a time on nothing but dates and water. When times became better, dates remained his favorite food, one of his own particularly loved dishes being pitted dates stuffed with sweet butter and eaten with quantities of camel's milk.

This recipe makes the best date bread I've ever eaten.

2 cups chopped, pitted dates	1½ cups white or brown sugar
1 teaspoon soda	½ cup soft butter
1 teaspoon salt	3 cups flour
2 cups boiling water	1 to 1½ cups chopped nuts
2 to 6 large eggs (depending on how rich a bread you wish)	

Combine in a bowl the dates, soda, and salt, pour the boiling water over, and set aside to cool. Beat the eggs until thoroughly blended. Add the sugar and the butter to the eggs and beat until light and fluffy. Sift the flour and stir into the egg mixture. Now add the date mixture and the chopped nuts. Blend well. Pour into 2 buttered loaf pans and bake in a 350° oven for 1 hour, or in cupcake tins at 350° for 30 minutes.

VARIATIONS. This basic bread lends itself well to many variations. None of the following requires any changes in the recipe other than that suggested. You can add 2 teaspoons vanilla extract. Or use 1 cup orange juice in place of as much water. Or add the grated rind of 2 large lemons. Or use 3 cups of chopped dates instead of 2. Or add ⅓ cup brandy to batter. Or use raw sugar and graham flour. Our favorite variation uses both the vanilla and the orange juice.

You can also make only half of the batter, omitting the nuts. Pour the batter into a buttered 8- by 12-inch shallow glass pan. Cover with a topping made by mixing ½ cup sugar, ½ cup chopped nuts, and 1 6-ounce package chocolate chips. Bake in a 350° oven for 1 hour.

RAISIN-NUT BREAD. Substitute raisins for dates in the basic recipe. This makes a bread so delicious that it can be served with hard sauce as a holiday pudding.

HOLIDAY DATE PUDDING

Follow the basic recipe for Basic Date-Nut Bread, except increase butter to 1 cup; decrease sugar to 1 cup; add 2 teaspoons baking powder and

1 cup chopped candied cherries. Turn batter into 4 buttered No. 2½ cans and bake at 325° for 1¼ hours, or until the puddings test done with a toothpick or cake tester. Turn out of cans and serve hot with Butter Sauce.

BUTTER SAUCE

½ cup butter	3 cups milk
3 tablespoons flour	1 teaspoon vanilla extract
1 cup white or brown sugar	

Melt the butter. Combine the flour and sugar and blend well, then stir into the melted butter. Cook slowly, stirring constantly, while you pour in the 3 cups milk. Bring just to a boil, then remove from heat and add the vanilla extract.

DUTCH APPLE BREAD

This delicious bread freezes well. We slice it thin and serve it with whipped cream cheese. The addition of ⅓ cup chopped cranberries is a flavor delight. And some good cooks sprinkle the top of the bread with a Streussel (see index) before baking.

½ cup butter	½ teaspoon salt
1 cup sugar	⅓ cup sour milk or
2 large eggs	orange juice
1 teaspoon vanilla extract	1 cup chopped apples
2 cups flour	⅓ cup chopped walnuts
1 teaspoon soda	

Cream the butter and sugar. Add the eggs and vanilla extract and beat. Add dry ingredients alternately with the sour milk or orange juice, and then fold in the apples and nuts. Bake in a buttered loaf pan in a 350° oven for 55 minutes, or until loaf tests done.

FIG-NUT BREAD

Dried figs add a marvelous flavor to quick breads. Chopped dates or slivered dried apricots could also be used.

2 large eggs	½ teaspoon soda
¼ cup brown sugar	2 teaspoons baking powder
½ cup honey	1 teaspoon salt
3 tablespoons melted butter	1 cup dried figs, chopped
1 cup bran	½ cup walnuts
2½ cups flour	1½ cups milk

Beat the eggs, sugar, honey, and butter until creamed. Combine the dry ingredients, figs, and walnuts, and stir into the creamed mixture alternately with the milk. Pour into a buttered loaf pan, let stand for 20 minutes, then bake in a 350° oven for 1 hour, or until bread tests done.

VARIATIONS. If desired 3½ cups of flour may be used, omitting the bran. Or a cup of whole-wheat or graham flour may be used, replacing either the bran or a cup of the flour. If you do not like honey it may be omitted and ¾ cup brown or white sugar used. Part orange juice may be used with the milk, substituting it for an equal amount of milk.

SWEET EGG BREAD

The flavor of this rich fruit bread is worth the 6 eggs.

1 cup butter	1 teaspoon baking powder
¾ cup sugar	1 cup candied fruits
6 large eggs	chopped walnuts or
2 cups flour	slivered blanched almonds

Cream the butter and sugar thoroughly. Add the eggs, 1 at a time, beating each egg in well. Sift the flour and baking powder together. Mix ¼ cup of the flour into the fruits. Fold the remaining flour into the creamed mixture, and then fold in the floured fruits. Pour into a well-buttered 8-inch loaf pan. Sprinkle the top with chopped walnuts or slivered blanched almonds. Bake in a 350° oven for 50 minutes.

IRISH SWEET LOAF

This traditional Irish sweet bread is good either hot or cold. Some cooks use half graham or whole-wheat flour, and other cooks shape the dough into buns and bake them in a 350° oven for about 25 minutes, or "bake" them on a griddle.

4 cups flour	grated rind of 1 lemon
1 cup sugar	2 eggs, beaten
1 tablespoon baking powder	1 cup milk
2 cups raisins	

Combine the flour, sugar, baking powder, raisins, and lemon rind. Beat the eggs and milk together and add to the dry ingredients. Mix carefully, until thoroughly moistened. Turn into a buttered 9- by 5-inch loaf pan and let stand for about 20 minutes. Bake in a 350° oven until done, about 1 hour to 1¼ hours.

GRAHAM BUTTERMILK BREAD

A delicious and nutritious tea bread.

3 cups white flour	1½ cups light molasses
¾ cup brown sugar	3 cups buttermilk
1 tablespoon soda	1 cup nuts
1 tablespoon baking powder	1 cup raisins, rinsed in hot
1½ teaspoons salt	water and drained
5½ cups graham flour	

Sift together the white flour, sugar, soda, baking powder, and salt. Mix thoroughly with the graham flour. Stir in the molasses and the buttermilk and mix well. Dredge the nuts and raisins with a small amount of flour and add. Pour into 2 buttered 9- by 5-inch loaf pans. Let stand for 15 minutes and then bake in a 350° oven for 1 hour, or until loaves test done. Cool 10 minutes in pans and then turn out on a rack.

ORANGE-SLICE BREAD

3 large eggs	¼ teaspoon salt
1¼ cups brown sugar	1 cup chopped nuts or moist
¼ cup soft butter	coconut
1 teaspoon vanilla extract	1 cup chopped candied orange
2 cups flour	slices
2 teaspoons baking powder	

Cream the eggs, sugar, and butter together. Beat until thick. Add the vanilla extract and stir to blend. Sift the flour, baking powder, and salt. Combine with the nuts or coconut and the orange slices. Blend into the creamed mixture. Turn into a buttered loaf pan and let stand for 20 minutes. Then bake in a 350° oven for 45 to 55 minutes. Cool in the pan, on a rack, for 10 minutes before turning out.

NOTE. Orange whipped butter or whipped cream cheese goes well with thin slices of this bread.

ORANGE-POTATO BREAD

The mashed potatoes in the batter add to the moistness and the keeping qualities of this bread, without affecting its flavor.

1 cup butter	5½ cups flour
1½ cups sugar	2 tablespoons baking powder
3 large eggs	1 teaspoon salt
⅓ cup orange marmalade or apricot preserves	1 teaspoon soda
	1½ cups orange juice
⅔ cup mashed potatoes	1½ cups chopped nuts

Cream the butter and sugar. Add the eggs and the marmalade or preserves and beat well, then beat in the mashed potatoes. Sift the flour, baking powder, salt, and soda and add to the creamed mixture alternately with the orange juice. Stir in the nuts last. Pour into 2 buttered loaf pans and bake in a 350° oven for about 50 to 55 minutes.

ORANGE-MARMALADE BREAD

Orange marmalade comes into frequent use in the good cook's kitchen. It's very good just swirled gently into a risen coffee cake dough which is then covered with a Streussel or with chopped bits of cold butter and some sugar. Spoonfuls of marmalade can be pressed gently into a plain coffee cake batter. In this rich marmalade bread, it's a family favorite.

3 cups flour (may be part graham flour or bran)	1 tablespoon grated orange rind
1 tablespoon baking powder	1 cup *hot* marmalade
½ teaspoon salt	2 large eggs
½ cup sugar	1 cup milk or orange juice
½ cup slivered blanched almonds	2 tablespoons melted butter

Put the dry ingredients, including the orange rind, into a large bowl. Blend in the marmalade. Beat the eggs into the milk or orange juice and add. Add the butter last. Put the batter into a large well-buttered loaf pan, and bake in a 350° oven 1 hour, or until bread tests done.

NOTE. The recipe is easily increased, and 1½ times the recipe (this uses 4½ cups flour, 4½ teaspoons baking powder, etc.) will fill two glass pans, as these are usually smaller. Bake in glass pans at 325° for about 45 minutes; test bread before removing from oven. Sour cream may be used instead of milk or orange juice; in that case omit butter, add ½ teaspoon soda, and use only 2 teaspoons baking powder.

PEACH NUT BREAD

This delicious and unusual nut bread uses canned peaches and their syrup. Diced very ripe papaya can be substituted, in which case use milk for the liquid.

1 pound 14 ounce can peach halves	½ teaspoon cinnamon
	½ cup butter
5 cups flour, plus 1 to 2 tablespoons	1 cup sugar
	3 large eggs
2 tablespoons baking powder	3 tablespoons grated orange rind
1 teaspoon salt	
½ teaspoon nutmeg	1 cup chopped walnuts

Drain the peaches thoroughly and reserve 1¼ cups of the syrup. Dice the peaches and set aside. Sift the dry ingredients. Cream the butter, sugar, and eggs. Add the orange rind and blend well. Add the sifted dry ingredients alternately with the reserved peach syrup. Stir until batter is well blended. Stir 1 or 2 tablespoons flour through the diced peaches and the nuts. Stir into the batter. Turn batter into 2 well-buttered glass loaf pans. Bake in a 350° oven for about 1 hour, or until loaves test done. Cool in pans for 10 minutes before turning out onto a rack. Cool completely, preferably overnight, before cutting.

PINEAPPLE-DATE NUT BREAD

This fruity and rich tea bread has good keeping qualities.

1 pound raisins	1½ cups sugar
2¼ cups water	2 large eggs
1 pound pitted, chopped dates	1 teaspoon salt
½ cup chopped, candied cherries	1 teaspoon vanilla extract
1 cup chopped nuts	1 pound 4 ounce can crushed pineapple, drained
5½ cups flour	2 teaspoons soda
½ cup butter	2 teaspoons baking powder

Simmer the raisins in the water for 15 minutes. Drain, reserving liquid. Add the dates, candied cherries, and chopped nuts. Stir in 1 cup of the flour. Cream the butter, eggs, sugar, and salt. Stir in the vanilla extract and the drained pineapple, reserving the juice. Sift the remaining flour, the soda, and the baking powder. Combine the raisin liquid and pineapple juice and add water to make 2 cups. Add to the creamed mixture alternately with the dry ingredients. Last, stir in the dried fruit mixture. Pour into 3 well-buttered loaf pans and bake in a 375° oven until done, approximately 50 to 60 minutes.

POTATO-CHOCOLATE LOAF

Another delicious loaf using mashed potatoes.

1 cup mashed potatoes	2 cups flour
¾ cup cocoa	1 tablespoon baking powder
½ cup soft butter	1 teaspoon each: salt and cinnamon
1½ cups sugar	
4 eggs	1 cup chopped nuts
½ cup milk	1 cup raisins (optional)

Heat the potatoes and the cocoa and stir until hot and thoroughly mixed. Cool. Cream the butter, sugar, and eggs and then add the milk. Stir in the cooled potato mixture. Sift dry ingredients together and add. Fold in the nuts and raisins (if used) last. Pour into 2 buttered 8-inch loaf pans and bake in a 300° oven for 1 hour, or until done. Cool in pans for 10 minutes before turning out onto racks. Cool overnight before cutting.

PRUNE NUT BREAD

This delicious bread is thickly studded with chopped nuts. The recipe can easily be doubled and the bread freezes well. It is excellent served with whipped cream cheese.

1¼ cups flour	1 large egg
1 cup sugar	1 cup sour milk or sour cream
½ teaspoon salt	½ cup thick prune juice
1 teaspoon baking powder	2 tablespoons melted butter
1 teaspoon soda	½ cup chopped, cooked prunes
1 cup graham flour or bran flakes	1 tablespoon grated orange rind
1 cup chopped nuts	

Sift the flour, sugar, salt, baking powder, and soda. Put into a large bowl and add the graham flour or bran flakes and the chopped nuts. Blend. Beat the egg with sour milk or sour cream and add the prune juice, butter, chopped prunes, and orange rind. Stir into the dry ingredients and blend. Pour into a well-buttered loaf pan and bake in a 350° oven for 50 to 60 minutes, or until bread tests done.

SPICE BREADS

DUTCH HONEY BREAD

This easy and delicious bread is very popular throughout Holland; it bears a striking similarity to the French Pain d'Épices (see page 175).

1 cup brown sugar	½ teaspoon ginger
½ cup butter	½ teaspoon cinnamon
2 large eggs	½ teaspoon cloves
1 teaspoon soda	¼ teaspoon salt
½ cup honey or corn syrup	¼ cup each chopped nuts,
½ cup buttermilk	chopped dried figs, raisins
2 cups flour	(all optional)

Cream the brown sugar and butter. Beat in the eggs. Stir the soda into the honey or corn syrup and combine with the buttermilk. Sift the dry ingredients together and stir into the creamed mixture, alternately with the liquid mixture. If the nuts, figs, and raisins are used, stir a small amount of flour through them and fold them into the batter. Pour the batter into a well-buttered loaf pan. Let stand at room temperature for 20 minutes, then bake in a 350° oven for 45 to 60 minutes. The bread should be 24 hours old before it is cut. Cut into thin slices to serve.

GINGERBREAD

This is our favorite Gingerbread, an old-fashioned one made with boiling water. Ginger is one of the oldest spices known to man and is thought to be a native of Asia. Most popularly known throughout the centuries as a spice, it has also been used as an aromatic and as a stomach medicine. Early American cookbooks include many recipes for "soft" and "hard" "gyngerbredde." We often use Gingerbread to make an apple, peach, or pineapple upside-down cake. The pineapple upside-down cake is especially good, using pineapple juice as the liquid in the Gingerbread, and including coconut in the topping as well as in the Gingerbread.

1 cup boiling water	2½ cups flour
1 cup butter	1 teaspoon salt
1 cup white or brown sugar	1½ teaspoons soda
1 cup molasses, maple syrup,	1 teaspoon cinnamon
or honey	1 teaspoon ginger
3 or 4 large eggs	1 teaspoon allspice

Pour the boiling water over the butter, sugar, and syrup. Stir until butter is melted. Cool slightly, add the eggs, and beat well. Sift the dry ingredients, stir in, and beat until smooth. Pour into a buttered 9- by 13-inch pan and bake in a 325° oven for 1 hour, or until done. Frost lightly, or serve with whipped cream.

CHOCOLATE GINGERBREAD.   Add 2 squares melted unsweetened chocolate to the preceding recipe.

COFFEE GINGERBREAD.   Old-time cooks used 1 cup of boiling coffee in place of the boiling water.

FROSTED GINGERBREAD.   A vanilla-, lemon-, or orange-flavored glaze is always good with Gingerbread, as is plain or whipped cream. A particularly delicious way of frosting Gingerbread is to lay halved marshmallows over the top of the bread as it comes from the oven. Place back in hot oven to soften and lightly brown the marshmallows. This will take just a few minutes, so watch carefully.

ORANGE GINGERBREAD.   Substitute orange juice for the boiling water, and use brown sugar. Heat the butter, syrup, juice, and sugar until butter is melted, but do not bring to a boil. Continue as in the basic recipe. To the spices used, add 1 tablespoon grated orange rind and 1 teaspoon grated lemon rind. Frost with an orange glaze.

⸱ GINGERBREAD.   Add 1 cup chopped dates to the
⸱ or to the Orange Gingerbread variation.

GINGERBREAD.   Use pineapple juice instead
a boil. Proceed as in the basic recipe. Add 1 cup

of moist fine coconut to the dry ingredients. Frost and sprinkle the top with more coconut.

SPICE BREAD.   In the basic recipe for Gingerbread cut sugar and butter to ½ cup each. Omit ginger and allspice. Add 1 teaspoon dry mustard. This bread makes a good snack, served hot with coffee and plenty of butter.

CANDIED-GINGER BREAD

Gingerbread made with spicy and delicious candied ginger. Be sure to cut the ginger into tiny pieces.

½ cup brown sugar
1 cup hot milk
1 large egg
2¼ cups flour
1 tablespoon baking powder

pinch of salt
⅓ cup candied ginger, cut in
    very small pieces
½ cup melted butter

Combine the sugar and milk. Cool. Stir in the egg. Sift dry ingredients and add the ginger. Stir into the milk mixture and then stir in the melted butter. Pour into a buttered coffee can with a cover, or into a pudding mold, filling the can or mold not more than two-thirds full. Cover and steam for 2 hours.

ORANGE-MARMALADE GINGERBREAD

½ cup butter
1 cup orange marmalade
½ cup molasses or maple
    syrup
2 cups flour

½ teaspoon salt
1 teaspoon ginger
½ teaspoon nutmeg
2 large eggs
1 teaspoon soda

Combine the butter, marmalade, and molasses or maple syrup. Sift the dry ingredients and fold into the creamed mixture. Add the eggs and soda. Turn into a well-buttered 8-inch square pan. Bake in a 350° oven for 30 minutes, or until bread tests done.

SOUR-CREAM GINGERBREAD

A very good Gingerbread. The dough is stiffer than that of the usual Gingerbread and lends itself well to the English variation which follows.

1 cup sugar	4 large eggs
½ teaspoon cinnamon	1 cup honey or corn syrup
½ teaspoon cloves or allspice	1 cup sour cream
½ to 1 teaspoon ginger	4 cups flour
½ teaspoon salt	2 teaspoons soda

Combine the sugar, spices, and salt. Beat the eggs into the sugar mixture. Add the rest of ingredients in order, sifting the flour and soda together. Bake in a 3-quart shallow glass pan, well buttered, at 325° for 1 hour to 1¼ hours. Test with a toothpick or cake tester before removing from the oven. Recipe may be halved and the Gingerbread baked in a 9-inch square pan if desired.

FILLED GINGERBREAD. The English use for this a Gingerbread that is firm enough to be rolled out, but the preceding recipe will do fine. Spread half of the dough in the buttered pan. Brush with melted butter and then spread with chopped nuts and candied fruit peels of your choice. Carefully spread the other half of the batter over the filling. Bake as directed in basic recipe. Cut into squares while hot. Fine for the holiday season.

HOLIDAY GINGERBREAD. Add ½ cup melted butter to the Sour-Cream Gingerbread recipe, and ¼ to ⅓ cup each golden raisins, chopped nuts, and candied fruit peels. (If desired you may replace the sour cream with buttermilk or sour milk, but this substitution is not necessary.) Bake in 2 square pans, as in basic recipe. Or use 2 buttered 8- by 4-inch loaf pans and bake in a 350° oven about 50 to 55 minutes, testing after 45 minutes. Sprinkle with powdered sugar and cool thoroughly before slicing.

PAIN D'ÉPICES

This excellent bread makes a wonderful Christmas gift. Cut into very thin slices and served with whipped butter (the French serve it with raspberry jam), it has an appealing sophisticated flavor. It's best when several days old. Some good cooks use hot coffee for all or part of the liquid. Others steep 1 teaspoon anise seed in the liquid and then strain the seeds out. Still other cooks decrease the water to 1 cup and add ¼ cup melted butter and 1 large egg. A very good fruit bread is made by simply adding 1 cup of any desired chopped, dried fruits, and/or nuts.

1½ cups boiling water	4 cups flour
¾ cup honey	1½ teaspoons soda
1 cup sugar (part or all may be brown)	1 to 2 teaspoons cinnamon
¼ teaspoon salt	¼ cup rum

Pour the boiling water over the honey and sugar. Stir to combine thoroughly. Sift the next 4 ingredients into a large bowl. Pour the liquid ingredients into the dry ingredients and blend well. Stir the rum in last. Pour into a 10- by 5- by 3-inch loaf pan, well buttered, and bake in a 350° oven for 1¼ hours, or until a toothpick or cake tester comes out clean. Cool the bread thoroughly and then wrap and store it carefully. If it is kept well wrapped, the bread will keep for a long time.

PAN NERO

This sweet chocolate bread is a great favorite served cold with coffee. Some Italian cooks separate the eggs and beat the yolks with the sugar, and then fold the stiffly beaten whites into the yolk-sugar-chocolate mixture. The other ingredients are then carefully folded in. Other Italian cooks omit the cinnamon, but we have found a natural affinity between chocolate and cinnamon,

¾ cup sugar, plus 1 tablespoon	½ cup plus 2 tablespoons flour
5 large eggs	½ teaspoon cinnamon
3 squares chocolate, melted	½ cup ground unblanched al-
¼ cup minced citron	monds

Beat the eggs and sugar until light and fluffy. Fold in the rest of the ingredients in order. Pour into an 8-inch square baking pan that has been buttered and sprinkled with 1 tablespoon sugar. Bake in a 350° oven for 20 to 25 minutes, or until bread tests done. Let cool thoroughly before cutting in squares to serve.

BAKING-POWDER COFFEE CAKES

BASIC COFFEE CAKE

This delicious cake changes character with the topping used and is very easy to make.

½ cup butter	1 teaspoon salt
½ to 1 cup sugar	2 teaspoons baking powder
3 large eggs	grated rind of 1 lemon
1¾ cups flour	½ cup milk

Cream the butter with the sugar until light and fluffy. Add the eggs and beat in. Sift flour, salt, and baking powder. Add the lemon rind to the milk and stir into the creamed mixture alternately with the dry ingredients. Pour into a 9-inch buttered pan, spread with desired topping, and bake in a 350° oven for 40 to 45 minutes.

TOPPINGS

CRANBERRY.   Spread 1 cup ground cranberries, or more if desired, over dough. Sprinkle with Streussel made with ⅓ cup each flour, sugar, and butter. If desired ½ cup of mincemeat or chopped apple, or a combination of the two, may be added to the cranberries.

MARMALADE.   Combine any favorite marmalade with an equal amount of coconut (about ½ cup each), and spread over the dough. Sprinkle with 1 tablespoon sugar.

MERINGUE.   Beat 2 or 3 egg whites with ½ cup white or brown sugar, until whites are stiff. Spread over dough and sprinkle with chopped walnuts or slivered blanched almonds.

PEANUT BUTTER.   Combine as for Streussel: 3 tablespoons butter, 3 tablespoons peanut butter, ⅓ cup brown sugar, and ⅓ cup flour. Spread over batter and bake as directed. If desired (and this is very good), spread a thin layer of any preferred jelly or jam over the batter before sprinkling it with the Peanut-Butter Topping.

PEACH COFFEE CAKE.   Into the Basic Coffee Cake batter fold 1 to 1½ cups of diced fresh peaches. Bake as directed and serve with cream. Other fruits or berries may be used, to make a delicious and simple cake.

BLITZ KUCHEN
(Quick Cake)

Since kuchen means cake, there is virtually no limit to the number of German yeast and baking-powder recipes so labeled. Blitz kuchen translates as "quick cake"; this one is both quick and delicious.

¾ cup soft butter	½ teaspoon salt
2 cups sugar	3 cups flour
4 large eggs, separated	3 teaspoons baking powder
grated rind of 1 large orange	1 cup milk
grated rind of 1 large lemon, or	sugar
1½ teaspoons vanilla extract	almonds

Cream the butter and sugar. Add the egg yolks and beat in. Blend in the flavorings. Sift the salt, flour, and baking powder and add the sifted dry ingredients alternately with the milk. Beat the egg whites until stiff and fold in. Spread the batter in a buttered 8- by 12-inch pan. Sprinkle with sugar and slivered blanched almonds, or with brown sugar, bits of cold butter and any chopped nuts preferred. Bake in a 325° oven for 1 hour, or until cake tests done. If desired, the cake may be baked in a loaf pan in a 350° oven for about 30 to 40 minutes.

VARIATION. Omit orange rind and lemon rind or vanilla extract. Add ¼ teaspoon cloves or nutmeg and ½ teaspoon cinnamon to batter. Fold in 1 cup raisins or currants that have been soaked to plumpen and then let dry. Let stand a day before cutting and slice very thin.

LAZY-DAY COFFEE CAKE

An emergency coffee cake, to be used on lazy days, or any time unexpected company drops in.

Use uncut bread, preferably homemade, and cut it into thick slices. Remove crusts. Dip each slice first in melted butter (you will need a good ½ pound for 1 loaf of bread) and then in a mixture of granulated sugar and cinnamon. Be sure that slices are well coated. Place on a buttered cookie sheet and heat in a 400° oven until golden brown and crisp. Serve with tea or coffee. Easy and delicious!

BLUEBERRY COFFEE CAKE

A popular and simple coffee cake. You could use almost any fresh berries or canned and drained berries.

¾ cup sugar	½ teaspoon salt
⅓ cup butter	2 cups berries
2 large eggs	½ cup sugar
⅓ cup milk	⅓ cup flour
2 cups flour	½ teaspoon cinnamon
2 teaspoons baking powder	¼ cup butter

Cream the ¾ cup sugar and the ⅓ cup butter together and add the eggs. Sift the 2 cups flour, the baking powder, and the salt and add alternately with the milk. Stir in the berries. Spread in a 9-inch square pan, well buttered. Blend the ½ cup sugar, ⅓ cup flour, the cinnamon, and the ¼ cup butter and sprinkle on top. Bake in 375° oven for 25 to 30 minutes.

CORN SALLY LUNN

The Americanization of a great English recipe brought about this delicious bread. It is too sweet to be served as a cornbread, classifying rather as a bread-cake. We serve it with fresh fruit in season.

1 cup coarsely ground corn-meal	1½ cups sugar
	4 large eggs, separated
2 cups white flour	1 cup rich milk or half-and-half
1 tablespoon baking powder	1 teaspoon vanilla extract
½ teaspoon salt	¾ cup melted butter

Combine the cornmeal, flour, baking powder, salt, and sugar. Combine the egg yolks, milk, vanilla extract, and melted butter. Stir into the dry ingredients until they are thoroughly moistened. Beat the egg whites until stiff and fold into the batter carefully. Pour into a 3-quart shallow baking pan that has been well buttered. Bake in a 350° oven for 30 minutes, or until it tests done. If desired, 2 8-inch square pans may be used.

FRESH-FRUIT COFFEE CAKE
(Baking-Powder Kuchen)

This delicious coffee cake can be made with any fruit in season.

1 cup butter	1¾ cups flour
1 cup sugar	2 teaspoons baking powder
4 large eggs	2 pounds fresh fruit (peaches,
1 teaspoon grated lemon rind	plums, apricots, or berries)

Cream the butter and sugar. Beat in the eggs. Sift the flour with the baking powder and blend in, along with the lemon rind. Butter and flour the bottom of a 9- by 13-inch cake pan. Spread the batter in the pan and arrange the fruit in rows over the top, cut side down. Peaches should be peeled and quartered; apricots and plums should be halved and pitted. Sprinkle the fruit with an additional ½ cup of sugar or with a Streussel. Bake in a 325° oven for 30 to 35 minutes. Cool and cut into squares.

NOTE.   If the eggs are separated, and the yolks and stiffly beaten whites folded in separately, the cake will be much lighter.

PEAR COFFEE CAKE.   Cover batter with thinly sliced fresh pears. Sprinkle with chopped walnuts and spread with Sour-Cream Topping, to which ½ teaspoon vanilla extract has been added. Bake as directed.

PRUNE COFFEE CAKE.   Bring batter up the sides of pan to form a rim. Spread thickly with Lekvar (prune butter, available in Jewish markets), sprinkle with chopped nuts. Bake as directed and serve with a sauce made by beating together equal amounts of cream cheese and sour cream, sweetened with 1 or 2 tablespoons sugar.

MERINGUE COFFEE CAKE.   For this excellent Hungarian variation, spread apricot preserves on the batter and bake as directed for 30 minutes. Then spread with a meringue, sprinkle with chopped nuts, and bake 10 minutes longer.

GATAH (Baking-Powder)

These fragile pastries are very popular with the Armenians; they are very similar to the Italian Neapolitan Bread. Usually served with tea or coffee, the pastries are a cross between a tea bread and a cookie. (See also yeast-raised Gatah, page 196.)

1 cup butter	1 tablespoon baking powder
1 cup sweet cream	1 teaspoon salt
1½ to 2 cups sugar	about 4 cups flour
4 egg yolks	sesame seed
1 whole egg	

Cream the butter, cream, sugar, egg yolks, and whole egg until thoroughly blended. Sift the baking powder and salt with 2 cups of the flour. Add to the creamed mixture and blend well. Now add just enough more flour to make a workable dough. If desired, chill the dough for an hour. When ready to bake, pinch off pieces of dough and roll into long, thin ropes. Braid the ropes and cut into 3-inch lengths. Put onto buttered cookie sheets, brush with milk or cream, and sprinkle with sesame seed. Bake in a 375° oven for 15 minutes, or until browned and done.

NEAPOLITAN BREAD. Make half of the preceding recipe, using about 1½ cups flour. Add the grated rind of 1 lemon and 1 cup grated blanched almonds. Braid as directed and brush the pastries with an egg yolk beaten with 1 tablespoon cream, then sprinkle with sugar. Bake in a 350° oven for 15 minutes, or until browned and done.

GERMAN COTTAGE-CHEESE STOLLEN

A German friend says that this very unusual Stollen is a tradition in parts of Germany. The dough is stiffer than usual, almost like a biscuit dough, so as to hold its shape. It's a good keeper. While it is traditionally studded with currants and chopped nuts only (2 cups of each), we much prefer the combination of golden raisins, chopped nuts, and candied fruits and peels. Brandy or rum can be drizzled over the top as soon as it comes from the oven, or a rum icing could be used. The bread makes delicious toast, even when slightly stale. If a lighter, fluffier bread is wished, decrease the flour to 4 cups and bake the bread in 2 buttered loaf pans at 350° for 1 hour. Either way it is delicious.

1 cup butter
1 cup sugar
2 tablespoons grated lemon rind
2 large eggs and 4 egg yolks
4 cups small-curd cottage cheese
5½ cups flour

4 teaspoons baking powder
1 teaspoon soda
1 teaspoon salt
¾ cup each golden raisins, chopped walnuts or slivered almonds, and candied fruit peels

Cream the butter and sugar and add the lemon rind. Beat in the eggs, egg yolks, cottage cheese, and 4 cups of the flour. Add the remaining ingredients and stir in enough more of the flour to make a stiff, biscuit-like dough. Shape the dough on a buttered cookie sheet into the traditional Stollen shape—a large oval, brushed with soft butter and then lapped over. Bake in a 350° oven for 1¼ hours, or until bread tests done when a cake tester or toothpick is thrust into the center. Cool on a rack and frost, or glaze, while warm. Makes 1 huge loaf, or 2 medium loaves. If desired, the dough may be baked in a 10- or 12-inch round cake pan. These cake pans are 2 inches deep and make a very attractive round loaf.

LAPLAND CAKES

These delicious little sweet rolls, with no leavening other than the whipped cream and beaten egg whites, were a popular delicacy almost a hundred years ago. *Miss Parloa's Kitchen Companion* of 1887 gives a good recipe for them, as does Mary Stuart Smith's *Virginia Cookery-Book* of 1885. I added the sugar and lemon rind to make a sweet roll; without them you have a delicate little breakfast muffin, easily made. Delicious either way. The recipe is easily doubled, using 5 large eggs, and twice the amounts of the other ingredients.

3 large eggs, separated	1 teaspoon grated lemon rind
1 cup whipping cream	1 cup flour
3 tablespoons sugar	¼ teaspoon salt

Beat the egg yolks until light. Beat the cream with the sugar and lemon rind, until thick. Sift the flour with the salt. Fold the cream into the yolks, alternately with the flour. Fold in the stiffly beaten egg whites last. Spoon the rather thick batter into small muffin cups and bake in a 375° oven for about 20 minutes, or until done. This will make 16 sweet muffins, delicious served with coffee.

PENNSYLVANIA DUTCH CRUMB CAKE

This is an excellent quick coffee cake, fine for Sunday breakfasts. Its origins are German, and the variations slight, but numerous.

3 cups flour	½ to ⅔ cup butter
1 tablespoon baking powder	3 large eggs
1 teaspoon salt	1 cup milk
1½ cups sugar	2 teaspoons vanilla extract

Sift the flour, baking powder, salt, and sugar. Cut in butter until the mixture has the consistency of coarse meal or small peas. Reserve about 1½ cups of this mixture. Combine the eggs, milk, and vanilla extract and stir into the remainder of the dry blend. Pour into 2 well-buttered 10-inch pie pans. Brush the top of the dough with butter and sprinkle with the reserved crumb mixture. Bake in a 350° oven for 25 to 30 minutes, or until cake is done.

NOTE. If desired the liquid mixture may be blended into all of the dry mixture, and the tops of the cakes sprinkled with a separately made Streussel, or dotted with chunks of cold butter and sprinkled liberally with sugar. If the dough is not moist enough when prepared this way, moisten it with another egg or a little milk.

BROWN SUGAR CRUMB CAKE. Use brown sugar in place of white, omit the vanilla extract and add 1 teaspoon cinnamon, or more if desired.

BUTTERMILK CRUMB CAKE. Use buttermilk, or heavy sour milk, in place of regular milk. Decrease baking powder to 1 teaspoon and add 1 teaspoon soda.

CHOCOLATE CRUMB CAKE. In the basic recipe, add 1 square bitter chocolate, melted, along with the eggs, milk, and vanilla extract. Very good.

DESSERT CRUMB CAKE. Omit the vanilla extract and use ½ teaspoon nutmeg and 2 teaspoons grated lemon rind. Do not reserve any of mixture for crumbs, but mix entire amount of dough. Use 4 large eggs, beating the yolks and whites separately, and fold the beaten whites into the dough last. Spread in buttered 10-inch pie pans, and sprinkle with Streussel made by combining: ½ cup brown sugar, 2 tablespoons flour, 1 teaspoon lemon rind, 2 tablespoons melted butter, and ⅓ cup chopped nuts. Bake as directed in the basic recipe.

FRUITED CRUMB CAKE. Make the batter as in Dessert Crumb Cake. Before sprinkling with Streussel, cover batter with sliced firm bananas, or with whole, washed berries.

SOUR-CREAM CRUMB CAKE. This is one of our favorites and is a delicious coffee cake. Use ⅔ cup butter, decreasing baking powder to 2 teaspoons, add ½ teaspoon soda. Reserve about 1½ cups of the mixture for crumbs. Omit milk and use 1½ cups sour cream in batter. Brown sugar may be used if desired, or chocolate added, or sliced fruit.

PROVINCIAL COFFEE CAKE

This coffee cake, like the Scotch shortbread which it resembles, depends on the goodness of its ingredients for its fine flavor. Made with butter and fresh lemon rind it is a delicious cake; with shortening and dried lemon rind it can be quite insipid.

1 cup butter (part may be a good margarine)	4 cups flour
1⅔ cups sugar	4 teaspoons baking powder
6 large eggs	½ teaspoon salt
1 tablespoon grated lemon rind	½ cup milk
1 teaspoon vanilla extract (optional)	

All ingredients should be at room temperature. With an electric mixer beat the butter and sugar until well creamed. Add the eggs, lemon rind, and vanilla extract (if used) and beat until blended. Sift the dry ingredients together and add to the beaten egg and sugar mixture alternately with the milk. Stir these ingredients in carefully. Pour into a buttered 9- by 13-inch pan. Bake in a 250° oven for 1½ hours.

NOTE. If desired the top of the cake may be sprinkled with chopped walnuts and chopped bits of cold butter before baking. Or the batter can be baked in a shallow 3-quart baking pan, to make a thinner coffee cake, with more of the delicious crust. Bake in a 250° oven for approximately 1 hour.

SOUR-CREAM COFFEE CAKE

One of the finest coffee cake recipes I've ever come across. Each of the variations is a delight. The keeping qualities are excellent, too.

2 cups sugar	½ teaspoon salt
1 cup softened butter	1 cup sour cream
5 eggs	1 teaspoon vanilla extract
4 cups flour	grated rind of 1 lemon
1 tablespoon baking powder	1 cup each chopped walnuts
½ teaspoon soda	and golden raisins

Cream the sugar and butter. Beat in the eggs. Sift the dry ingredients and add alternately with the sour cream. If mixture is too thick add a tablespoon or two of milk. Add the remaining ingredients. Turn into a well-buttered tube pan, or Bundt cake pan, and bake in a 350° oven for 1 hour. Remove from pan, spread top with butter, and sprinkle with powdered sugar.

CHRISTMAS COFFEE CAKE. Omit the lemon rind. Add 1 teaspoon rum flavoring or 2 tablespoons rum and 1 cup candied fruits.

EXTRA-RICH COFFEE CAKE. Omit the butter and use 2 cups sour cream. Pour batter into 2 buttered square pans, and cover with a topping. Bake at 400° for 40 minutes, or until done. For our favorite topping, spread batter with more sour cream, using 1½ cups for both cakes, and sprinkle with chopped nuts, brown sugar, and cinnamon. You could omit the sour cream in the topping, and use just the brown sugar, nuts, and cinnamon.

BROWN-SUGAR COFFEE CAKE. Substitute brown sugar for 1 cup of the granulated sugar called for in the basic recipe. Pour into 2 buttered square pans. Beat 1 cup sour cream with ¼ cup brown sugar and pour over batter. Sprinkle thickly with chopped nuts.

LEMON SOUR-CREAM COFFEE CAKE. Omit the vanilla extract and add 3 to 4 tablespoons lemon juice. Bake in a tube pan. Or spread in buttered square pans and spread with any of the preceding toppings, adding 1 tablespoon grated lemon rind.

10. *Yeast-Raised*
Coffee Cakes and Sweet Rolls

Sweet breads and coffee cakes, sliced and served, say a warm "welcome" to friends and neighbors. The coffee klatch has become a popular custom in the Western world, and indeed the very word "coffee cake" testifies to the excellence of the marriage between hot coffee and sweet bread. In many countries—notably Austria, America, and the Spanish-speaking world—coffee is seldom drunk at any time of day or night without a rich pastry to accompany it.

Each country has its favorite sweet breads and coffee cakes to serve with cups of steaming coffee. But, since the basic ingredients are the same the world over, it is the spice used, or the simple shaping of the unbaked product, that marks the boundary lines of national cuisine. And for neighboring countries, which often share a common cuisine along with flexible borders, the difference may be only in the name. Thus the rich rolled pastry that the Polish housewife calls Potica is the same that the Hungarian cook calls Makos Es Dios Kalacs. The Hungarian Belés, and the Bohemian Kolache are the same, and the Finns make a pastry so similar that a different recipe is not needed.

Because of a common cuisine between bordering countries, many recipes have such similarity that I have included them as variations of a basic recipe. But at no time has authenticity been discarded for convenience. Where necessary, even similar recipes have been listed separately. In other instances, the similarity is mentioned in the note preceding the recipe.

The recipes for these traditional sweet breads are rich, using much butter and many eggs. The Hungarian or Bohemian cook adds sour cream to make an even richer dough. Although American cooks sometimes protest the number of eggs and the amount of butter, the less-rich, cut-down versions just aren't the same. I would rather make Pan de Huevo (which requires 8 large eggs) only during the spring and summer when eggs are cheap than make a "type" of Pan de Huevo with 2 eggs; while this may be very good in its own right, it is still not what it's supposed to be.

From a purely practical viewpoint, the seeming preference for 1- and 2-egg recipes is difficult to understand. For much of the year eggs are reasonable in price, and extra eggs add much in nutrition as well as flavor. By using the Cornell Triple-Rich Formula (1 tablespoon soy flour, 1 tablespoon skim-milk powder, and 1 teaspoon wheat germ in the bottom of each cup before measuring in the flour) for every bread baked, including the sweet breads, and by using recipes that call for many eggs, you are giving your family a bread or a coffee cake that is what it is supposed to be—the "staff of life." Whether sweet breads are daily fare or are served only on rare occasions, this point is worth keeping in mind. Another point not to be overlooked is that the Spanish and the Hungarians, the finest bakers in the world, use many eggs in every bread recipe, whether sweet bread or dinner bread.

Egg yolks make the finest dough for sweet breads and coffee cakes, but whole eggs can always be substituted by using 1 whole egg for each 2 egg yolks called for.

The mixture for many of the sweet breads—Gugelhupf, for example— is not actually a dough but more of a heavy batter. This is as it should be, but kneading, which is necessary to make a fine-textured bread, is virtually impossible. If you have a heavy-duty mixer with a dough hook, this can be used. Otherwise the batter has to be mixed with the hands, and the "kneading" is accomplished with a combination of pulling, stretching, and slapping the heavy batter in the bowl.

Most sweet breads freeze well, so a variety can be kept on hand. Thinly sliced, spread with flavored butters, and served with strong coffee, they make excellent company fare.

FLAVORED SUGARS

Flavored sugars are excellent to sprinkle on the tops of sweet breads after first brushing the loaves with soft or melted butter. To use Lemon, Orange, or Tangerine Sugar in baking, substitute 1 tablespoon of the flavored sugar for each teaspoon of grated rind called for. Vanilla Sugar has such a delicate flavor that it is best used for dusting the tops of sweet breads, or for making thin glazes and frostings; in baking the flavor is usually lost.

ANISE SUGAR. Grind 1 tablespoon anise seed, or pound in a mortar, and blend into 1 cup sugar. Keep in a covered jar. Sprinkle on some of the Italian breads before baking. Imparts a delightful flavor.

CINNAMON SUGAR. Combine 1 tablespoon cinnamon and 1 cup granulated sugar. Store in covered jar. Will keep indefinitely.

LEMON SUGAR. Follow recipe for Orange Sugar, using the rind of 6 large lemons.

ORANGE SUGAR. Grate the thin outer rind of 4 large oranges. Add to 1 cup granulated sugar and blend. Keep refrigerated. Will keep for months.

TANGERINE SUGAR. A very delicate and pleasing flavor change. Follow recipe for Orange Sugar, using the rind of 6 tangerines.

VANILLA SUGAR. In a canister, bury 3 vanilla beans cut in half in 1 pound of powdered sugar. Keeps almost indefinitely.

FLAVORED BUTTERS

These are very simply made and are delicious with thinly sliced tea breads, or with muffins, pancakes, waffles, and toast.

LEMON, ORANGE, OR TANGERINE BUTTER. Simply whip softened butter in an electric mixer, and flavor with 1 teaspoon or more grated lemon, orange, or tangerine rind.

MAPLE BUTTER. Whip softened butter with crushed maple sugar.

CINNAMON BUTTER. Whip softened butter with brown sugar and 1 teaspoon cinnamon.

APRICOT BUTTER. Combine 2 tablespoons apricot preserves with ½ cup of soft butter.

MARMALADE BUTTER. Combine 2 tablespoons lime, grapefruit, orange, or kumquat marmalade with ½ cup softened butter.

GLAZES (FROSTINGS)

Breads should be brushed with melted butter just before baking. The baked breads may be brushed again with butter and sprinkled with sugar, or they may be frosted. If no frosting is desired, a most excellent before-baking glaze for sweet breads is made by brushing the bread with cream and then sprinkling it heavily with sugar.

APRICOT GLAZE. One of the best for coffee cakes. Simply heat apricot preserves until very hot, or boiling, and brush on the coffee cake. If desired sprinkle very lightly with sifted powdered sugar.

APRICOT-ORANGE GLAZE. Heat ½ cup apricot preserves with 1 teaspoon grated orange rind and 1 tablespoon orange juice.

CHOCOLATE GLAZE.   Over low heat, melt ½ cup semisweet chocolate pieces with ¼ cup water. Stir constantly. Add 1 tablespoon white corn syrup and cool.

HONEY GLAZE.   Blend thoroughly: ¼ cup soft butter, ¾ cup powdered sugar, 1 egg white, and 3 tablespoons honey. Sprinkle with nuts after spreading on sweet bread, rolls, or coffee cake.

ORANGE GLAZE.   Blend thoroughly 1½ cups powdered sugar, 2 tablespoons soft butter, 2 tablespoons orange juice, 1 teaspoon lemon juice, the grated rind of ½ large orange, and ½ teaspoon grated lemon rind.

SWEET GLAZE.   Blend thoroughly 1 cup powdered sugar, 1 tablespoon soft butter, 1½ tablespoons milk and ½ teaspoon vanilla extract.

SOUR-CREAM FROSTING.   Boil together equal amounts of white sugar and sour cream, stirring all the time, until mixture is thickened. Remove from heat, add 1 teaspoon vanilla extract or ½ teaspoon grated nutmeg, or some grated lemon or orange rind. Beat the mixture with an electric mixer until thick. If you boil the mixture just to the thickened stage, the frosting will remain creamy and will spread easily.

YEAST-RAISED COFFEE CAKES

BUTTER SLICES

This rich, crumbly coffee cake almost classifies as a cookie. The dough is very rich and will not rise very much. If desired the dough may be kept refrigerated for several days.

2¼ cups flour
1 cup soft sweet butter
3 egg yolks
3 tablespoons sugar
1 cake yeast
¼ cup scalded, cooled milk

FILLING AND TOPPING
apricot preserves
¾ cup ground almonds
3 teaspoons sugar
1 egg white

Combine dough ingredients in the order given and work together thoroughly. Cover the dough and let stand at room temperature for several hours. Now divide dough into three parts. Roll each part to fit an 8- by 12-inch glass pan. Fit 1 part into the buttered pan; spread with apricot preserves and then sprinkle the preserves with 3 or 4 tablespoons ground almonds and 1 teaspoon sugar. Fit the second part over this and repeat the filling. The third part won't quite fit over the second layer, so lay pieces of dough in a patchwork pattern over the filling, letting the filling show through. Brush the top with 1 slightly beaten egg white and then sprinkle liberally with ground almonds and another teaspoon of sugar. Put immediately into a 350° oven and bake 30 minutes. Cool in the pan and serve in small slices.

CUSTARD-FILLED COFFEE CAKE

The dough for this attractive and unusual cake is made somewhat like that for cream puffs, in that the flour is stirred into a boiling liquid and the eggs are then beaten in. It is easier than it sounds. A custard cream filling recipe is given here but other fillings could be used.

½ cup milk
½ to ¾ cup flour
1 cup whole eggs (about 4
   large eggs)

1 cup melted butter
1 cake yeast
¾ cup sugar

Bring the milk to a boil and stir in ½ cup flour (as in cream puffs, but add the butter later). Beat in the eggs gradually, with electric mixer. Then add the butter, the yeast (first dissolved in a very small amount of water), and the sugar. Beat well and let the spongy mixture rise. When the mixture has doubled, punch or stir it down, and add enough more flour to make a stiff dough. Knead mixture lightly and let it rise again until doubled. Then, punch the dough down and shape it into 2 round loaves. Place in buttered round 9-inch cake pans. Brush each cake with butter and spread with the Topping. Let the cakes rise again and then bake in a 350° oven for 30 minutes, or until done. Cool the cakes completely. Then cut each cake into 2 layers and spread the bottom layer with Custard Cream. Put the top layers back on. Cut the cakes into wedges for serving.

TOPPING. Combine thoroughly ½ cup sugar, 1 cup chopped nuts, ½ cup melted butter, and ¼ cup heavy cream.

CUSTARD CREAM. Combine 3 egg yolks, ½ cup sugar, and 2 tablespoons cornstarch. Add 2 cups milk very gradually, stirring constantly. Pour into the top of a double boiler and cook, stirring, over hot water, until thickened. Cool completely before using.

KAREN'S DANISH KRINGLE

This delicious Kringle is the specialty of a friend. The Danes, who love raspberry jam, sometimes use that and chopped nuts as a filling.

4 cups flour	3 egg yolks
2 tablespoons sugar	1 cup butter
1 teaspoon salt	3 egg whites, beaten until stiff
1 cake yeast	1 cup sugar
1 cup cold milk	1¼ cups chopped nuts or more

Sift the flour, 2 tablespoons sugar, and the salt. Dissolve the yeast in the milk. Beat the egg yolks and add to the milk and yeast. Blend the flour mixture and the butter as for pie crust. Add the liquid and mix well. Refrigerate overnight. Cut the dough into 3 parts and roll each part into a thin rectangle. Mix the stiffly beaten egg whites with the sugar and 1 cup nuts and spread on each part. Roll up as for jelly roll. Carefully lift the rolls onto buttered cookie sheets and turn the ends to make them horseshoe-shaped. Let the rolls rise for an hour and then bake in a 350° oven for 30 to 40 minutes. Frost while warm and sprinkle with remaining chopped nuts. If desired, the Kringle may be decorated with candied fruits and halved blanched almonds.

ENSAIMADE
(Spanish Coffee Cake)

These are known as Concha Rolls in Mexico, but they were originated by the Spanish who are among the world's most masterly breadmakers. The coffee cake is sometimes rolled into one huge wheel, the size of a pizza pan at least. One well-known cookbook author claims to have eaten one that was 2 feet across.

4½ cups flour	¾ cup soft butter
1 teaspoon salt	1 cup water
4 large eggs	more soft butter as needed
1 cake yeast dissolved in ¼	honey
cup water	chopped nuts
½ cup sugar	

Combine all ingredients through the 1 cup water in a large mixing bowl. Mix with a spoon as long as you can, and then knead thoroughly with the hands. Brush with butter, cover, and let rise until doubled. Then knead the dough down, and place it on a floured board. Roll it out very thin and spread with a thin layer of soft butter. Fold the dough over, roll it out again, and spread with another layer of soft butter. Now fold it over again and roll it out. Cut into strips and roll each strip into a rope. Shape each rope into a snail-like curlicue about 4 or 5 inches in diameter. Place on buttered cookie sheets and let rise until doubled. Brush the rolls with honey and sprinkle thickly with chopped nuts. Bake in a 400° oven 20 minutes.

DOUGHNUTS USING RISEN BREAD DOUGH

Cooks in the old days, to save time, used once-risen bread dough to make other delicacies. When making a batch of bread, it is a simple matter to remove 2 cups of the dough after the first rising, and work other ingredients into it to make doughnuts or coffee cake.

For Doughnuts, work into 2 cups once-risen bread dough 3 eggs, ½ cup melted butter, ½ cup sugar, ½ teaspoon cinnamon or nutmeg, and approximately 2 cups flour, or enough to make a dough that is soft but workable. Roll the dough out and cut with a floured doughnut cutter. Let the doughnuts rise until light and then deep-fry them.

COFFEE CAKE USING RISEN BREAD DOUGH

Into 2 cups of once-risen bread dough work ¾ cup sugar and ⅓ cup soft butter. No extra flour will be needed. Roll the dough to fit a 10-inch square pan. Brush the top with butter and cover with a Streussel or simply with sugar and cinnamon. Let it rise and bake in a 350° oven for about 35 to 40 minutes. One delicious variation is made by spreading the top of the dough with apricot preserves and topping the preserves with a meringue. Bake as directed. This is European and very, very good.

FRENCH COFFEE-RING DOUGH

If you use sour cream instead of milk, you will have a rich Kuchen dough, tender, light, and fluffy. Either way, it is an excellent recipe, adapted from the 1911 edition of *Malzbender's Practical Recipe Book for Bakers and Pastry Cooks*. The variations you can make with it are endless, and any listed with other coffee cakes or rolls may be used with this dough. The recipe doubles or halves easily, and the dough may be refrigerated for 4 or 5 days.

1 cup milk or sour cream, scalded	½ cup egg yolks, beaten
1½ teaspoons salt	1½ yeast cakes, dissolved in ¼ cup warm water
½ to 1 cup sugar	6 cups flour
½ to 1 cup butter	

Pour scalded milk or sour cream over the salt, sugar, and three-fourths of the butter (either ⅓ cup or ¾ cup; use the same total amount of sugar as of butter). Stir to melt the butter. Let cool to lukewarm. Add the beaten egg yolks and the dissolved yeast. Beat well. Gradually work in the flour. Knead in a bowl or on a lightly floured breadboard. Place in a bowl, brush with butter, cover, and let rise until doubled. Then punch the dough down and roll it out on a lightly floured board. Shave the remaining butter over the dough. Fold the dough over the shaved butter and roll out again. Now place the dough in a buttered bowl and let it rise for 30 minutes. When risen, roll out again and cut into rounds with a biscuit cutter. Place on buttered cookie sheets and let rise again. Bake in a 400° oven for 20 minutes. Frost.

BUNDT KUCHEN. "Bundt Kuchen" literally means any bread or cake baked in a Bundt pan, but more usually it is this sweet bread-cake. Add all the butter to the scalded milk. Add to dough the grated rind of 1 large lemon and of 1 large orange. After the first rising turn the dough into a buttered Bundt pan, or a large tube pan. Cover and let rise. Bake in a 350° oven for 1 hour, or until done. Turn out of pan and drizzle with a thin white or chocolate icing. This bread keeps well and freezes well. If desired, the Bundt pan may be well buttered and then sprinkled liberally with slivered blanched almonds or slivered almonds mixed with breadcrumbs. An American innovation uses slivered blanched almonds and chocolate chips. With the almonds and additions no frosting is needed.

CHOCOLATE-FILLED KUCHEN. You may follow the basic recipe, or add all the butter to the scalded milk. After rising, roll dough out on lightly floured board. Chip and melt a 6-ounce package of semisweet chocolate. Spread the dough with the chocolate and then sprinkle the chocolate with ¼ cup sugar and, if desired, raisins or nuts. Roll tightly and place in a buttered tube pan. Let rise. Bake at 350° for 1 hour. When done, turn out of pan and drizzle with a thin chocolate icing.

CHOCOLATE BRAIDS. Delicious and unusual! Use only ½ cup each of butter and sugar. Work all the butter into the scalded milk. After the first rising, divide dough in half. Into one half work 1 or 2 squares of unsweetened chocolate, melted. Roll each piece of dough into a thick rope. Braid the two ropes together making a thick braid. Place on a buttered cookie sheet, or in a large loaf pan (10 by 5 inches), or coil the braid in a 10-inch tube pan. Let rise until doubled and bake in a 350° oven for 1 hour, or until done. The bread may be brushed with cream and sprinkled with sugar before baking, or frosted after baking.

DOUGHNUTS. The recipe for French Coffee-Ring Dough makes delicious doughnuts—as is, or with the addition of ¼ teaspoon mace, or 1 teaspoon crushed cardamom seed, or 1 tablespoon grated lemon rind.

Frost as desired. To make Bismarcks, roll the dough thin and cut into rounds. Top half of the rounds with 1 teaspoon stiff jam or conserve. Cover with the rest of rounds and pinch the edges together, using a little water to seal. Let rise and deep-fry.

FILLED TWIST. This is a simply fabulous holiday recipe! First make the filling by combining ¾ cup sugar, 2 cups cake crumbs, 1½ cups coconut, ½ cup butter, 3 large eggs, 2 tablespoons brandy, ¾ cup candied cherries, ⅓ cup candied orange rind, ⅓ cup finely chopped dates, ⅓ cup candied pineapple, ⅓ cup candied lemon rind, and ½ cup golden raisins. Then roll out the dough and spread with all of the filling. Roll as for a jelly roll. When tightly rolled, cut the roll lengthwise, being careful not to cut completely through one end. Now, starting at the connected end, twist the two strips of filled dough over and over, with the cut side up. Put onto a buttered cookie sheet and let rise until doubled. Bake in a 350° oven until done, 35 to 45 minutes.

HOLIDAY COFFEE CAKE. Make the less rich version of the dough, using only ½ cup each of butter and sugar. After the first rising, roll the dough out and spread it with sugar, nuts, and chopped candied fruit peels which have been soaked in brandy and then drained. Roll up and place in 2 buttered loaf pans, or in 1 large tube pan. Let rise and bake in a 375° oven. While still warm, frost and decorate with more candied fruits.

VIENNA CARNIVAL BALLS. A famous delicacy. Make French Coffee-Ring Dough, using 1 cup each butter and sugar and adding 1 tablespoon grated lemon rind. Cut the dough with a doughnut cutter and fry in deep fat at 375°.

GATAH (Yeast-Raised)

You won't find the country called Armenia on any modern map or in any world atlas. Its origins are lost in antiquity, and its current domain is only in the hearts and traditions of its people, who keep alive its songs, folklore, and proud heritage. The breadbasket of America has benefited from the generous sharing of the Armenian people. As I mentioned earlier (page 62), Armenian Peda and Lavash are so similar to Arabic Bread (which could also be called Syrian or Lebanese Bread), that separate recipes are not needed. Gatah, however, is uniquely an Armenian recipe. It is flaky, rich, and delicious, without being too sweet. The pastries go well with coffee or tea at any time of day. Tradition demands rolling the dough to a thickness of 1 inch; we like it rolled as thin as suggested in the following recipe. The recipe makes from 3 dozen to 5 dozen pastries, depending entirely on how thick or thin you roll the dough. (See also baking-powder Gatah, page 180.)

½ cup melted butter	4 to 4½ cups flour
2 large eggs	1 cup warm water
1 cake yeast	sesame seed
½ cup sour cream or yogurt	melted butter
½ teaspoon salt	Filling

Beat together the melted butter and the eggs. Add the yeast and stir to dissolve. Now add the sour cream or yogurt, the salt, flour, and warm water. Blend well and then turn the dough out onto a lightly floured board and knead thoroughly. When you are convinced that you've kneaded the dough enough, knead it some more. Place the dough in a bowl, brush with butter, cover, and let rise until doubled. Then punch the dough down and divide it into 4 or 5 pieces, shaping each piece into a ball. Place each ball on a floured board and roll it with a rolling pin until *very* thin; again, when you think it is thin enough, roll it a little thinner. Now brush the dough with melted butter and fold in half. Again brush with melted butter and fold in half, so that you have folded it as you would a square handkerchief and the dough is now a quarter of its former size and consists of four layers. Open the top layer as you would a pocket and spoon in ½ cup of the filling. Cover the filling with the dough and pinch the edges slightly, so that the filling is sealed in. Now roll the dough again, rolling it into a rectangle about ⅓ to ½ inch thick. Cut with a very sharp knife into squares or oblongs. Place them on buttered cookie sheets, brush with melted butter, and sprinkle with sesame seed. Bake immediately in a 375° oven for 15 to 20 minutes.

FILLING. Combine ½ cup sugar and 1 cup flour, and cut in ⅓ cup butter until butter-flour mixture resembles coarse cornmeal.

HONEY COFFEE CAKE

This coffee cake is actually better the second day. You can use almost any filling you wish: thinly sliced apples mixed with cinnamon and sugar; nuts and candied fruits that have been soaked in brandy and well drained; or a can of well-drained crushed pineapple added to the Filling given in the recipe. One of my favorite variations is made by pouring hot water to cover over ¾ cup each dried apricots and figs. Let stand and then drain and chop the fruits. Add to the dough with the last of the flour. Let rise, and then for a filling use ¾ cup brown sugar, ½ cup chopped nuts, and 2 teaspoons cinnamon.

¾ cup heavy cream	2 egg yolks
⅓ cup honey	2 yeast cakes dissolved in ½
2 tablespoons butter	cup warm water
1 tablespoon sugar	4 cups flour or more
2 teaspoons salt	Filling

Heat the cream to lukewarm and pour over the honey, butter, and sugar. When cooled add the salt and the egg yolks and blend well. Add the yeast mixture and enough flour to make a stiff dough. (You may need another ½ cup flour.) This dough is so rich that, like that for many coffee cakes, it requires no kneading. Cover and let rise until doubled. Then turn out on a floured board and roll into an oblong. Spread with the filling. Roll as for a jelly roll and coil in a well-buttered round 10-inch pan. Cover and let rise again. Bake in a 375° oven for 30 to 45 minutes, or until nicely browned. Serve hot with butter, or cool and spread with a glaze and sprinkle with more chopped nuts.

NOTE.   A delight to the family, and not much more work, is to make individual rolls and bake them in tiny individual loaf pans.

FILLING

2 egg whites, beaten stiff	1 cup chopped walnuts
¾ cup sugar	1 teaspoon cinnamon

Combine ingredients and spread over the dough.

KAFFEE KAKA
(Swedish Tea Ring Dough)

The most famous of the many excellent Swedish tea breads.

2 cups hot milk	12 to 20 cardamom seeds, or
1 cup sugar	1 tablespoon vanilla extract,
1 cup butter	or 2 teaspoons almond ex-
2 teaspoons salt	tract
2 cakes dry or compressed	2 large eggs
yeast	7 to 8 cups flour

Combine the milk, sugar, butter, and salt. Cool just to lukewarm. Dissolve the yeast as directed in a small amount of warm water. Add to milk mixture. Add the flavoring (if cardamom seeds are used be sure to crush fine) and the eggs and beat in. Stir in enough flour to make a soft dough. Put the rest of the flour on the breadboard. Turn the dough out and knead in enough flour so that the dough is not sticky, but be sure not to add too much. Place in a buttered bowl, cover, and let rise until doubled. Punch down and let rise again. This amount of dough will make 2 large tea rings or 2 dozen Semlor.

SWEDISH TEA RING. Take half of the dough and roll into a rectangular shape. Brush with melted butter and sprinkle liberally with brown or white sugar, currants or raisins, and chopped dates, chopped nuts, and candied fruits if desired. I sometimes use a very little chopped candied ginger. Roll up the dough the long way to make a ring, tuck the edges under, and seal. Place on a well-greased cookie sheet or pizza pan. Make cuts in the dough with scissors, about 1 inch apart, but do not cut all the way through. Lay each layer over on its side. Let rise and then bake in a 375° oven just until done, about 45 minutes. Be sure not to overbake. While still warm, frost just the edges so that the fruit shows through. Decorate as desired.

SEMLOR. These sweet buns are traditional Shrove Tuesday eating throughout Sweden and are also eaten on all the Tuesdays in Lent. After the Kaffee Kaka dough has risen the second time, punch it down again and shape into small rolls. Place on buttered cookie sheets. Cover and let the rolls rise until doubled. Bake in a 400° oven for 15 minutes, or until done. Cool. Cut the tops off the buns. On the bottom of each spread a little almond paste and over the almond paste place 1 or 2 tablespoons of sweetened whipped cream. Replace the tops and dust with powdered sugar. The traditional Semlor contain cinnamon. If you are making the sweet dough to use entirely for Semlor, add 1½ teaspoons cinnamon to dough and omit the cardamom seeds.

KUCHEN

There are as many recipes for Kuchen as there are German and Jewish housewives. Each uses her own favorite topping, a favorite dough, or a particular variation that makes hers different. For baking-powder Kuchen dough see page 177. All the toppings may be used interchangeably. Kuchen, like many European coffee cakes, is made in at least two ways: plain for everyday use, and rich for company, using more eggs, more butter, and sweet or sour cream in place of water or milk. I am including three recipes for yeast Kuchen Dough, two rich and one plain.

SOUR-CREAM KUCHEN DOUGH

1 cake yeast
1 tablespoon warm water
1 cup salted butter or sweet butter
¾ cup sugar
3 large eggs
1 cup sour cream
3 to 3½ cups flour
pinch of salt
1 tablespoon grated lemon rind

Dissolve the yeast in the water. Cream the butter and sugar. Beat in the eggs and then the sour cream. Blend in the rest of the ingredients. The dough may be refrigerated overnight or for several days. To use, press the dough into 2 lightly buttered 9- by 13-inch pans. Spread with fruit and topping of your choice. Let rise at room temperature for 1 to 1½ hours. Bake in a 350° oven for approximately 30 minutes, or until done.

KUCHEN BRAID. Use half the dough made by the preceding recipe. After dough has risen once, turn half of it onto a breadboard that has been sprinkled with 1½ cups flour. Knead this flour into the dough by turning and folding the dough gently. Now roll the dough into a rectangle and spread with 2 tablespoons soft butter. Sprinkle with 2 tablespoons brown sugar and 2 tablespoons each golden raisins and chopped walnuts. Now fold the dough in half, enclosing the brown-sugar mixture. Roll out again very gently. Cut the dough into 3 long strips and roll the strips with your hands to form 3 ropes of dough with the filling completely enclosed. Braid the ropes. Butter a 9-inch loaf pan. Holding the braid with one hand on each end, gently turn the ends under just enough to let the braid fit into the loaf pan. Cover the pan and let the dough rise until it just comes to the top of the pan. Brush with milk, sprinkle with sugar, and bake in a 350° oven for approximately 1 hour, or until done.

RICH KUCHEN DOUGH

This recipe calls for milk but scalded sour cream or sweet cream may be used. The number of egg yolks may also be varied from a minimum of 5 to as many as 8, depending on the richness desired.

1 cup scalded milk	5 egg yolks
1 cup butter	½ teaspoon salt
½ cup sugar	grated rind of 1 lemon
2 cakes yeast dissolved in 2 tablespoons warm water	5 cups flour

Pour the scalded milk over the butter and sugar. Stir to melt the butter. Let cool to lukewarm. When cooled add the dissolved yeast. Then blend in the rest of the ingredients in order. Blend the dough thoroughly. No kneading is required. Brush the dough with melted butter, cover the bowl, and let rise until doubled. When the dough has doubled, punch it down and use for any of the variations. This amount of dough will make 3 9- by 13-inch cakes. The dough may be kept in the refrigerator for several days if necessary.

FILLED COFFEE CAKE. The preceding recipe will make 2 of these cakes. Divide the dough in half. Roll each half into a rectangle. Taking one rectangle at a time, sprinkle with brown sugar and shavings of butter, then with chopped walnuts. Fold the rectangle over, covering the filling. Roll out, spread with filling, and fold over twice more, making three times in all. Roll out once more. Now fit the rectangle into a 9- by 13-inch lightly buttered pan and cover. Let rise until doubled. Repeat the procedure for the second rectangle. Bake in a 350° oven for 30 to 45 minutes, or until done. Either before or after baking, brush with melted butter and sprinkle with sugar. Cut into squares to serve. Makes 2. This recipe may also be made with Plain Kuchen Dough (see below).

LAYERED COFFEE CAKE.   Take part of the dough and roll to fit a lightly buttered 9- by 13-inch pan. Cover dough with slivers of butter, chopped nuts and/or raisins, sugar, and cinnamon. Now cover with another layer of dough. Let the dough rise until doubled. Then brush with milk and sprinkle with sugar. Bake at 350° for 30 to 45 minutes, or until done. Cut into squares to serve. This could also be made with Plain Kuchen Dough.

GERMAN ALMOND WREATH.   Roll the dough out and spread with a filling made of 2 cups slivered or ground almonds, 1 cup sugar, 2 egg whites beaten and folded into the nuts and sugar, and ¼ cup raisins. Roll as for jelly roll, seal the edges, place on a cookie sheet, and bake at 350° or 375° about 45 minutes.

NAPF KUCHEN.   Butter a Bundt pan or large tube pan thoroughly and sprinkle lavishly with slivered blanched almonds. More slivered blanched almonds and golden raisins may be added to the dough or not, as preferred. Turn the dough into the pan. Let rise until doubled and then bake at 350° for about 1 hour, or until done.

PLAIN KUCHEN DOUGH

1½ cups scalded milk or boiling water	¼ cup butter
	1 cake yeast
½ teaspoon salt	2 eggs
½ cup sugar	6 cups flour

Pour the scalded milk or boiling water over the salt, sugar, and butter. Let cool to lukewarm and then stir the yeast in. Then add the eggs and flour, blending carefully and thoroughly. The dough may now be placed in the refrigerator for several days and used as needed, or it may be let rise until doubled. In either case, the dough should rise once before using. Knead it after rising and then use in any variation preferred. Recipe makes 3 cakes.

FRUIT AND STREUSSEL KUCHENS

I have listed these separately because they may be made with any of the yeast Kuchen doughs, or with the baking-powder Kuchen Dough. It is impossible to give hard-and-fast rules for fruit kuchens, as they are entirely a matter of personal taste. Some people sprinkle the fruit lavishly, some frugally, adding sugar, chopped bits of butter, and cinnamon. Some add ground almonds, or chopped walnuts to the sugar topping. Some omit the cinnamon and use Vanilla Sugar instead or add grated lemon rind. Some people prefer a Streussel, perhaps with different proportions of ingredients than I give. The recipes given are our favorites but may easily be adjusted to other tastes.

TOPPINGS

These toppings are for 1 cake only, so increase proportions if you are making more.

STREUSSEL.   In the words of a German friend, "The better the Streussel is, with real butter." Combine ½ cup each sugar and flour with the grated rind of 1 lemon and ½ teaspoon vanilla extract. Rub ½ cup melted butter into this. If desired you may add ½ cup ground unblanched almonds. The lemon rind and vanilla extract may be omitted and 1 teaspoon cinnamon used instead.

CUSTARD TOPPING.   Blend ½ to ¾ cup sweet or sour cream with 2 whole eggs and ¼ cup sugar. One German friend uses 3 egg yolks, omitting the egg whites; another beats the whites separately and folds them into the custard.

SWABIAN TOPPING.   This topping, very little known in this country, appears to be found only in German-language cookbooks. It is a delicious cross between Streussel and Custard Topping and is preferred by many German cooks to either. It is especially good with rhubarb, cherry, or any berry filling. This recipe includes flour, but as some cooks do not use it, the flour may be omitted without any other changes. Combine ½ cup ground almonds, ⅓ cup sugar, ⅓ cup flour, 3 tablespoons lemon juice, and 4 large egg yolks. Beat the 4 egg whites with 2 tablespoons sugar until stiff. Fold into the flour-almond mixture and spread over the fruit. Bake as directed.

KUCHENS

FRUIT KUCHENS. Any fruit desired may be used. If canned fruit is used, be sure to drain it well. I have used strawberries, blueberries, blackberries, raspberries, plums, grapes, peaches, apricots, and sour or sweet cherries. The sour cherries, grapes, and plums require about ½ to ¾ cup sugar *before* adding the topping. The berries and sweet cherries do not need any extra sugar. With peaches and apricots it depends on personal taste. Children love Kuchens covered with fruit, dotted with butter, and sprinkled with sugar and cinnamon, with or without the addition of ground almonds or chopped walnuts. For company I always add a Streussel or Custard Topping. Line the buttered pans, bottom and sides, with the preferred Kuchen Dough, then spread with the desired fruit and topping. Let rise 30 to 45 minutes, or until the dough seems puffy. If a custard topping is used, pour it over the dough just before baking. Bake as directed.

APPLE STREUSSEL KUCHEN. Wash, peel, and core baking apples and slice over the top of the raised Kuchen Dough. Brush apples with melted butter and cover with Streussel. Bake in a 350° oven for 35 to 45 minutes.

CHEESE KUCHEN. Line the bottom and sides of the pan with dough. Combine 1½ cups cottage cheese, 3 or 4 eggs (some good cooks beat the egg whites separately and fold into the mixture), ½ teaspoon vanilla extract or 1 teaspoon grated lemon rind, 2 tablespoons flour, and ½ cup sugar. Place in dough-lined pan and bake immediately in a 375° oven for 15 minutes, then reduce heat to 325° and bake until done, about 20 to 30 minutes longer. If desired use only 2 medium eggs and add ⅓ cup cream. Some cooks add ½ teaspoon cinnamon to the mixture, or

½ cup raisins, or ½ cup crushed pineapple. We sprinkle the top of the cheese mixture with slivered blanched almonds before baking.

CINNAMON KUCHEN. A very simple and delicious Kuchen. Make holes at 2-inch intervals in the raised Kuchen Dough. If you do this very gently, the dough will not fall. Put a piece of butter in each depression. Sprinkle the cake lavishly with sugar and cinnamon. Bake in a 350° oven for 35 to 45 minutes. If desired—and this is excellent—put marmalade or jam in the depressions. A Streussel could be spread over the top.

MINCEMEAT KUCHEN. Line the bottom and sides of the pan with dough. Spread dough with brandied mincemeat, then with custard, made with 1 egg and ¼ cup each sour cream and sugar. Bake in a 350° oven 35 to 45 minutes.

PINEAPPLE KUCHEN. Use Rich Kuchen Dough, making the entire amount, and bake in a shallow 3-quart glass pan, well buttered. First make a filling by cooking together until thickened ½ cup sugar, 3 tablespoons cornstarch, ¼ teaspoon salt, 1 egg yolk, beaten, and 1 No. 2½ can crushed pineapple. Cool filling. Divide dough into 2 balls, one a little larger than the other. Roll the larger part out and fit it into the bottom of the pan, stretching it up the sides. Spread the cooled filling over the dough. Then roll out remaining dough and fit it over the filling, pinching the edges together to seal. Slash the top in several places so that steam can escape. Let rise, but do not let dough double. Bake in a 375° oven for 35 to 40 minutes, or until done.

RHUBARB KUCHEN. Cover the dough with ½-inch pieces sliced rhubarb. Sprinkle with ⅓ to ½ cup sugar, then add Custard Topping. Bake in a 350° oven 35 to 45 minutes.

OLD-TIME BAKING-DAY COFFEE CAKE

This recipe and the next are good examples of baking-day coffee cakes from two entirely different cultures. This one can be made with any bread dough but a French Bread or Italian Bread dough is preferable.

Le⸱ ᴛhe dough rise once, then punch it down and roll into a rectangle about ½ inch thick. Place on a buttered cookie sheet. Pat or roll the dough until smooth. Let rise until light, and then bake at 375° until done, about 25 minutes. While bread is hot, split it and butter both side generously. Sprinkle the bottom half with brown sugar and replace the top. Cut into squares and serve hot. It's a deliciously crusty coffee-time snack.

KHOOBZ SUMSUM
(Sesame Bread)

Khoobz is Lebanese for bread, and *sumsum* means sesame. In Lebanon the housewife uses oil, but for American tastes, we use butter.

This should be made with Arabic Bread dough, but any bread dough will be good. Spread the dough in a ¼-inch-thick sheet on a buttered cookie sheᴇᴛ or in a pan. Spread each cake with a mixture of approximately ¾ cup sesame seed, ⅓ cup sugar, and enough soft butter to make it spreadable. Let the dough rise and then bake as above. Eat while hot.

NOTE.   For a crustier bread, roll the dough ⅛ inch thick.

OLD COUNTRY COFFEE ROLL

The use of sour cream and egg yolks shows this recipe to be of German, Hungarian, or Romanian origin. The dough freezes very well, and the filling will keep almost indefinitely in a covered container in the refrigerator. It makes a rich, flaky, and very tender coffee cake.

¼ cup sugar
5 to 6 cups flour
¼ teaspoon salt
1 pound soft butter or
   margarine
4 to 6 egg yolks
1 teaspoon vanilla extract, or
   the grated rind of 1 large
   lemon

2 or 3 cakes of yeast dissolved
   in 3 tablespoons warm water
1 cup sweet or sour cream
jam, Nut Filling, or a mixture
   of cinnamon, sugar, and raisins

Sift the sugar, flour, and salt. Cut in the butter. Add the egg yolks, and vanilla extract or grated lemon rind, yeast, and cream. Stir all to a smooth dough, adding a little more flour or cream if needed. The dough will be fairly soft and sticky. Put the dough into a large buttered bowl and refrigerate for 4 to 6 hours or overnight. Divide the dough in half and roll each part on a lightly floured breadboard to a thickness of ¼ inch. Spread with jam, Nut Filling, or the cinnamon mixture. Roll lengthwise as for jelly roll and seal the edges. Form into a ring on an ungreased cookie sheet, sealing where ends meet. Do not let the rolls rise, but bake immediately in a 375° oven for 35 minutes. The outside edges may be slashed before baking, but not if jam is used. Makes 2 rolls.

KIPFELS I
(Hungarian Sweet Crescents)

Crescents were named after the crescent on the Turkish flag, when, in 1686, Hungarian bakers heard the noise as the invading Turks dug tunnels under Budapest, and warned the people, thus saving the city. Rogelach is another name for the same sweet roll.

Make the dough as for Old Country Coffee Roll. Sprinkle sugar instead of flour on the breadboard. Separate the dough into 8 to 12 balls. Take 1 ball at a time, keeping the rest refrigerated, and roll it into a circle 8 to 10 inches in diameter. Brush with melted butter and spread thinly with filling. Cut into 8 triangles and roll each triangle from the outside to the center of the circle, to form a crescent. Place on foil-lined cookie sheets and bake immediately in a 350° oven for 20 to 25 minutes, or until golden brown. Repeat until dough is finished, unless you wish to save some for another day. Recipe makes 5 dozen to 8 dozen crescents.

NUT FILLING.   Combine ¼ cup butter, 1 cup finely ground nuts, 1 cup sugar, ½ cup raisins (optional), juice and rind of ½ lemon. Beat 4 egg whites until stiff and fold into mixture.

NUT-CHOCOLATE FILLING.   Combine 3 stiffly beaten egg whites, ¼ cup sugar, 1½ cups ground nuts and ¼ pound tiny chocolate chips.

NUT-COFFEE FILLING. Cream ½ cup butter with ½ cup sugar. Stir in 2 cups of ground or finely chopped walnuts, ¼ cup of coffee, and the grated rind of 1 orange.

NOTE. Plain sugar and cinnamon may also be used as a filling, or use any of the fillings listed with Hungarian Poppy-Seed Rolls.

KIPFELS II

There are other recipes for basic Kipfel dough, each rich and delectable. This one is too good to be omitted.

3 cups flour	4 or 5 egg yolks from large
1 cake yeast (packaged dry	eggs
yeast won't do)	grated rind of 1 lemon
1 cup butter	¼ teaspoon salt
1 cup heavy sweet cream, or	
½ cup sour cream	

Combine the flour, yeast, and butter. Cut the yeast and the butter into the flour as for pastry, until the particles are like coarse cornmeal. Stir in the rest of the ingredients and blend well. Cover the dough well and chill in the refrigerator overnight. When ready to use, turn a portion of the dough out onto a sugared breadboard. Any part of the dough not used immediately should be kept refrigerated. Roll the dough out and cut, fill, and bake as for Kipfels I. The dough is so rich and soft that it must be kept chilled.

VARIATIONS

1. If desired, and this is delicious, roll the dough out on a board that has been liberally sprinkled with sugar and chopped almonds. Roll the dough tightly, as for a jelly roll. Cut into slices and bake in a shallow pan or in muffin tins. These are a melt-in-the-mouth coffee-time treat.

2. The Hungarians are very fond of apricot and prune jams (called Lekvar) and of meringue toppings. They take this same Kipfel dough and

divide it into 2 portions, one larger than the other. The larger portion is put into a buttered 9- by 13-inch pan and spread with Lekvar. Over the jam a thick meringue, usually with ground walnuts in it, is spread. The smaller portion of dough is then rolled out and cut into strips, which are placed lattice fashion over the meringue. The cake is then baked in a 350° oven for 45 to 50 minutes.

MERINGUE.   Beat 4 large egg whites with ¼ cup sugar. When stiffly beaten, fold in 1 teaspoon vanilla extract, juice and rind of ½ lemon, and 1 cup chopped or ground walnuts or almonds.

RICH SOUR-CREAM DOUGH

This rich, eggy dough is an excellent basis for almost any coffee cake. The variations given for it are especially good, but remember that most variations may be used interchangeably with almost any coffee-cake dough.

1 cup egg yolks	grated rind of 2 lemons
1 cup melted butter	½ to ¾ cup sugar
1 cup sour cream	½ teaspoon salt
2 cakes yeast	8 cups sifted flour or more
2 tablespoons lukewarm water	

Combine the first 3 ingredients. Dissolve the yeast in the water and add. Stir in the rest of the ingredients and knead until the mixture forms a stiff dough. Now put the dough in a clean tea towel or flour sack, tie, and place in a bowl of cold water. Let stand until the dough bag rises to the top. Knead the dough, adding a little more flour if necessary. It is now ready to be used as the basis of a variety of coffee cakes. If you wish to refrigerate the dough, use ¾ cup sugar and 3 cakes of yeast. Punch the dough down each time it rises. It will keep for 3 days in the refrigerator.

LAYER TORTE.   Take half the Rich Sour-Cream Dough and divide into 3 parts. Roll or pat each part into a round about the size of a dinner plate. Pinch the edges of each piece to form a rim. Place on greased cookie sheets, cover, and let rise until puffy, but not doubled. Spread one round with ⅓ cup jam, one with Cheese Filling, and one with Walnut Filling I. Bake at 350° for 30 minutes. Place the cheese layer on the bottom, then the jam layer, and top with the walnut layer. Serve hot or cold, but preferably hot. If desired, drizzle the edges of the finished cake with a thin icing.

CHEESE FILLING. Combine 1 cup cottage cheese, drained, with 2 tablespoons sugar and the rind and juice of 1 lemon.

WALNUT FILLING I. Combine ⅓ cup chopped walnuts, 2 tablespoons sugar, and ½ teaspoon cinnamon.

WALNUT ROLL. Roll half the dough into a thin rectangle. Spread with Walnut Filling II (see following recipe), being sure to spread the filling right to the edges. Now roll the dough as for a jelly roll, fairly tightly. Pinch the edges to seal. Coil the roll loosely on a greased cookie sheet, cover and let rise until nearly but not quite doubled, about 45 minutes. Bake in a 325° oven for 40 to 45 minutes. Cool on a rack. Slices and serves beautifully.

WALNUT FILLING II. Combine ½ cup soft butter, ¾ cup brown sugar, 1 egg, ⅓ cup cream, 1 teaspoon vanilla extract, and 1 teaspoon cinnamon. Add 3 cups finely chopped walnuts.

YEAST STRUDEL DOUGH

This is our favorite Strudel dough. Made with yeast, it is flaky and tender without the tedious stretching, folding, and rolling necessary with other Strudels. If desired, a simple jam or preserve may be used as a filling, or a mixture of 4 stiffly beaten egg whites, ½ cup sugar, 1 teaspoon cinnamon, and 1 cup chopped or ground nuts. Any filling used with Strudels in other cookbooks may also be used.

2½ cups flour	½ cup sour cream
1 cup butter (or margarine)	3 large egg yolks
pinch of salt	1 cake yeast

Cut the flour, butter, and salt together as for pastry. Have the sour cream and egg yolks at room temperature. Dissolve the yeast in the sour cream and add to the flour-butter mixture along with the egg yolks. Stir all together and knead with the hands until mixture is smooth. Brush the dough with butter and chill for 8 hours, or overnight. When ready to use, place dough on a lightly floured board, pat it down, and then turn it over so that both sides are floured. Using a rolling pin, roll the dough as thin as possible. It will make a long, very thin sheet of dough which may be cut in two to make two Strudels. Spread dough with filling, keeping filling short of the edges. Fold the sides of the dough over the filling, then roll the dough carefully and seal the edges so that the filling does not seep out. Lift the roll carefully and place in a buttered shallow baking pan. Bake immediately in a 350° oven for 50 to 60 minutes, or until browned and done. Strudels are best eaten fresh. However, a rolled and filled meat or cabbage Strudel can be kept in the refrigerator for several days before baking. Fruit Strudels should be kept no longer than 24 hours before baking. Makes 1 large Strudel or 2 small ones.

APPLE FILLING. Canned apple-pie filling may be used. Or about 1 pound thinly sliced apples may be combined with ⅔ cup sugar, ¼ cup golden raisins, ½ cup chopped walnuts, the grated rind of 1 lemon, and a pinch of salt.

CHEESE FILLING. Combine and blend thoroughly 1 pound drained cottage cheese, ½ pound cream cheese, 2 whole eggs or 3 egg yolks, ½ cup sugar, the grated rind of 1 lemon, and ½ teaspoon vanilla extract. If desired the egg whites may be stiffly beaten and folded into the mixture last.

PINEAPPLE FILLING. Combine 1½ cups pineapple preserves (apricot preserves are also excellent), 1 cup coconut, and 1 cup chopped walnuts or more.

ONION-CHEESE FILLING. For a good main-dish Strudel, use as a filling 2 large onions, minced and sautéed, and combined with 2 cups cottage cheese, and salt and pepper to taste. Sprinkle with sesame seed.

SWEET-POTATO ROLL

A delicious and unusual sweet roll. If you don't like sweet potatoes you won't appreciate it, but if you do, the flavor will be most appealing.

Instead of fresh hot boiled and mashed sweet potatoes, you may use the canned variety, which can be mixed cold. To get 2½ cups of mashed sweet potatoes you will need the 2-pound 8-ounce size can. Use the whole can. You may use the liquid from the can, or plain water, or sweet cream, rich milk, or half-and-half. If desired, omit the filling; add chopped nuts, dates, and grated orange rind to the dough; drop spoonfuls of dough into buttered muffin tins; and bake at 375° for 20 to 25 minutes, making certain that rolls are done by testing with a toothpick or cake tester. Or roll the dough as suggested in the recipe, then cut it into slices. Place slices cut side down in large buttered muffin tins, or side by side in a buttered jelly-roll pan. Glaze with an orange-flavored frosting.

⅓ cup soft butter	1 cup liquid
2½ cups hot boiled, mashed sweet potatoes	1 cake yeast
⅓ cup sugar	2 large eggs
1 teaspoon salt	3½ to 4 cups flour

Combine the butter, hot sweet potatoes, sugar, salt, and liquid. Let cool to lukewarm. Stir the yeast into the mixture and stir to dissolve the yeast. Now add the eggs and half the flour. Beat thoroughly. Add rest of flour and blend well. At this point the dough may be refrigerated for several days. Punch it down as it rises. If you do not refrigerate the dough, brush it with soft or melted butter, cover, and let rise until doubled. Then punch down and turn out onto a floured breadboard. Roll the dough out and brush with melted butter. Sprinkle with brown sugar, cinnamon, nuts, and raisins; or with chopped dates, chopped nuts, brown sugar, and grated orange rind. The appeal of this roll is in the dough itself, so a simple, uncomplicated filling is best. Roll the dough as for a jelly roll. Pinch the edges to seal and then carefully lift the roll into a buttered 10-inch tube pan. Cover and let rise until doubled. Bake in a 350° to 375° oven for 1 hour and 15 minutes, or until the roll is browned and tests done. Glaze with a light orange-flavored frosting.

DINNER ROLLS. Cut sugar and butter to ¼ cup each. Use ½ cup wheat germ in place of that amount of flour. Spoon the dough into buttered muffin tins, let rise, and bake.

SWEET ROLLS

BASIC SWEET DOUGH USING ROLLED OATS

This basic sweet dough can be used in variations listed with other recipes.

½ cup butter
½ cup brown sugar
1 teaspoon salt
1 cup scalded milk
1 cup flour
2 large eggs

1 cake yeast dissolved in ¼ cup warm water
1 cup rolled oats
3 cups flour
soft butter, brown sugar, cinnamon, chopped nuts (optional)

Combine butter, brown sugar, and salt. Pour scalded milk over the mixture. Cool. Beat in 1 cup flour and the eggs. Blend. Add the dissolved yeast and rolled oats. Stir in the rest of flour using only enough to make a soft dough. Let rise. Punch down and turn out onto a floured board. Knead dough lightly and then divide into 2 parts. Roll each part and spread with soft butter. Sprinkle liberally with brown sugar and cinnamon, and chopped nuts if desired. Roll the dough as for jelly roll. Cut into slices and place the slices, cut side down, in buttered muffin pans. Let dough rise until doubled. Bake in a 375° oven for 20 to 25 minutes. Turn out immediately. If desired, 1 teaspoon each of brown sugar and melted butter may be put into each muffin tin and the dough sprinkled with nuts.

NOTES.   If desired, 1 cup each golden raisins and chopped nuts may be added to the dough. The dough may also be shaped into rolls, baked, and frosted.

You may also make the basic recipe and just before baking pour over the rolls a mixture of 1 cup brown sugar and ½ cup heavy cream, well blended. Delicious.

ORANGE ROLLS. Make dough as in basic recipe, but add 1 tablespoon grated orange rind and substitute orange juice for the milk. When dough has risen, punch it down and roll out. Cut into round rolls. Brush rolls with melted butter and place a piece of sugared, diced orange in the center of each. Fold dough into Parker House shapes and press lightly to seal orange into dough. Place the rolls on buttered cookie sheets and let rise. Bake in a 400° oven for 20 minutes, or until done. Frost with an orange glaze.

ORANGE STICKY BUNS. Roll dough out as for basic recipe, brush with soft butter, and sprinkle with brown sugar and grated orange rind. Roll up and slice. Place slices, cut side down, in a buttered shallow baking pan. Rolls should be just touching. Let rise and bake in a 400° oven for 15 minutes. Spoon Orange Syrup over rolls and bake for 10 minutes longer.

ORANGE SYRUP. Combine ⅔ cup sugar and ⅓ cup orange juice, bring to a boil, and simmer 5 minutes. Remove from heat and stir in ½ cup orange juice and 2 tablespoons butter.

BATH BUNS

These rich and delicious buns originated in the city of Bath, England, many generations ago. With a recipe as old as this one no one can claim originality, since housewives and bakers down the years have put their own stamp on it by varying the flavoring or the shape, or by using raisins in place of currants, candied cherries in place of citron, etc. The original Bath Buns were less sweet and were sprinkled with caraway "comfits" (seeds) instead of currants and sugar.

1 cup butter	4 cups flour
1 cup sugar	½ cup citron, minced
1 teaspoon salt	½ cup currants
4 large eggs	½ cup slivered almonds (op-
⅔ cup milk	tional)
2 cakes yeast dissolved in ⅓ cup warm water	

Cream the butter, sugar, and salt. Beat the eggs and the milk until blended. Add to creamed mixture along with the dissolved yeast. Dust the fruits and nuts with ½ cup flour and add the rest of the flour to the dough. Stir in the fruits and nuts last and knead the dough thoroughly. Cover and let rise until doubled. Punch the dough down and turn out onto a floured board. Divide dough into 20 pieces and shape pieces into round buns. Place on buttered cookie sheets and brush with cream. Sprinkle with sugar and press a few raisins or currants on top of each bun. Let rise again until doubled. Bake in a 375° oven 25 to 30 minutes.

ROHRNUDELN IN DER AUFLAUFFORM
(Baked Rolls in Pudding Form)

This German recipe deserves to be better known in this country. Served with a thin custard sauce, this "pudding" makes a nice dessert after a light meal. The dough isn't very rich, so you may prefer to serve the rolls without the sauce, as slightly sweet dinner rolls. In this case use milk in place of cream in the mixture poured over the rolls, but don't omit it, as it is necessary to provide moisture.

1 pound sifted flour	¼ teaspoon salt
1 package yeast, dissolved in	grated rind of 1 lemon
¼ cup lukewarm milk	3 eggs
¼ cup sugar	¼ pound soft butter

Be sure that all ingredients are at room temperature. Combine all ingredients in the order given and mix with your hands (be sure they are clean). Add the butter last, working it in carefully. When all has been kneaded into a smooth dough, cover with a towel and let rise until doubled, about 1½ hours. Now form the dough into small rolls and place them side by side in a well-greased shallow 3-quart pan. Cover and let rise again until doubled, about 1 hour. When the rolls have risen and are ready to bake, pour over them a mixture of 1½ cups cream, ¼ cup sugar, ¼ cup melted butter and 1 teaspoon vanilla extract (omit vanilla extract if serving as dinner rolls). Bake in a 375° oven until browned and done, about 45 minutes. At the end of the baking time the liquid will have been absorbed by the rolls.

BABA AU RHUM

This famous French specialty was supposedly invented by King Stanislas Leczinski and named by him after Ali Baba of *The Arabian Nights.* At first a large leavened cake was simply sprinkled heavily with rum and then set aflame. Later the dough was made into individual cakes and brushed with a heavy rum syrup, which practice then evolved into dipping the cakes into the syrup several times, and letting them drip dry. The Baba became so popular throughout France that pastry cooks used it as a foundation from which to build other eventually famous delicacies. The Gorenflot is the same pastry, only baked in a hexagonal mold. The Savarin, named after Brillat-Savarin, originally differed in shape, in the kind of syrup used, and by the omission of raisins, but the pastry is the same. The Baba became Americanized with the addition of orange rind to the syrup, and in some cases the rum was omitted altogether and an orange or coffee syrup used.

1 cake yeast	½ cup melted butter
¼ cup scalded and cooled milk	1 cup raisins or currants
3 cups flour	1 teaspoon vanilla extract or
4 large eggs	½ teaspoon almond extract
¼ cup sugar	

Dissolve the yeast in the milk. Sift the flour into a large bowl and make a well in the center. Into the well drop the eggs, sugar, melted butter, raisins or currants, flavoring, and the yeast. Blend ingredients well, cover, and let rise until doubled. Brush a Bundt pan or a 10-inch tube pan well with butter and sprinkle with slivered blanched almonds or with slivered Brazil nuts and/or bits of candied fruits. Pour the Baba dough into the mold and let rise again. Bake in a 350° oven for 45 minutes, or until done. Cool in the pan on a rack for 10 minutes. Then turn out of pan and spoon hot Rum Syrup over the hot cake, letting it sink in slowly. If desired the cake may be pricked all over with a fork, thus letting the syrup sink in quicker. Serve either hot or cold, with whipped cream.

SYRUPS

RUM SYRUP. Bring 1 cup sugar and ½ cup water to a rolling boil. Remove from heat and stir in ½ cup rum. Brandy or cognac could be used.

ORANGE SYRUP. Bring to a boil 1 cup orange juice, 1 cup sugar, 1 tablespoon lemon juice, and the grated rind of 1 orange. Boil for several minutes, then remove from heat and spoon over the Baba.

COFFEE SYRUP. Cream ½ cup butter with 1 cup sugar until light and fluffy. Slowly add ⅓ cup very strong, very hot coffee and 2 tablespoons brandy or rum. Spoon over the hot Baba letting the sauce sink into it.

SAVARIN

Make Baba au Rhum (omitting the raisins) with the Rum Syrup. Cool the cake completely and then paint it with hot apricot preserves. Whip 1 cup of heavy cream with ¼ cup sugar and 1 teaspoon vanilla extract. Fold ¼ to ⅓ cup finely chopped candied fruits into the whipped cream. Pile the cream in the center of the cake and serve cold. Delicious.

BUTTER BOWS

These sweet coffee rolls, very popular wherever they are known, are a Jewish specialty. Teflon-lined cookie sheets or lining paper for regular cookie sheets make the cleaning job much easier. The dough will keep in the refrigerator for several days.

1 cake yeast	pinch of salt
1 cup scalded and cooled milk	4 cups flour
⅓ cup sugar	1 cup brown sugar
½ cup butter, melted	Almond Filling
2 medium eggs	

Dissolve the yeast in the cooled milk, with the sugar. Add butter, eggs, salt, and flour and beat thoroughly. The dough will be soft. Cover the bowl and let the dough rise twice, punching down after each rising. Spread a breadboard with 1 cup brown sugar. Take out 1 spoonful of the dough at a time and fold it over the filling, then roll the piece of dough into a 5-inch length. Now knot, or fold, the piece of dough into the shape of a bow. Place on buttered cookie sheets. Cover and let rise about 20 to 30 minutes. Bake in a 400° oven for 15 minutes, or until done.

NOTE. The dough can be dropped, by spoonfuls, into a mixture of ¾ cup chopped nuts, ½ cup sugar, and 1 teaspoon cinnamon. The pieces can then be twisted into any shape desired, and baked as directed. The rolls are equally good and much simpler to make.

ALMOND FILLING. Combine 1¼ cups ground almonds, ⅓ cup sugar, a pinch of salt, 1 tablespoon melted butter, and 1 stiffly beaten egg white. If desired, a little chopped candied ginger may be added to the filling.

BUTTER BOWS WITH BUTTER FILLING. When the dough has been punched down after its second rising, work into it not less than ¾ cup and not more than 1 cup ice-cold butter that has been chopped into small pieces. Work the butter in with your hands, but do not let it melt or soften too much, as the pieces of butter should still show. Now take out spoonfuls of the dough and roll on both sides in the brown sugar. Roll or flatten into 5-inch lengths and shape into bows. Place on cookie sheets and let rise for 20 to 30 minutes in a cool room. These are better made in the winter and should not be attempted in hot weather. Bake in a 400° oven as directed in the basic recipe. These are especially delicious.

CINNAMON ROLLS

Cinnamon rolls may be made with any sweet yeast dough, but this combination is best. There is no mistake in the liquid ingredients; some people prefer to use all milk so milk is included twice.

1 cup hot mashed white potatoes or sweet potatoes	1 cup soft butter
1 cup warm water, potato water, or scalded milk	1 cup sugar
	1½ teaspoons salt
1 cup scalded milk	4 large eggs
7 cups flour, or more	soft butter, brown sugar, cin-
1 or 2 cakes yeast	namon, chopped nuts (op-
	tional)

Combine the potatoes, liquids and 1 cup of the flour. Beat until thoroughly blended. Let cool until lukewarm, then stir the yeast into the mixture. Cover and let rise until light. When mixture is light, stir it down with a wooden spoon. Cream the butter and sugar, add the salt and eggs, and beat until thoroughly blended. Stir into yeast mixture with the remaining flour, using enough flour to make a firm dough. Knead, place in a bowl, brush with butter, and let rise again. When dough has risen, punch it down and turn it onto a floured board. Roll the dough out, adding a little more flour if necessary. Spread the dough with soft butter and sprinkle thickly with brown sugar and cinnamon, adding some chopped nuts if desired. Roll as for a jelly roll and cut into 1-inch slices. Place the slices, just touching, in a buttered pan with sides. Let rise again and bake in a 375° oven for about 20 minutes. Glaze rolls. These keep well.

NOTE.   If desired the dough may be spread with Grape-Nuts or Raisin-Bran Flakes, or chopped dried fruits.

FRUITED LOAF.   To the dough you may add ½ cup each cooked dried pears, apricots, and prunes; ¼ cup minced candied lemon or orange peel; ½ cup chopped nuts, and 1 teaspoon cinnamon or other desired spice. Bake in 2 loaves at 375° until done, about 45 minutes. Frost loaves while warm.

MORAVIAN SUGAR CAKE.   A wonderful variation. Spread dough in 3 buttered 9-inch round cake pans. Let rise. Now carefully make indentations in each cake. Blend 1 cup brown sugar and ½ cup soft butter to a paste and put a bit of this paste in each indentation. Sprinkle the tops of the cakes with brown sugar and cinnamon. Bake in a 375° oven until done, about 25 to 30 minutes.

MORAVIAN CHRISTMAS CAKE.   Add to the basic dough 1 cup golden raisins and 1 cup slivered blanched almonds. Place in 2 buttered loaf pans, brush with melted butter, and sprinkle with sugar and more slivered blanched almonds. Let rise. Bake in a 375° oven until done, about 40 minutes.

KUCHEN. This dough is excellent in any of the Kuchen recipes on pages 200-205.

COTTAGE-CHEESE ROLLS

The recipe for these flaky, tender rolls is one of the most requested in my files. The recipe doubles easily and, if desired, half of the dough may be formed into buns and baked as dinner rolls and the other half filled and baked as a sweet roll.

2 cakes yeast	1½ pounds cottage cheese
½ cup warm water	2 large eggs
5 cups flour	
½ cup sugar	FILLING
1½ teaspoons salt	1½ cups brown sugar
1 cup butter	½ cup butter
	1 teaspoon cinnamon

Dissolve the yeast in the water. Sift the dry ingredients into bowl. Cut in the butter until the dough has the consistency of very coarse cornmeal. Blend in the cheese, eggs, and dissolved yeast. When well mixed, turn the dough onto a floured board, shape it into a ball, and let it rest for 10 minutes. Blend the filling ingredients until crumbly. Roll the dough into a rectangle. Sprinkle with filling and roll as for jelly roll. Cut into 1-inch slices. Place slices, cut side down, on buttered cookie sheets. Let rise until doubled and then bake in 375° oven for 20 minutes, or until done.

VARIATION. Add ¼ cup rum and some chopped pecans to the filling. Roll out the dough and spread the filling on it. Roll tightly and fit the roll into a buttered 10-inch tube pan. Let rise. Slash top in several places and bake in 375° oven approximately 45 minutes to 1 hour. Test before removing from oven. Very good.

CORNISH SPLITS

These rich little buns are a traditional teatime treat; they are served hot, split open, with butter, jam, or clotted cream.

1 cake yeast	½ teaspoon salt
2 tablespoons warm water	⅔ cup scalded, cooled milk
⅓ cup butter	2 large eggs
⅓ cup sugar	4 cups flour

Dissolve the yeast in the water, or if desired, cream the yeast with 1 tablespoon of the sugar, until syrupy, omitting the water. Stir together the yeast mixture, the butter, sugar, salt, milk, eggs, and 2 cups of the flour. Beat until smooth. Then stir in the rest of the flour. Knead the dough until smooth, and then let it rise until doubled. Then punch the dough down and turn it out onto a floured breadboard. Roll dough into a rectangle about ½ inch thick. Cut with a biscuit cutter and place on buttered cookie sheets. Let rise until doubled. Brush with milk and bake in a 350° oven for 25 to 30 minutes. Serve hot. If a softer crust is desired, wrap the Splits in a towel before serving.

DANISH PASTRY

This excellent pastry is the basis for numerous sweet rolls and coffee cakes.

6 cups flour	⅓ cup sugar
2 cups butter or margarine	2 large eggs
2 cakes yeast	6 or 7 cardamom seed, crushed
1¼ cups scalded and cooled milk	(optional)

Blend ½ cup of the flour and the butter or margarine as for pastry. When thoroughly blended mold it into a large square, wrap in waxed paper, and chill. Now dissolve the yeast in the milk and add the sugar. Stir in the rest of the flour, the eggs, and the cardamom seed if used. Knead to make a firm dough. Now roll the dough out on a lightly floured bread-board into a long rectangle. Place the chilled butter-flour mixture on the dough and fold part of the dough over to cover it. Roll the dough out into a long rectangle again. Now fold both ends of the dough over the center so that you have three layers. Roll out again, fold again, and then repeat the procedure a third time. Chill the dough until ready to use. When ready to use, cut off portions of the dough and roll and fill as desired.

NOTE. The dough may be cut into squares, a spoonful of any desired filling placed in the center, and the edges folded toward the filling. Let rise. Bake in a 400° oven for about 20 minutes, or until done. For crescents cut the dough into triangles and place a roll of almond paste at the wide end. Fold the dough over the filling and roll toward the thin end. Place on buttered cookie sheets, let rise, and bake as for buns. For sweet square buns, cut the dough into 2-inch squares, let rise, and bake the same way. Frost while hot and sprinkle thickly with chopped walnuts or slivered almonds. The dough may also be used as the foundation of Kuchen or other coffee cake.

ALMOND-PASTE FILLING. In a blender, blend 1 cup grated blanched almonds until fine. Add 1 egg, ½ cup sugar, and 1 tablespoon lemon juice and mix well.

CREAM FILLING. Put 1 cup milk, 2 tablespoons flour blended with 2 tablespoons sugar, 2 egg yolks, and 1 teaspoon vanilla extract into the top of a double boiler and cook over boiling water, stirring constantly, until thickened. Cool before using.

FILLING VARIATIONS. A cottage-cheese filling, as for Kuchen, or prune Lekvar, or apple pie slices all make good fillings. The canned berry pie fillings are also good.

KOLACHES
(Bohemian Filled Buns)

Delicious little yeast buns, which change character with the filling used. If you prefer a less rich dough, any coffee-cake dough may be used. This recipe is traditional as well as exceptional.

1 cup soft butter
4 to 6 egg yolks
1 cake yeast dissolved in ¼
   cup warm milk
4 stiffly beaten egg whites
4 cups flour

2 cups scalded, cooled sweet
   cream
½ cup sugar
grated rind of 1 lemon
pinch of salt

Cream the butter and egg yolks. Add the dissolved cake of yeast and fold in the beaten egg whites and 1 cup of the flour. Let rise until bubbly. Then stir the sponge down and stir in the rest of the flour, using only enough to have the dough soft but not sticky. Stir in the remaining ingredients. Let rise until doubled. (This dough does not require kneading.) When dough has doubled punch it down. Pinch off pieces and press each out to a thickness of about ½ inch, using 3 fingers to make the indentations. Spread with desired filling. Brush the dough lightly with melted butter or with 1 egg yolk beaten with a little milk. Bake on buttered cookie sheets in a 375° oven for approximately 20 to 25 minutes.

NOTE. Some cooks roll the dough out and cut it into small squares. They then place 1 tablespoon filling in the center of each square and fold the corners over the filling so that the filling peeks through the sides. Sprinkle the baked rolls with sugar.

COOKED FILLINGS

APPLE-RAISIN. Combine 1 cup thick applesauce, 2 tablespoons brown sugar, 1 tablespoon melted sweet butter, a pinch of nutmeg, and ½ cup each raisins and chopped nuts. Place 1 teaspoon, or a little more, in center of each piece of dough and draw the edges up and over the filling. Bake these in buttered muffin tins. Sprinkle with powdered sugar when done.

APRICOT. Use thick apricot preserves. Or simmer ½ pound dried apricots, ⅓ cup sugar, and 1 cup water or orange juice for 45 minutes, or until thick. Cool before using.

CHEESE. Combine 1 tablespoon melted butter, 1 pound cottage cheese or ½ pound softened cream cheese, 4 egg yolks, ⅓ cup sugar, rind of ½ lemon, dash of salt, and ½ cup golden raisins or slivered almonds.

DATE BUTTER. Use the date butter that is sold commercially. Or simmer 2 cups pitted finely chopped dates, ⅓ cup sugar, ¼ cup butter (sweet butter preferably), ¼ cup water or orange juice, stirring constantly to prevent scorching. When thickened, add ½ teaspoon vanilla extract or 1 teaspoon grated orange rind. Cool before using. If desired, chopped nuts may be added. If you use slivered almonds, flavor the Date Butter with ¼ teaspoon almond extract.

FIG. Follow the recipe for Date Butter, using chopped dried figs in place of dates.

NUT. 2½ cups chopped walnuts, 1 cup sugar, ½ cup butter (sweet butter preferred), ½ cup thick sweet cream. Simmer over low heat just until butter melts.

POPPY SEED. ¾ cup poppy seed, crushed or ground, combined with ½ cup heavy sweet cream, 2 tablespoons butter (sweet butter preferred), ⅓ cup honey (or sugar, if preferred), and 1½ tablespoons cornstarch. Bring ingredients to a boil and let boil for just 1 minute. Cool before using. Or use the canned poppy-seed filling.

PRUNE. Use ¾ pound prunes. Pit and chop the prunes and combine with the grated rind of 1 small lemon, ¼ cup sugar, ¾ cup water, orange juice, or apple juice, and a pinch each of cloves and cinnamon. Simmer these ingredients for about 30 to 45 minutes, or until thick. Stir to keep from scorching. If necessary, thin the filling with a little more juice, or with 1 tablespoon sweet butter.

UNCOOKED FILLINGS

The cooked fillings are traditional for Kolaches, but any desired filling may be used. I have on occasion spread the dough with a thin layer of jam and then topped the jam with a not too sweet meringue. Sprinkle with sugar before baking. Canned fillings may be used. Fillings listed with other European coffee cakes may be used also. For another nut filling, cream 3 egg yolks with ⅓ cup sugar and add the grated rind of 1 lemon and ½ cup blanched almonds, ground; then fold in 3 stiffly beaten egg whites.

NOTE.   If you have an electric blender, the ground nuts or seeds called for in so many European recipes are no problem. Just spin the desired amount in the blender.

JAM OR MARMALADE.   Use any preferred thick jam or marmalade. Place a perfect walnut half or blanched almond half on top of jam or marmalade. Sprinkle buns with powdered sugar while warm.

MERINGUE.   Make a thick meringue using 6 egg whites and ⅓ cup sugar. Spread on top of Kolaches. Sprinkle with powdered sugar and place a candied cherry half or a walnut half or almond half in the center of the meringue. Bake.

RICH REFRIGERATOR ROLLS (SWEET)

The following recipe makes quite a large quantity and may easily be halved if desired. But it is an easy-to-make recipe, with results that are so sure fire and delicious that even so large a batch of dough is quickly used. The dough will keep, in the refrigerator, for up to a week, but be sure to punch the dough down as it rises. You will have to do this several times the first day; after that, once a day should be enough. If you wish a richer roll, the liquid may be cut to a total of 3 cups and the eggs increased to 8. The dough is rich either way. Braid it, twist it, make pinwheels, or make it into buns. Brush with milk and sprinkle with sugar before baking. Or use in any variations listed with this or other recipes.

2 cups boiling water or	4 large eggs
scalded milk	4 cakes yeast
1 pound butter or margarine	2 cups warm water or scalded,
2 to 3 cups sugar	cooled milk
1 tablespoon salt	12 to 13 cups flour

Pour the boiling water or scalded milk over the butter, sugar, and salt. Blend well and cool to lukewarm. Add the eggs and beat. Dissolve the yeast in the 2 cups warm water or scalded, cooled milk. Add to the butter mixture along with half the flour. Beat thoroughly. Stir in the rest of the flour and blend well. Refrigerate overnight. Shape the rolls 2 hours before baking, to let them rise. Bake rolls in a 400° oven for 20 minutes.

NOTE. This dough will stand a good bit of handling and thus is ideal for shaping into somewhat intricate patterns. Some good cooks like to experiment with flower shapes or with making chickens, etc., with dough. Baked and frosted, these always bring praise.

HOLIDAY BREADS. Pieces of the dough may be shaped into small rolls and then shaped on a buttered cookie sheet into Christmas trees, New Year's Eve bells, etc. Let the dough rise and bake as for rolls. Frost thickly and decorate with almond halves and candied fruits.

FILLED TWISTS. Take any desired portion of dough and roll into a thin rectangle. Spread half the rectangle with any desired filling (chopped nuts, sugar, butter, and cinnamon) and fold the other half over the filling. Roll out again lightly and cut into strips. Twist the strips of dough, place on buttered cookie sheets, let rise, and bake as directed for rolls.

PENCIL ROLLS. Roll one-fourth of the dough out on a floured board. Spread with melted butter and brown sugar. Cut into 4- by 3-inch rectangles. Roll these into pencil shapes and place them seam side down in a buttered loaf pan. Stack the rolls on top of one another, brushing each layer of rolls with melted butter. Let rise and then bake in a 375° oven for approximately 35 to 45 minutes. The rolls will break off into individual pieces.

ROSE-GERANIUM ROLLS. Using one-fourth of the dough, roll it out on a floured board. Spread with a filling made by combining 1 cup sugar, ½ cup melted butter, grated rind of 2 oranges, and 10 medium rose-geranium leaves, finely minced. Roll the dough as for a jelly roll and cut into 1-inch slices. Place in large buttered muffin tins, or side by side in a shallow baking pan. Let rise until doubled and bake in a 375° oven for about 20 to 25 minutes. These are delicious rolls, and the fragrance is nothing short of divine, but be sure that you are using the herb rose geranium, which is a member of the geranium family but is *not* the bush geranium that is so popular. Rose-geranium leaves were frequently used by American housewives of a century ago. A leaf was placed at the bottom of each cake tin before the batter was poured in, or several leaves were used in a sponge cake or angel cake. The delicate flavor permeated the cake. Rose-geranium leaves are still used in some apple-jelly recipes, but other uses have been forgotten. A few leaves in any recipe using orange juice or having a pronounced orange flavor does a great deal to enhance the flavor.

ORANGE ROLLS. Make the Rose-Geranium Rolls variation, using rose geranium leaves or not, as desired. Roll and cut into 1-inch slices. Place, cut side down, in buttered muffin tins or a shallow baking pan. Let rise and bake in a 375° oven for 20 to 25 minutes, or until done. As soon as the rolls are removed from the oven, turn them out of the pan onto a large dish or tray. Pour over the hot rolls a mixture of powdered sugar and orange juice, about ½ cup orange juice to a cup of sugar. Cool before serving.

CHERRY RINGS. Use half of recipe. Roll into two 14- by 7-inch rectangles. Spread with 1½ cups well-drained canned sour pie cherries and a mixture of ½ cup each brown sugar, flour, and walnuts or almonds. Form the dough into rings, sealing the edges well. Coil in large buttered cake pans or fit the dough into buttered loaf pans. Cover and let rise and then bake in a 375° oven until done, about 45 minutes. Frost with a powdered-sugar frosting.

FRUIT ROLLS. Pinch off pieces of dough and work each piece around a well-drained canned peach slice, a canned apple slice, a pitted, soft date, a piece of fresh orange that has been rolled in brown sugar, or any other fruit you choose. Place in buttered muffin tins and let rise. Bake in a 375° or 400° oven until done, about 20 minutes.

APRICOT-ORANGE ROLLS. To one-third of the dough add 1 cup chopped dried apricots that have been softened in water or orange juice, and 1 tablespoon grated orange rind. Form the dough into round buns. Let rise and bake at 375° or 400° for about 20 minutes, or until done. Frost lightly with an Orange Glaze.

DATE-FILLED ROLLS. Use one-fourth of the dough. Roll into a rectangle and cut into 12 3-inch squares. In the center of each square place 1 tablespoon of filling. Fold the corners over the filling, and then turn them back slightly so that the filling shows through the pocket. Place on buttered cookie sheets, or in buttered muffin tins if desired, and let rise. Bake in a 375° oven for about 15 to 20 minutes. For the filling combine 1 cup pitted, chopped dates with ½ cup orange juice or pineapple juice, ½ teaspoon orange rind or lemon rind, 2 tablespoons lemon juice, and 1 tablespoon butter. Simmer about 5 minutes, or until mixture is thick. Cool before using.

CHOCOLATE-COCONUT ROLLS. Use one-third of the dough. Roll into a rectangle and spread with filling. Fold one-third of the rectangle over the center of the filling and then fold the other third back over the second part, making 3 layers. Cut into oblong buns and place on buttered cookie sheets. Let rise. Bake in a 400° oven about 20 minutes. For the filling combine ⅓ cup sugar, 1 tablespoon soft butter, 1½ cups coconut, 2 tablespoons flour, and 1 tablespoon cocoa. Blend and add 1 large egg. If filling is not soft and smooth enough to spread, soften it with a little more butter.

COCONUT ROLLS. Take one-quarter of the dough and work into it 1 cup moist coconut and 2 teaspoons vanilla extract. Place pieces of the dough in buttered muffin tins and let rise. Bake in a 375° oven for about 20 minutes, or until done. Frost and sprinkle with more coconut. If desired, add ¼ cup cocoa with the coconut. Or omit the vanilla extract and use 2 tablespoons grated orange rind.

FRUIT AND NUT BUNS. Use one-fourth of the dough. Work into the dough 1 cup of any combination of raisins, chopped figs or prunes, chopped nuts, and candied fruits. Form into buns or place in buttered muffin tins. Let rise and bake at 375° or 400° until done, about 20 minutes. Frost.

PEANUT-BUTTER ROLLS. Using half the dough, work 1 cup of crunchy peanut butter into it. Place pieces of the dough in buttered muffin tins and let rise. Bake at 375° until done, about 20 minutes. Frost with a thick frosting and sprinkle with chopped peanuts.

TWISTS. Shape one-fourth of the dough into a long rope. Coil this rope into a buttered round cake pan, about 9 or 10 inches in diameter, beginning at the outside edge. Brush the coil generously with honey and then spread thickly with chopped nuts, pressing them into the honey slightly. Let rise until doubled in bulk and then bake in a 375° oven until browned and done, from 30 to 45 minutes.

WHOLE-WHEAT ROLLS. If you prefer a whole-wheat sweet roll, substitute whole-wheat flour for half of the white flour and use half brown sugar in place of granulated white sugar.

SCHNECKEN

These are the delicious German sweet snails. Many different fillings may be used; a few are included here.

½ cup scalded milk	1½ teaspoons salt
1 cup butter	6 cups flour or more
2 large eggs	
1 cup sour cream	FILLING
1 teaspoon vanilla extract or grated lemon rind	⅔ cup brown sugar
	1 teaspoon cinnamon
1 cake yeast	¼ cup cold butter
1 or 2 tablespoons warm water	⅓ to ½ cup chopped nuts
½ cup sugar	

Pour the scalded milk over the butter and stir to dissolve the butter. Let cool to lukewarm and then beat in the eggs, sour cream, and vanilla extract or lemon rind. Dissolve the yeast in the warm water and add. Stir in the rest of the dough ingredients and beat thoroughly. Cover and refrigerate overnight. In the morning remove the dough from the refrigerator and let rise until doubled. Punch down and turn out onto a board which has been spread with 1 cup flour. Knead this flour into the dough. Use more flour on the board if necessary. Roll the dough into a thin rectangle and sprinkle with a mixture of the brown sugar, cinnamon, cold butter (chopped into bits), and chopped nuts. Roll as for a jelly roll and cut into ½-inch slices. Place on buttered cookie sheets or in buttered muffin pans. Let rise until doubled and bake in a 375° oven for 20 to 30 minutes. Frost rolls while warm.

APPLE SCHNECKEN.   For filling use 2 large apples, pared, cored, and chopped, ½ cup chopped walnuts, ¼ cup cold butter, 1 teaspoon cinnamon, and ¾ cup brown sugar.

STICKY BUNS.   Make Schnecken as directed, but use baking pans with sides, and before putting in the rolls spread the pans with a mixture of 1 cup brown sugar, ⅓ cup melted butter, and 1 tablespoon corn syrup. Sprinkle this brown-sugar sauce thickly with chopped nuts. Lay the Schnecken over the sauce and nuts, let them rise, and bake as directed. Turn out of pans carefully and serve hot.

ORANGE STICKY BUNS. Make and bake Schnecken as directed in basic recipe. Turn the rolls out while hot, but instead of frosting them pour the following sauce over the hot rolls. Combine 1 cup sugar and ½ cup frozen concentrated orange juice. Bring to a boil and boil for 1 minute. Into the hot mixture stir ¼ cup butter, stirring until it melts, then add 1 cup chopped nuts.

TWISTS. These are delicious! Make dough for Schnecken, omitting the sugar. Refrigerate dough overnight, let rise, and roll. Combine 1 cup sugar with 2 teaspoons cinnamon. Spread the rolled dough with 1 tablespoon butter and ¼ cup of the sugar and cinnamon mixture. Fold in half and roll the dough out again. Repeat procedure of sprinkling with sugar mixture, folding, and rolling, until sugar mixture is all used. This requires 4 foldings and rollings. Then cut oblong strips of dough, shape into twists, place on buttered cookie sheets, sprinkle with more sugar, let rise, and then bake in a 400° oven for 20 minutes, or until done.

SUGAR ROLLS. Make Twists as directed and following the directions for sprinkling, folding, and rolling the dough. When dough has been rolled out 4 times, roll it up as for a jelly roll. Cut into 1-inch slices. Dip the slices, cut side down, in more sugar, and place on buttered cookie sheets. Now press or roll the slices until they are not more than ¼ inch thick. Let rise for 15 to 20 minutes, and then bake in a 350° oven about 15 to 20 minutes.

PRUNE SCHNECKEN. Make Schnecken as directed, but for filling combine 1 cup cooked, chopped, drained prunes, ½ cup brown sugar, ½ cup chopped walnuts or slivered almonds, 1 teaspoon cinnamon, and ½ cup golden raisins (optional).

SOUR-CREAM SWEET ROLLS
(Refrigerator Type)

An excellent recipe for making either rich dinner rolls or sweet rolls good enough to use in any variation you prefer. The dough makes especially tasty pecan rolls. Or you can just add some grated orange rind and chopped nuts and/or chopped candied fruits to the dough, shape into rolls, let rise, bake, and frost with an orange glaze. For rich dinner rolls, brush the unbaked dough with an egg-white glaze and sprinkle heavily with poppy seed or sesame seed.

2 cakes yeast	2 large eggs
¼ cup warm water	1 cup heavy sour cream
½ cup sugar	about 5½ cups flour
¾ cup butter	1 teaspoon salt
¼ cup milk, scalded	

Dissolve the yeast in the warm water. Combine the sugar, butter, and milk and stir until butter is melted. Add the yeast. Stir the eggs and sour cream together and add to the mixture. Add 4½ cups flour and the salt and blend thoroughly. Place in a buttered bowl, cover, and place in the refrigerator. Punch down dough about three times as it rises. Next day, or when needed, turn the dough out onto a well-floured board and knead thoroughly, kneading in about 1 more cup of flour. Make into dinner rolls or any desired sweet rolls, let rise, and bake in a 400° oven about 20 minutes. Or roll dough out, spread with more sour cream, and sprinkle liberally with chopped nuts and brown sugar. Roll as for a jelly roll, slice, and place slices, cut side down in a greased jelly-roll pan. Let rise and bake at 350° to 375° for 45 minutes to 1 hour. Frost with a plain glaze.

Some people have a foolish way of not minding, or of pretending not to mind, what they eat. For my part I mind my belly very studiously and very carefully, for I look upon it that he who does not mind his belly will hardly mind anything else.

—SAMUEL JOHNSON

11. *Holiday Breads and Other Sweet Yeast Breads*

It is in the holiday breads and coffee cakes that good cooks around the world give vent to their imaginative artistry. In some European countries, the rich pastries full of chopped nuts and candied fruits, fancifully braided or baked in ornate molds, make their appearance on just two or three occasions a year.

Holiday breads, either rich or plain, date back to antiquity and are replete with religious symbolism and superstition. Made in the shapes of animals, sacrificial breads were baked as symbolic offerings to various gods. Other breads were buried with the dead, either as offerings or as food to help the dead on their journey.

Later in history, certain breads became associated with particular holidays, and a Russian Easter would be as incomplete without the rich Kulich as a German Christmas without the fruit-studded Stollen. The European peasant, whose daily bread was black and coarse and for whom the white flour breads were only a holiday event, anticipated holidays as much for gustatory pleasure as for religious commemoration. Even in

232

America, where we take a plenitude of rich foods for granted and have adopted breads from all over the world, certain breads are reserved for holiday use. It is then that our daily bread, richly studded with jewels of fruits, spices and nuts, becomes the crown of our culinary achievement.

However, while our holiday creations are beautiful to look at as well as good to eat, neither the peasant housewife of an earlier era nor the modern housewife with numerous outside interests would have the time to compete with the master bakers of the Renaissance who, influenced by the great architecture of the era, vied to see which of them could produce the most complicated and intricately decorated loaves. Nevertheless, it is fun to experiment with different shapes, and an Easter bread baked in a lamb mold, or a Christmas bread baked in the shape of a tree and decorated with frosting and chopped bits of candied fruit adds interest, as well as visual pleasure. Experience in handling rich doughs leads to more courage in their use and in time, while offering no competition to the Renaissance craftsmen, we can at least delight our families and friends.

HOLIDAY BREADS

AUSTRIAN STRIEZEL

Big, braided loaves very similar to this are made in most European countries. In Austria this is the traditional Christmas bread. In some countries chopped nuts or candied fruits are added, or a slightly different flavoring is used. Braided loaves are very common throughout Europe for the simple reason that loaf pans, as such, are little used. And the big braids, glistening with sugar or frosting, are lovely to look at as well as delicious to eat.

1 cake yeast	2 whole eggs
¼ cup warm water	2 egg yolks
⅔ cup scalded, cooled milk	4½ to 5 cups flour or more
½ to ⅔ cup sugar	1 teaspoon grated lemon rind
½ teaspoon salt	1 cup golden raisins
½ cup melted butter	

Dissolve the yeast in the warm water. Pour the scalded milk over the sugar, salt, and butter. Let cool until lukewarm, then stir in the yeast. Add whole eggs, egg yolks and about 2½ cups of the flour. Beat thoroughly. Stir in 2 more cups flour, lemon rind, and raisins. Turn dough out onto a floured breadboard, and stir in more flour, if necessary, to make a firm dough. Place in a bowl, cover, and let rise until doubled. Divide dough into 6 parts, 2 of the parts being smaller than the others. Roll each part into a long rope. Braid 4 of the ropes together and place on a buttered cookie sheet. Twist the 2 smaller ropes together and place over the braid. Let rise until almost doubled and then bake in a 350° oven for approximately 45 to 50 minutes.

NOTE.   Traditionally, the unbaked braid is sprinkled with coarse salt and caraway seed. We prefer brushing the braid with milk or cream and then sprinkling it with 1 tablespoon sugar and 2 tablespoons slivered blanched almonds.

CHILEAN TRENZAS

This delicious braid from Chile shows the European influence; it is the same as Striezel with the following exceptions. Omit the raisins and lemon rind. Use ½ cup sugar and use 5 egg yolks instead of 2 whole eggs and 2 egg yolks. The bread is braided in the same way. Brush with an egg-yolk wash or glaze and sprinkle with 1 tablespoon sugar.

RICH GERMAN COFFEE BRAID

This bread, one of our favorites, is again the same as Striezel, except that the sugar is increased to 1 cup, the raisins are omitted and 2 teaspoons vanilla extract are added. The big braid is placed on a buttered cookie sheet and brushed with a topping of 1 egg yolk beaten with 2 tablespoons sugar and 2 tablespoons milk.

FINNISH PULLA

The same as Striezel, omitting the raisins. Sprinkle braid with sugar and slivered almonds.

BARMBRACK

In Ireland this rich, sweet bread is also known as "speckled" or "freck-led" bread, with the "speckles" and "freckles" being the fruits in the dough. It is a traditional Halloween bread-cake and is *always* served during that season of the year. The Irish use all currants, but I prefer to use all or half raisins.

1 cup scalded milk	1 teaspoon allspice
½ cup soft butter	¾ cup currants
3 large eggs	¾ cup golden raisins
⅔ cup sugar	½ cup candied orange or
1 cake yeast dissolved in ⅓	lemon peel
cup warm water	grated rind of 1 lemon or 1
5 cups flour	orange
1 teaspoon salt	

Pour the scalded milk over the butter and stir until butter is melted. Let cool until lukewarm. Then add the eggs, the sugar, and the yeast mixture, blending thoroughly. Stir in the rest of ingredients in order, dusting the fruits with a little flour before adding them. Knead the dough thoroughly. Place in a buttered bowl, cover, and let rise until doubled. Then turn out again and punch down. Place dough into 2 small buttered loaf pans, or into a buttered oven-proof bowl or casserole, 2-quart size. Cover and let rise again until doubled. Bake in a 350° oven 30 minutes for the smaller loaves, or 45 minutes for the larger loaf, or until browned and done. Brush hot loaves with melted butter and then sprinkle with sugar.

CHALLAH
(Jewish Egg Braid)

Challah is always served after Yom Kippur, the Jewish Day of Atonement. This solemn day occurs ten days after the Jewish New Year and is a day of fasting, penitence, and prayer. At the end of the day the fast is broken with some light food, and then later there is a heavier meal of which this excellent bread is always a part.

1 cake yeast
1½ cups warm water
1 tablespoon sugar
5 to 6 cups flour

½ teaspoon salt
1 egg
1 tablespoon oil

Dissolve the yeast in the warm water, adding the sugar. Place the flour and salt in a large bowl and make a well in the center. Into this well pour the yeast mixture, the egg, and the oil. Blend well before turning out onto a floured board. Knead the dough thoroughly. Place in the bowl again, brush with oil, cover, and let rise until doubled. Punch down and turn out onto the floured board again. Divide into 3 parts and roll each part into a long rope. Braid the ropes and then place the braid in a buttered long loaf pan. Cover and let rise again until doubled. Brush with beaten egg and sprinkle with poppy seed. Bake in a 375° oven for 45 to 60 minutes, or until done.

CHRISTMAS FRUIT BRAIDS

The cardamom seed brands this bread as a Scandinavian specialty. If the flavor of cardamom is not liked, 1 teaspoon vanilla extract may be substituted.

2 cups milk, scalded
½ cup butter
⅔ cup sugar
1 teaspoon salt
½ teaspoon crushed carda-
    mom seed
1 teaspoon cinnamon, or
    1 tablespoon grated lemon
    rind

2 cakes yeast
¼ cup warm water
2 large eggs
8 cups flour
1 cup white raisins
1 cup candied fruits
1 cup maraschino cherries
1 cup chopped nuts

Pour the scalded milk over the butter, sugar, salt and spices. Let cool to lukewarm. Dissolve the yeast in the warm water and add to the cooled milk mixture. Beat in the eggs and half the flour. Beat well. Stir the remaining flour through the fruits and nuts. Stir into the flour mixture and blend well. Let dough rise until doubled. Punch down and turn out onto a floured board. Knead lightly, then divide dough into 8 parts. Roll each part into a long rope. Using 4 ropes for each loaf, braid tightly. Place on buttered cookie sheets, let rise and then bake in a 350° oven for 45 minutes, or until browned and done. Frost while warm, and decorate with candied fruits and nuts.

NOTE. If desired the milk may be decreased to 1¾ cups and ¼ cup brandy added to the dough.

CHRISTMAS FRUIT BREAD

This recipe makes 2 large loaves, which will keep for 3 or 4 weeks. We cut it in thin slices and serve it with whipped orange butter or whipped cream cheese.

8 large eggs	1½ cups golden raisins
2 cups sugar	1½ cups chopped walnuts
4⅓ cups flour	¾ cup candied fruits
4 teaspoons baking powder	1 tablespoon grated lemon rind

Beat the eggs and sugar for 10 minutes with an electric mixer. Fold in 4 cups of the flour and the baking powder. Combine rest of ingredients with the remaining ⅓ cup flour and add to the mixture, folding in gently. Pour into 2 buttered loaf pans and let stand at room temperature for 20 minutes. Bake in a 325° oven for 1 hour, or until loaves test done. To prevent overbrowning, place loaves on the lower shelf of the oven.

VIENNA CHRISTMAS FRUIT BREAD. To the preceding recipe add ⅓ cup cognac or brandy, 2 teaspoons vanilla extract, and, if desired, 1 or 2 teaspoons anise seed.

OLD HARTFORD ELECTION CAKE

This cake, or a variant of it, was always served on Election Day in early New England. Actually it is just a raised raisin bread with the addition of some spices and a little brandy, although some recipes don't include this last ingredient. Many modern recipes start from scratch with the yeast and flour, but traditionally the cake was always made by adding butter, sugar, eggs, etc., to an already raised bread dough. Because we like this version best, it is the one presented here.

2 cups bread dough (prefer-   ¼ cup brandy, rum, or cognac
ably non-rich dough)   2½ cups flour
1 cup soft butter   1 teaspoon cinnamon
2 large eggs   ½ teaspoon mace
2 cups brown sugar   ½ teaspoon nutmeg
1 cup sweet cream   ½ teaspoon salt
2 cups golden raisins

Take out 2 cups of bread dough after it has risen once. Put the dough into a large bowl and knead in the rest of the ingredients, working them in very well. Put into 2 buttered loaf pans and let rise until doubled. Bake in a 350° oven for about 1 hour. While bread is still hot, drizzle 1 additional tablespoon brandy, rum, or cognac over each loaf, letting it sink into the hot bread. Cool the loaves and glaze lightly.

NOTE. Sour milk or buttermilk may be used instead of cream; add ½ teaspoon soda with either.

GÂTEAU DES ROIS
(Twelfth Night Cake)

This delicious French cake is also called Cake of the Magi. It honors the three kings or Magi, who, led by a star, came to offer gifts to the Christ child, traditionally on Twelfth Night.

2 cups flour   4 large eggs
½ cup soft butter   1 teaspoon salt
½ cup sugar   grated rind of 1 lemon, or 1 tea-
1 cake yeast, or 1 package or 1   spoon vanilla extract
    tablespoon dry yeast

If yeast cake is used, cream it with 1 or 2 teaspoons of the sugar. If dry yeast is used, dissolve it in as little water as possible, preferably no more than 1 tablespoon. Stir all ingredients together thoroughly, and then chill the dough in the refrigerator overnight. In the morning remove it from refrigerator and put it into a buttered 9-inch square pan. Cover and let rise until doubled, about 3 or 4 hours. Bake in a 350° oven for 30 to 35 minutes, or until browned and done. Cool the cake in the pan for about 10 minutes then remove from pan and cool on a rack. Frost with a light glaze and decorate with citron, candied cherries, and almond halves.

GREEK EASTER BREAD

This is not Greek Lambropsomo, an Easter bread that has hard-cooked colored eggs set into the dough, but another Easter bread which traditionally represents the Trinity. The bread should not be cut until it is presented at the table, and each person is supposed to be served a thin slice from each of the 3 combined loaves. If you wish, you may add a cup of maraschino cherries, drained and chopped. Frost the finished loaves with a powdered-sugar frosting, and decorate with nuts and candied fruits.

1 cup rich milk or	2 cakes yeast
half-and-half	5 to 6 cups flour
½ cup butter	4 large eggs
½ cup sugar	grated rind of 2 large lemons
¼ teaspoon salt	

Scald the milk or half-and-half and pour it over the butter, sugar, and salt. When cooled to lukewarm, stir in the yeast and add the rest of the ingredients in order. Blend thoroughly and then turn out onto a floured board. Knead well. Place in a buttered bowl, cover with a towel, and let rise until doubled. Punch the dough down and knead again. Now divide the dough into three parts and shape each into a round loaf. Put the loaves together on a buttered cookie sheet in the shape of a clover leaf. Let rise until doubled. Bake in a 425° oven for 10 minutes and then reduce heat to 350° and bake for another 40 minutes, or until the bread is browned and done.

VARIATION. Another version of this bread adds 2 teaspoons mahlepi, a spice that is much used in Syrian baking and is available in some specialty shops. The dough is divided into 3 parts, but each part is rolled into a long rope. The ropes are then braided, or sometimes just twisted, together. Placed on a buttered cookie sheet, the flat braid is allowed to rise until doubled and then is brushed with beaten egg and sprinkled liberally with sesame seed. Bake in a 350° oven for 40 minutes, or until browned and done. This makes a very attractive rich dinner bread for any occasion.

Good Friday comes this month, the old woman runs
With one-a-penny, two-a-penny, hot cross buns,
Whose virtue is, if you believe what's said,
They'll not grow moldy like common bread.

—OLD ENGLISH FOLK CHANT

HOT CROSS BUNS

By the early part of the eighteenth century the Hot Cross Bun was traditional Good Friday eating throughout England. Until modern times it
was available there *only* on Good Friday, but in America the buns were
sold throughout the Lenten season. The imprint of the cross on rolls and
breads dates from pre-Christian cultures, when such imprinted breads
were offered as sacrifices to various gods. Many good cooks today make
the cross with frosting instead of cutting it into the buns before baking.
The frosting may be flavored with lemon juice or vanilla or almond
extract.

2 cups scalded milk	8 cups flour
1 cup butter	½ teaspoon salt
1 cup sugar	2 cups currants or raisins
2 cakes yeast dissolved in ⅓ cup warm water	½ cup candied fruit peels
2 large eggs	½ teaspoon cinnamon or nutmeg

Pour the scalded milk over the butter and sugar and stir to dissolve the
butter and sugar. Let cool to lukewarm. Add the dissolved yeast and the
eggs and blend well. Add the flour and salt gradually, reserving a small
amount of flour to dust the fruits. Add the floured fruits and the spice to
the dough and knead in thoroughly. Place in a buttered bowl, cover, and
let rise until doubled. Punch the dough down and turn it out onto a
floured board. Shape dough into 30 buns and place on buttered cookie
sheets. Cover and let rise for 30 minutes, then very carefully press the
shape of a cross into each bun, using a spatula or the back of a knife.
Bake in a 375° oven for 10 minutes, then reduce heat to 350° and continue baking until buns are browned and done, about 10 to 15 minutes
longer. Frost either the entire bun or just the shape of the cross.

FROSTING.   Beat 1 egg white until stiff, adding powdered sugar gradually until mixture is thick. Flavor with 1 teaspoon lemon juice or vanilla extract, or ¼ teaspoon almond extract. If the frosting thins, add more powdered sugar.

ITALIAN EASTER BREAD

This is Cresca, the traditional Easter bread in parts of northern Italy.

1 cake yeast	¾ cup grated Parmesan or
6 tablespoons warm water	Romano cheese
4 cups flour	3 large eggs, beaten
½ teaspoon salt	2 tablespoons olive oil
½ teaspoon black pepper	

Dissolve the yeast in the warm water. Sift the flour, salt, and pepper into a large bowl and stir in the cheese. Make a well in the center of the mixture and into it pour the yeast solution, beaten eggs, and olive oil. Blend well and then turn out onto a lightly floured breadboard. Knead thoroughly, adding flour if necessary to make a stiff dough. Place in a buttered bowl, cover, and let rise until doubled, about 1½ to 2 hours. Punch dough down, and then let it rise again until doubled, about 30 to 45 minutes. Turn the dough out onto a breadboard again. Knead and shape it into a round loaf. Fit the loaf into a 10-inch pie pan, cover, and let it rise again until doubled. Brush the top with olive oil and bake it in a 350° oven for 1 hour, or until loaf sounds hollow when tapped.

KULICH
(Traditional Russian Easter Bread)

This is a delicious light bread, always served in Russia at Easter time with Pashka, a rich mixture of cottage cheese, cream, eggs, butter, and sugar. Beating the egg yolks and whites separately and folding the whites into the sponge is traditional *and* I think improves the texture of the bread. However, many cooks just add the whole eggs to the sponge. The cake-bread will be just as delicious.

6 to 6½ cups flour
1 cup cream
1 cake yeast
¾ cup sugar
½ teaspoon salt
5 large eggs, separated (eggs must be at room temperature)

½ cup soft butter
1 tablespoon vanilla extract, or 1 tablespoon grated lemon rind, or 2 tablespoons brandy or cognac

Put 1 cup of the flour in a large bowl. Scald the cream and blend into the flour. Cool just to lukewarm and then stir the yeast into the flour-cream mixture. Beat ½ cup of the sugar, and the salt, into the egg yolks. Stir into the yeast mixture. Beat the egg whites until stiff, gradually adding the remaining ¼ cup sugar. Fold the stiffly beaten whites into the yeast-egg yolk mixture. Place the bowl over a pan of hot but not boiling water and let mixture rise until light and full of bubbles. Stir down. Beat the soft butter with the flavoring and add. Add remaining flour gradually, using just enough to make the dough firm enough to be kneaded. Knead the dough lightly and then place in a buttered bowl. Place the bowl again over hot but not boiling water. Let rise until doubled. Punch the dough down and place in a well-buttered 3-pound coffee tin. (This makes the traditional shape; if desired you may use two 8- by 4-inch loaf pans.) Cover and let rise again until doubled. Bake in a 350° oven for about 1 hour, or until done. Turn the coffee tin on its side to cool, then carefully turn out the Kulich. This should be cut into round slices and is traditionally served with Pashka. Any whipped butter spread is delicious, though.

NOTE.   One friend reserves enough dough from the Kulich recipe to make 2 small braids, which she crisscrosses on top of the loaf to make the shape of a cross. She brushes the top of the loaf with cream and sprinkles it with sugar before baking. When sliced, this sugar-crusted piece goes to the guest of honor or to the oldest member of the family.

FINNISH EASTER BREAD.   The Finns make a very similar and very delicious Easter Bread, by substituting 1½ cups rye flour for the same amount of white flour, and adding 1 teaspoon crushed cardamom seed, 1 tablespoon each grated lemon rind and orange rind, and 1 cup each golden raisins and slivered blanched almonds. Bake in a 350° oven for about 1 hour. Cut loaf into quarters before slicing. Serve with whipped cream cheese.

LUCIA CATS
(Swedish Lussekatter)

These Swedish buns are traditional eating on December 13, the official start of the Christmas season in Sweden. The name is in honor of St. Lucia, a fourth-century martyr.

2 cakes yeast	½ cup butter, melted
¼ cup warm water	4½ cups flour
1 cup evaporated milk	1½ cups rolled oats
⅔ cup sugar	1 teaspoon crushed cardamom
3 large eggs	seed
1 teaspoon salt	

Dissolve the yeast in the warm water. Combine the evaporated milk, sugar, eggs, salt, and melted butter and blend thoroughly. Stir in the yeast mixture, half the flour, all the rolled oats, and the cardamom seed. Beat well and then stir in enough more flour to make a soft but workable dough. Turn onto a floured breadboard and knead until smooth. Place in a bowl, brush with butter, cover, and let rise until doubled. When dough has doubled, punch it down, turn it out onto the breadboard again, and let it rest for 10 minutes. Take a portion of the dough at a time and roll into a rope. Cut the ropes into 5-inch strips, each strip about ½ inch wide. Using 2 strips for each roll, cross them to form the letter X, and turn each end out slightly. Place on buttered cookie sheets and let rise. Decorate the rolls with raisins and brush with butter. Or brush with cream and sprinkle with sugar and slivered almonds. Bake in a 350° oven for about 15 to 20 minutes, or until rolls are done.

NOTE.   If desired the rolls may be shaped into S's, or coiled. This good sweet roll dough is usable in any sweet roll variation, and especially good as cinnamon or orange rolls.

FINNISH CHRISTMAS ROLLS.   The Finns make a Christmas sweet bread using the same dough, which is shaped into figures of boys and girls. Pieces of the dough are pinched off and, using several pieces for each girl or boy, shaped directly on the cookie sheets. Eyes, mouth, and nose are made with raisins.

PAN DE PASQUA
(Argentine Easter Bread)

As in any sweet bread, you may vary the candied fruits to suit your own taste, but the angelica is different and pleasing. I use golden raisins in this recipe but they could be omitted. French Easter Bread and the Italian Christmas bread, Panettone, although it uses honey instead of sugar, are both so similar that separate recipes are not needed.

1 cup milk, scalded and cooled
1 cake or 1 package yeast
6 egg yolks
5 cups flour
½ teaspoon salt
½ cup sugar
½ cup butter, melted
2 tablespoons finely chopped angelica

2 tablespoons finely chopped citron
2 tablespoons finely chopped candied orange or lemon peel
½ cup golden raisins (optional)

Pour the cooled milk over the yeast and stir until dissolved. Beat in the egg yolks, half the flour, the salt, sugar, and butter. Combine the rest of the flour with the fruits, and then blend into the dough. Turn out onto a floured board and knead until smooth and elastic. Place in a buttered bowl, cover, and let rise until doubled. Turn out onto a lightly floured breadboard and knead again. Shape into loaves, or rings, or chickens, or anything you desire. If you shape the dough into loaves, place them in buttered bread pans; otherwise use a buttered cookie sheet. Cover and let rise again. When ready to bake, brush, if desired, with an egg yolk mixed with a little cream or milk and sprinkle with sugar or colored shot. Bake in a 375° oven for about 35 minutes, or until browned and done.

NOTE. You may omit the egg-yolk wash and sugar or shot and glaze the warm, baked loaves with a thin icing, then decorate as desired.

BRAZILIAN EASTER BREAD. In Brazil the same Easter Bread is made with the addition of 1 teaspoon each cinnamon and grated lemon rind and ½ cup slivered or ground Brazil nuts. The dough is made into 1 large loaf, with a little of the dough reserved. Into the loaf 3 hard-cooked eggs are set. Then the reserved dough is twisted into 2 ropes and these ropes are crossed over the loaf, from corner to corner, in the shape of a large X. The bread is brushed with cream and sprinkled with sugar before baking.

PORTUGUESE EASTER BREAD

The Portuguese make this bread only at Easter, and always give a loaf to friends. To the basic recipe I add the grated rind of 3 large lemons. If desired, add 1 cup each blanched slivered almonds and golden raisins, but the bread is sweet and delicious enough without such additions. A powdered-sugar glaze, flavored with the rind and juice of 1 large lemon, is excellent. Any way you slice it, it makes excellent toast. The recipe as given makes 4 large loaves but is easily cut down to make 2 loaves.

3 yeast cakes	3 cups sugar
1 cup lukewarm water	12 eggs, well beaten
12 cups flour	1 pint lukewarm milk
1 tablespoon salt	½ pound butter, melted

Dissolve the yeast in the lukewarm water and set aside. Sift the flour and salt together into a large pan. Mix the sugar and eggs with the lukewarm milk. Add the mixture to the flour. Stir in the yeast. Knead until dough has the consistency of bread dough. Now add the melted butter, kneading a little more, and adding more flour as necessary. Cover and let rise until doubled. Divide dough into round, slightly flattened loaves, roll the loaves in flour, and place in buttered pie pans. On top of each loaf, if desired, press into dough a raw egg in its shell. Place 1 or 2 strips of dough over the egg and let loaves rise again until doubled. Bake in a 350° oven until golden brown and done, about 45 minutes.

ROSCA DE REYES
(Mexican Kings' Bread Ring)

In Mexico, Twelfth Night, the twelfth day after Christmas, is always a festive occasion. This bread, also called Three Kings' Bread, is a must. A small china doll is always placed in the dough before baking, and whoever gets the doll must give a party on Candlemas Day (February 2).

⅔ cup scalded milk
⅓ cup sugar
1 teaspoon salt
½ cup soft butter
2 cakes yeast dissolved in 2
tablespoons warm water

5 medium eggs
4 to 4½ cups flour
2 cups candied fruits, or 1 cup
each candied fruits and nuts

Pour the scalded milk over the sugar, salt, and butter. Stir to melt the butter. When cooled add the dissolved yeast. Beat in the eggs and then the flour, using enough to make a soft but not sticky dough. Knead lightly and then roll the dough out on a floured board. Spread the candied fruits or fruits and nuts over the dough. Fold the dough over and work the fruits and nuts into the dough. Place in a large bowl, brush with butter, cover, and let rise until doubled. Now turn the dough out onto a floured board and shape into a long roll. Pinch the ends together to form a ring and carefully place on a buttered cookie sheet or in a large buttered ring mold. Cover and let dough rise until almost doubled. Bake in a 375° oven 30 to 45 minutes, or until done. Cool the loaves and frost with a powdered-sugar frosting. Decorate with candied fruits and nuts.

NOTE. If desired, increase milk to 1 cup and use only 3 eggs.

DRIEKONIGENBROOD
(Dutch Kings' Bread)

Follow the recipe for Rosca de Reyes, omitting the fruits and nuts. Add 1 whole almond to the dough. Let the dough rise once, then punch down and shape into a round loaf, not a ring. Place on a buttered cookie sheet or in a round deep buttered cake pan. Let rise and bake in a 425° oven for 10 minutes, then reduce heat to 350° and bake about 45 minutes longer. Frost the cake and decorate with almond halves and candied fruits.

OLIEBOLLEN
(Dutch Filled Doughnuts)

Follow recipe for Rosca de Reyes, omitting the fruits and nuts and using instead 1 cup currants or raisins, ¼ cup candied fruit peels, and 2 cups grated firm apples. Let the dough rise until doubled. Punch down and pinch off pieces of dough. Place the pieces on a lightly floured board and let rest for 10 to 15 minutes. Fry in deep hot fat. Sprinkle with powdered sugar and serve hot.

STOLLEN

This is the wonderful German Christmas bread called Christollen. The bread should be kept for 2 or 3 days before cutting, to allow it to mellow. It's a good keeper and, well wrapped, will last the Christmas season. We slice it thin and serve it with whipped butter.

2 cups milk, scalded and cooled	grated rind of 1 lemon
1 teaspoon sugar	1 pound chopped walnuts or
2 teaspoons salt	slivered blanched almonds
11 cups flour or more	1 pound assorted candied fruits
2 cakes yeast dissolved in ¼	and peels
cup warm water	1 pound golden raisins or cur-
1 pound butter or margarine	rants
1½ cups sugar	½ teaspoon nutmeg (optional)
6 large eggs	½ teaspoon mace (optional)
¼ cup rum or brandy	

Combine the scalded and cooled milk, the 1 teaspoon sugar, the salt, 1 cup of the flour, and the dissolved yeast. Blend, cover, and let stand until the sponge is bubbly. Cream the butter and 1½ cups sugar until fluffy, then add the eggs and the rum or brandy and beat thoroughly. Stir in 5 cups of the flour and then the yeast mixture. Blend 1 cup of the flour into the nuts and fruits. Add the rest of the flour and the other remaining ingredients to the dough, using enough flour to make a firm dough. Turn out onto a floured breadboard and knead quite thoroughly. Place in a large bowl, brush with butter, cover, and let rise until doubled. Then punch the dough down and turn out onto a floured board again. Divide the dough into 3 or 4 parts and shape each part into a thick oval shape. Lap the ovals over so that you have the traditional Stollen shape. Place on buttered cookie sheets and let the loaves rise until doubled. Brush with melted butter or with cream. Bake in a 350° oven for about 1 hour to 1 hour and 20 minutes, depending on the size of the loaves. If the tops of the loaves seem to be browning too fast, lay a piece of brown paper over them. While the loaves are still hot, brush them liberally with melted butter, allow it to soak in, and then sprinkle thickly with powdered sugar. Or if desired use a powdered sugar frosting. Makes 3 or 4 Stollen.

NOTE. This is very rich and if desired the amounts of nuts and candied fruits and peels may be cut in half. The rum or brandy may be increased to ⅓ cup and, after brushing the hot loaves with melted butter, a little more brandy or rum may be spooned over the top and let soak in. For those who prefer not to use rum or brandy, 2 tablespoons vanilla extract may be substituted. A large loaf of this placed on a pretty breadboard and wrapped in colored cellophane makes a lovely gift.

STOLLEN MADE WITH HOT-ROLL MIX

The commercial hot-roll mixes may be used, with a few very simple changes, for many of our favorite Easter and Christmas breads. The dough may be braided to make a bread similar to the Czech Vanocka. This recipe makes such a small amount that I recommend doubling it. The package of mix includes yeast.

1 box hot-roll mix
3 large eggs
¼ cup softened or melted
   butter
¼ cup sugar

⅓ cup skim-milk powder
grated rind of 1 lemon
candied fruits and nuts of your
   choice

Prepare the mix as directed, but decrease the water called for, using only ⅓ cup warm water. Work the eggs, butter, sugar, skim-milk powder, and lemon rind into the flour mix with the yeast. Knead to blend ingredients thoroughly. Place the dough in a bowl, brush the top with butter, cover the bowl, and let dough rise until doubled. Then punch down and add fruits, raisins, and nuts of your choice in the amount desired. Work the fruits and nuts in by kneading. Now turn the dough onto a floured board and press it out into a wide oval. Brush all over with softened or melted butter. Fold half of the dough over the other half, but not to the edge. Use your hands to shape the dough into the traditional Stollen shape. This is best done right on the buttered cookie sheet on which it is to be baked. Cover and let rise until almost doubled and then bake in a 350°

oven for about 40 minutes, or until well browned and done. Cool slightly and frost. Decorate with candied fruits and almond halves if desired.

NOTE.   Without the addition of the fruits and nuts, this dough makes a good base for any coffee cake, doughnut, or sweet roll recipes. For some of the richer European rolls and coffee cakes, such as Kuchen or Kolache, dissolve the yeast in heavy sweet cream, scalded and cooled.

VANOCKA MADE WITH HOT-ROLL MIX.   The traditional recipe for Vanocka is given on pages 252-53. For this version make dough as in the preceding recipe, divide into 3 ropes, and braid these together. Let rise on a buttered cookie sheet or in a buttered loaf pan. Or—and this is nearer the traditional Vanocka—use 2 boxes of hot-roll mix and double all other ingredients. Make one large loaf by braiding in the traditional manner, using 4 ropes for the bottom braid, 3 for the middle braid, and 2 ropes twisted together for the top. Bake on a cookie sheet and drizzle a thin icing over the top while warm.

EUROPEAN COFFEE BREAD.   Make the hot-roll mix as directed in Stollen recipe, omitting the fruits and nuts. Let rise once. Butter a 9-inch tube pan or a Turk's head mold. Sprinke the bottom of the pan liberally with slivered almonds and lay candied cherry halves over the almonds. Turn the dough into the pan and let rise again. Bake in a 350° oven until done, about 45 minutes. Turn out of pan and brush lightly with a thin icing.

SWISS PEAR BREAD

In Switzerland, this bread is made each fall from summer-dried fruits. The dried fruits used may be varied according to individual tastes. I often use equal quantities of dried apricots, prunes, figs, raisins, and dates. You may use any other candied fruits in place of the citron, or omit it entirely, or use more than the quantity called for. Some cooks —and this works quite well—use fresh, firm apples and pears, chopped and cooked along with the other fruits. The only difference between Swiss Pear Bread and the German "stuffed" bread is that in the latter ¼ pound melted sweet chocolate is added to the filling. If the recipe quantity seems too large, it is easily halved to make 2 small loaves. In Alsace-Lorraine, where this bread is a Christmas specialty, it is known as *Pain de Fruits*.

½ pound dried pears
½ pound dried apples
½ pound figs
½ pound dates
½ pound prunes
1 pound raisins
½ cup finely diced citron
½ cup soft butter
½ to ¾ cup sugar
1 tablespoon anise seed
  (optional)

1 teaspoon cinnamon
  (optional)
1 teaspoon nutmeg (optional)
½ pound mixed nuts
2 cakes yeast
2 large eggs
1 teaspoon salt
8 to 10 cups flour

Cook the fruits in just enough water barely to cover them. Simmer until tender. Drain the fruits and add enough water to the liquid to make 1 quart liquid. To the hot fruits, add the butter, sugar, and spices (if used). Stir to melt the butter. Let the mixture stand until it cools, or overnight. Then stir in the nuts. Warm a little of the liquid and dissolve the yeast in it. Stir the dissolved yeast into the remaining liquid and then add the eggs, salt, and flour, using enough to make a firm dough. Brush butter over the dough, cover the bowl, and let the dough rise until doubled. When dough has doubled, punch it down, turn it out onto a floured board, and knead well. Now put the dough back into the bowl. Take out 3 pieces of dough, each about the size of a cup. Work the fruits and nuts into the larger mass of dough. Work the fruits in so thoroughly that no white remains. The dough will be quite sticky. Divide this fruited mass into 3 portions and on a floured board shape each portion into a long, narrow loaf. Set aside. Take the small pieces of dough and roll each into a thin sheet. Place a roll of the fruited dough in the center of each sheet of plain dough. Wrap the plain dough around the fruited dough and seal the edges. Place in well-buttered loaf pans. Cover and let rise until almost doubled. Bake in a 375° oven for 15 minutes, then reduce heat to 325° and continue baking for approximately 1 hour to 1 hour and 15 minutes. Use a thin icing on the warm loaves.

NOTE. Some good cooks do not separate the mixture but work the fruits and nuts into all of the dough. The loaves are baked as in the recipe. Traditionally Kirsch is used as part of the liquid, with some recipes calling for as much as 2 cups of Kirsch. If desired you may use brandy or cognac in any desired amount up to 1 cup, or ½ cup dark rum. The German Hutzelbrot uses at least 1 pound of dried pears, cutting down on the other fruits; adds ½ cup each candied orange peel and lemon peel; uses equal quantities of hazelnuts and almonds; and always includes the spices. The breads, however mixed, keep well and freeze well.

VASILOPETA
(Greek New Year's Cake)

The original recipe for this bread calls for 1 teaspoon of mahlepi, a spice that is difficult to find in the United States, but is sometimes obtainable in specialty shops. In some parts of Greece Vasilopeta is made with a sweet cookie dough and is more cakelike. Whether it is made with a rich bread dough or a sweet cookie dough, the custom is to place a silver coin in each cake for luck.

½ cup milk	1 cake yeast dissolved in ¼
½ cup butter	cup warm water
4 egg yolks	2½ cups flour
⅓ cup sugar	beaten egg, sugar, sesame seed,
grated rind of 1 lemon	blanched almonds

Scald the milk, add the butter, and cool. Beat the yolks with the sugar and lemon rind. When the milk mixture has cooled, add the dissolved yeast and stir until smooth. Add to the egg mixture along with 1½ cups of the flour. Beat for 10 minutes. Add remaining 1 cup flour. Mix thoroughly, cover, and let rise until doubled. Then chill the dough overnight. Grease 2 9-inch layer-cake pans. Divide the dough into the pans and let rise again. Brush the tops with beaten egg, sprinkle with sugar and sesame seed, and decorate with blanched almonds. Bake in a 375° oven for 30 minutes, or until loaves are a deep golden brown. Cool.

OTHER SWEET
YEAST BREADS

APPLESAUCE-NUT BREAD

An applesauce bread made with yeast is somewhat unusual. It appears
to have originated with the French. If desired, 1 teaspoon cinnamon may
be added to the dough. The bread, immediately upon being removed
from the oven, may be brushed with butter and sprinkled with Cinnamon
Sugar.

1 1-pound can (2 cups) apple-	1 cake yeast
sauce	1 cup scalded, cooled milk
½ cup sugar	6 cups flour
¼ cup butter	1 cup chopped walnuts
1 teaspoon salt	

Heat the applesauce until very hot. Pour it over the sugar, butter, and
salt. Cool mixture to lukewarm. When the mixture has cooled, stir in the
yeast. Add the milk and half the flour. Beat until mixture is smooth. Now
add the rest of the flour and the chopped nuts. As this dough is too soft
to be kneaded on a breadboard yet is not quite a heavy batter, knead it in
the bowl by folding the dough over and over, and pressing with the palms
of the hands. Brush the dough with melted butter, cover with a towel,
and let rise until doubled. When doubled, punch dough down and put
into 2 well-buttered glass loaf pans. Brush the top with butter again,
cover the pans, and let the dough rise again. Bake in a 375° oven for
about 45 minutes, or until done.

VANOCKA

The Czechoslovakian Vanocka is one of the world's great breads. Czechoslovakian breads aren't as rich as those of Germany or Hungary but

they are imaginative and lovely to look at, besides being delicious. The traditional shape for Vanocka is a braid, starting with a four-strand braid on the bottom, topped with a three-strand braid, then a two-strand braid and finally a single twist. Dust each braid with flour to keep the braids from running into each other and losing their shape. The Polish Hola and the Czechoslovakian Houska are very similar but less rich.

2 cakes yeast	8 to 10 cups sifted flour
¼ cup warm water	½ to 1 cup chopped raisins
6 beaten egg yolks	½ to 1 cup chopped citron
⅔ cup sugar	½ to 1 cup chopped blanched
1 cup melted butter	almonds
2 cups scalded and cooled milk	1 tablespoon grated lemon rind
½ teaspoon salt	(optional)

Add the water to the yeast and set aside. Mix the egg yolks, sugar, melted butter, milk, salt and 2 cups of the flour. Add to the yeast mixture and beat thoroughly. Set aside and let rise until doubled, about 1 hour. Add 6 more cups of the flour and the fruits, almonds, and the lemon rind, if desired (this is optional, but good). Knead thoroughly, using more flour if necessary. Let rise until doubled in bulk. Braid as directed above and place on a lightly buttered cookie sheet. Let rise until doubled in bulk. Bake in a 425° oven for 10 minutes, then reduce heat to 350° and continue baking for 40 minutes, or until bread is browned and done. Frost while warm with a light powdered sugar glaze. Makes 1 huge braid.

BABKI

The name means "delicious cake," which it is. The poppy-seed filling is an acquired taste, so you may substitute ground nuts, or use any of the fillings listed with Rich Sour-Cream Dough, or Old Country Coffee Roll.

⅓ cup warm water	¼ cup sugar
1 cake yeast	1 teaspoon salt
1 teaspoon sugar	¼ teaspoon powdered ginger
6 egg yolks plus evaporated	(optional)
milk to make 1 cup	¼ pound sweet butter
3 cups flour	Poppy-seed Filling

Combine the water, yeast, and sugar. Set aside for 5 minutes. Beat the egg yolks and evaporated milk and add to the yeast mixture. Sift the dry ingredients together and cut in the butter. Add the yeast mixture and beat well. Chill overnight. Set the dough in a warm place and let rise until light, punch down, and let rise again. Roll the dough into a rectangle ½ inch thick and spread it with filling. Roll as for a jelly roll and place in a very well greased Bundt pan. Let rise until light, and then bake in a 350° oven until done, about 1 hour. Invert on a rack, cool, and sprinkle with powdered sugar, or brush with a thin glaze. Serve warm.

POPPY-SEED FILLING I.   Combine ½ pound ground poppy seed, ¾ cup sugar, 1 cup raisins, 1 teaspoon cinnamon, grated rind of 2 lemons, 1 apple, grated, and ¼ cup sour cream. Spread on dough.

POPPY-SEED FILLING II.   Combine ¾ pound ground poppy seed, ½ cup honey, 1½ cups half-and-half, ½ cup sugar, ¼ cup chopped golden raisins, 2 tablespoons sweet butter, and ¾ pound ground nuts. Place all ingredients in a heavy iron pan over a low heat. Cook, stirring constantly, until thick, about 30 minutes. Be sure to stir constantly as this mixture will burn easily. Cool before spreading on dough.

CHOCOLATE YEAST BREAD

This unusual bread is both delicious and easy to make. If desired, chopped dried apricots may be added, and/or a rum icing used.

1 cake yeast	½ cup butter
¼ cup warm water	½ cup cocoa, preferably
1 tablespoon sugar	Dutch cocoa
2 cups milk, scalded and cooled	5 cups flour
3 large eggs	1 teaspoon vanilla extract
½ cup sugar	½ cup chopped nuts

Dissolve the yeast in the warm water with the 1 tablespoon sugar. Add the yeast mixture to the cooled milk along with the eggs, ½ cup sugar, butter, cocoa, and half the flour. Beat thoroughly. Now add the vanilla extract, nuts, and remaining flour and knead lightly. Place in a bowl, brush with melted or softened butter, cover, and let rise until doubled. Punch the dough down and shape into 2 loaves. Put into buttered loaf pans, cover, and let rise again until doubled. Bake in a 350° oven for 40 to 45 minutes, or until done.

BEEF BREAD

This is an early pioneer recipe for what is really nothing more nor less than a mincemeat bread. It's fruity and good without being too sweet. If desired, use a half cup of wheat germ in place of as much flour. Other dried fruits, or even some candied fruits, may be substituted for the variety called for in the recipe. A cup of leftover cooked meat may be used in place of the fresh ground steak. Do be careful, however, to have the meat ground fine so that it will be evenly distributed. Makes 2 large loaves.

1 cup coarsely ground round steak	1 cup water
1 cup raisins	1 cup sugar
4 or 5 dried pear halves, chopped	2 cakes yeast dissolved in ½ cup water
4 or 5 dried peach halves, chopped	1½ cups water
4 or 5 dried apple slices, chopped	½ cup melted butter
4 or 5 dried apricot halves, chopped	2 cups bran flakes
	1 cup graham flour
	4 cups white flour
	1 tablespoon salt
	1 cup chopped nuts

Combine the meat, dried fruits, 1 cup water, and ⅓ cup of the sugar in a saucepan. Bring to a boil, reduce heat, and simmer for 10 to 15 minutes, or until meat is thoroughly cooked. Cool completely. Combine the yeast mixture, the 1½ cups water, the melted butter, bran flakes, remaining ⅔ cup sugar, graham flour, 2 cups white flour, and the salt. Add the meat-fruit mixture, stir it in thoroughly, and then add the rest of the white flour and the nuts. Knead thoroughly, adding a little more flour if necessary to make a dough that is soft, but not sticky. Cover and let rise until doubled. Punch down and let rise another 20 minutes. Shape into loaves and place in 2 large buttered bread pans. Cover and let rise until doubled. Bake in a 350° oven for 50 to 60 minutes, or until browned and done.

ENGLISH CURRANT BREAD

This is a specialty in England. English cooks always use currants, but we prefer raisins, which can be substituted for currants in any recipe.

2 cups milk, scalded	2 large eggs
1 cup butter	1½ cups currants, soaked in
1 teaspoon salt	rum and drained
2 cakes yeast	½ teaspoon mace
¼ cup warm water	½ teaspoon cinnamon
1 teaspoon sugar	1 cup sugar
7¾ cups flour	

Pour the scalded milk over the butter and salt. Let cool to lukewarm. Dissolve the yeast in the warm water with the 1 teaspoon sugar, then add to milk mixture. Stir in 4 cups of the flour, beat until smooth, cover, and let rise until bubbly. When sponge is bubbly, stir it down and beat in the rest of the flour and all the remaining ingredients. Let rise again until doubled. Punch the dough down and put into 2 buttered 9- by 5- by 3-inch loaf pans. Cover the pans and let the loaves rise until doubled. Bake in a 400° oven for 15 minutes, then reduce heat to 325° and bake until loaves are browned and done, about 45 minutes. Brush warm loaves with a light glaze.

NOTE. If desired, make a rum frosting by thinning powdered sugar with a little rum and brush it on the loaves. This bread makes wonderful toast and keeps well.

ENGLISH SAFFRON BREAD

The English have always liked the color and flavor of saffron in their breads and rolls. When saffron was in short supply, English housewives used dried marigold petals, soaking them first in boiling water or milk and then straining the petals out. The liquid, either saffron- or marigold-flavored, may be used in any sweet bread or roll, as you wish. In this recipe, you can leave out the nutmeg and cinnamon if you wish, and in place of the candied lemon peel use the grated rind of 3 large lemons.

2 teaspoons saffron	1 teaspoon salt
½ cup boiling water	½ teaspoon nutmeg
1½ cups scalded milk	1 teaspoon cinnamon
1 cup butter	6 cups flour or more
1 cup sugar	2 cups currants or raisins
1 or 2 cakes yeast	½ cup candied lemon peel
2 large eggs	

Steep the saffron in the boiling water for 5 minutes. Drain and reserve the liquid. Pour the hot scalded milk over butter and sugar and stir to melt the butter. Let cool to warm, then stir in the yeast first and then the saffron liquid and the eggs. Blend well. Now add the dry ingredients, reserving a little flour to dust the fruits with. Stir in the floured fruits last. The dough should be fairly stiff, so add a little more flour if necessary. Knead the dough, then place it in a buttered bowl, cover, and let rise. Knead down and shape into 2 loaves, or braid the dough. Let rise again until doubled. Bake in a 350° oven for 45 minutes to 1 hour, or until browned and done.

FEDERAL LOAF

This recipe is America's own; it is adapted from *Miss Parloa's Kitchen Companion* of 1887. Miss Parloa suggests that the bread be formed into rolls and placed close together in a loaf pan. After baking the rolls are pulled apart and spread with butter. Her recipe may not be complete, and the flour in that distant day was doubtless different from ours, but the dough is more batter than dough and impossible to shape. It is an excellent tea bread, however, has a good flavor, and makes wonderful toast.

1 cup milk	¼ cup butter
1 cake yeast	4 eggs, separated
1 cup warm water	1 teaspoon grated lemon rind,
4 cups flour	or 2 teaspoons grated orange
1 teaspoon salt	rind
¼ cup sugar	

Scald the milk and set aside to cool to room temperature. Dissolve the yeast in the warm water. Sift the dry ingredients and then cut the butter into the dry ingredients as for pastry. Beat the egg yolks until thick and lemon-colored and add to the yeast mixture. Stir this into the flour mixture and add the milk. Blend thoroughly. Beat the egg whites until stiff and fold them into the batter along with the grated rind. Pour the batter into 2 buttered 8-inch loaf pans. Cover and let rise until doubled. Bake in a 400° oven for 30 to 35 minutes.

WHOLE-WHEAT FEDERAL LOAF. Increase the butter to ½ cup, use brown sugar in place of white, and whole-wheat flour in place of white flour. If desired, use 2 cups whole-wheat flour and 2 cups of white flour.

GREEK RAISIN BREAD

Most nationalities have a raisin bread which they consider their own. Most of the recipes, however, are very similar. The Belgian raisin bread is almost the same as this. You may use brown sugar in place of the white sugar, use 1 or 2 cups of whole-wheat flour in place of as much white flour, or brush the loaves with light cream instead of milk, and sprinkle with sugar and cinnamon. And don't forget the wheat germ— keep it on hand in the refrigerator, and use ⅓ or ½ cup in place of as much flour.

2 cakes yeast	3 large eggs, beaten
½ cup cold milk	6 cups flour
½ cup scalded, cooled milk	½ teaspoon salt
½ cup water	½ teaspoon cinnamon
½ cup sugar	1½ cups raisins
½ cup melted butter	

Dissolve the yeast in the cold milk. Add the scalded milk, water, sugar, melted butter, and beaten eggs. Beat in 4 cups of the flour, cover the bowl with a clean towel, and let rise until doubled. Then stir in the salt, cinnamon, raisins, and remaining 2 cups of flour. Knead thoroughly on a floured board. Shape into 2 loaves and place in buttered loaf pans. Cover and let rise again. Brush with milk or cream and bake in a 375° oven until browned and done, approximately 45 minutes to 1 hour. Glaze with a light frosting.

WILTSHIRE DOUGH CAKE. This hearty and delicious loaf from England is made by substituting brown sugar for white, 1 teaspoon nutmeg for the cinnamon, and ½ cup candied fruits for ½ cup of the raisins in the preceding recipe. Sliced thin, it makes excellent cream-cheese sandwiches.

GUGELHUPF (or KUGELHUPF)

This recipe is Viennese, but the pastry is found under a variety of names throughout Europe.

1 teaspoon salt	1 teaspoon vanilla extract, or 1
14 egg yolks (or 7 large eggs)	tablespoon grated lemon rind
2 cakes yeast	1 tablespoon brandy or rum
1 cup lukewarm milk	1 cup golden raisins
5 to 6 cups flour	½ cup plus 2 tablespoons
1 cup butter, melted	slivered blanched almonds
1 cup sugar	2 tablespoons sugar
¼ teaspoon almond extract	

Add the salt to the egg yolks and beat until thick and lemon-colored. Add the yeast, the milk, and 2½ cups of the flour. Blend thoroughly and let rise until doubled in bulk. Add another 2½ cups flour, the butter, sugar, flavorings, and raisins. Knead thoroughly, adding more flour if necessary, and let rise again until doubled in bulk. Punch the dough down and let rise again. Now butter a 10-inch tube pan and turn half the dough into the pan. Sprinkle over the dough ½ cup of the slivered blanched almonds and cover with the rest of the dough. Over the top sprinkle 2 tablespoons each slivered blanched almonds and sugar. Let rise about 1 hour and bake in a 350° oven for about 1 hour, or until browned and done. Two small tube pans may be used instead of one large one.

NOTE. Sour cream could be used in place of the milk in the preceding recipe. Egg yolks make a better Gugelhupf, but if you lack the required number of yolks, the whole eggs may be used.

MONKEY BREAD

This very popular bread may be served as a rich dinner bread, or the dough may be used as the basis for any number of sweet bread variations. Serve hot, with a light meal, and just pull off the buttery delicious diamonds.

1½ packages or cakes of yeast	1 teaspoon salt
1 teaspoon sugar	¾ cup scalded milk
¼ cup warm water	5 cups flour
½ cup butter	3 large eggs
½ cup sugar (⅓ cup for dinner bread)	

Dissolve the yeast and the 1 teaspoon sugar in the warm water. Combine the butter, ⅓ to ½ cup sugar, and salt. Pour the scalded milk over these ingredients and stir to melt the butter. Cool and then add the yeast and half the flour. Beat in the eggs and beat the batter thoroughly. Add the rest of the flour to make a soft but nonsticky dough. Turn the dough out onto a floured breadboard and knead well. Place in a buttered bowl, cover, and let rise until doubled. Punch the dough down and turn it out onto a floured board again. Roll the dough to a thickness of no more than ¼ inch. Cut the dough into diamonds, or any shape preferred. Dip each piece of dough into melted butter and then arrange them in a buttered 10-inch tube pan. Cover and let the dough rise again until almost doubled. Bake in a 375° oven for approximately 45 minutes, or until browned and done.

HUNGARIAN GOLDEN DUMPLINGS. Follow the preceding directions, using ½ cup sugar. Roll the dough and cut with a cookie cutter or biscuit cutter. Dip each of the pieces of dough into melted butter and then into a mixture of brown sugar and cinnamon. Put the pieces in layers in a buttered 10-inch tube pan. Sprinkle each layer with more melted butter, chopped walnuts or slivered almonds, and with raisins if desired. Sprinkle the top layer with more melted butter and nuts. Let rise and bake as directed.

NOTE. If desired, the dough may be shaped into balls and dipped into the butter and sugar. Chocolate chips may be sprinkled between the layers. Or the pieces of dough could be butter-dipped and layered as directed, and jam or preserves spread between layers. Two glass loaf pans may be used instead of the tube pan.

LEMON DUMPLINGS. Add 1 tablespoon grated lemon rind to the dough. Follow directions, using more grated lemon rind between layers.

APPLE DUMPLINGS. Follow directions for the dough and shape into diamonds or balls. Layer the pieces of dough, spreading Apple Filling between the layers. Let rise and bake as directed. Drizzle the top layer with melted butter before baking.

APPLE FILLING. Combine 2½ cups applesauce, 1 teaspoon cinnamon or nutmeg, ¼ cup sugar, and as many nuts or raisins as desired.

PINEAPPLE BUBBLE LOAF. Make the coffee cake as for the Apple or Golden Dumplings, but between the layers spread well-drained canned crushed pineapple. Use chopped nuts and a little less sugar than would ordinarily be used. Let rise and bake as directed.

FILLING VARIATIONS. The same basic idea can be used with a variety of fillings. Finely chopped apples could be used, or drained mincemeat, with the addition, if desired, of chopped apples or pears. A combination of chopped dates and candied orange slices is good. Another very good idea is to drizzle each layer with 1 or 2 tablespoons brandy or rum. Drizzle the top layer also. This may be used with any filling and is especially good at holiday time.

BUTTERHORNS. Make the dough the same way as for Monkey Bread; the only difference is in the shaping. Let the dough rise once. Punch dough down and turn out onto a floured board. Divide dough into 2 parts. Roll each part into a circle and spread with soft butter (Garlic butter or grated Romano cheese sprinkled over regular butter is a tasty addition). Cut each circle into 16 wedge-shaped pieces. Roll each wedge, starting with the wide part and rolling to the point. Arrange on buttered cookie sheets with the points underneath. Let rise until light and then bake in a 400° oven for 15 to 20 minutes.

APPLE BUTTERHORNS. Make Butterhorns as directed. Sprinkle the rolled-out dough with melted butter and spread with canned apple-pie slices (drained), and chopped nuts. Cut each circle into 8 to 12 pieces. Roll, let rise, and bake as in the preceding recipe. Frost the rolls while warm.

T W I S T S. Make the dough as directed for Monkey Bread and let rise once. Turn dough out and pinch off pieces of dough. Pull each piece into a rope and dip it in melted butter, then in sugar and chopped nuts. Fold each rope in half and twist. Place on buttered cookie sheets, cover, and let rise until doubled. Bake in a 350° oven for 15 to 20 minutes. Recipe will make about 3 dozen twists.

ITALIAN FRUITED BREAD

This unusual bread is the only yeast bread I've found which has jam as one of the ingredients in the dough. It is a delicious heavy bread that is easily varied. If cocoa is not liked, it can be left out, or grated sweet chocolate used. We prefer apricot preserves; however, one Italian friend uses grape jam, another black-cherry preserves, and still another prefers a stiff quince jam. The recipe calls for candied fruits but chopped dried fruits can easily be substituted. We sometimes use a mixture of chopped dried apricots and figs, but chopped dates and/or prunes could also be used. The recipe calls for just enough flour (5 cups) to make a heavy batter. However, an attractive as well as delicious loaf can be made by adding enough more flour (about 2 cups more), to make a firm dough, which is braided, the ends tucked under, and the loaves baked in 2 loaf pans.

1 cup flour	1 cup candied fruits
2 cakes yeast	1 cup chopped nuts
⅓ cup warm water	⅓ cup cocoa
4 cups flour	1 egg
2 cups apricot preserves	½ cup soft butter

Combine the first 3 ingredients and mix together to make a stiff paste. Cover and let rise for about 2 hours, or until almost doubled. Now add the rest of the ingredients, in order, and work together thoroughly. Cover the dough and let it rise until doubled. Then punch it down and put the heavy batter into a well-buttered tube pan. Let the dough rise again (because it is such a heavy dough, it will take some time to rise), and then bake in a 350° oven for 1 hour, or until bread is done. Brush the bread, while hot, with a mixture of hot apricot preserves and rum and then sprinkle with powdered sugar.

NOTE.   The bread may be baked in 2 well-buttered glass loaf pans. Bake in a 350° oven for 45 minutes, or until done.

ORANGE BREAD

This delicious bread makes excellent toast. It is also good frosted and decorated. If desired, the dough may be rolled with a filling of more sugar, grated orange rind, and chopped nuts. It also makes a very attractive braided loaf, which is best when glazed with an orange frosting and decorated with chopped nuts.

1 cake yeast	½ cup sugar
1¼ cups orange juice	2 tablespoons grated orange
1 large egg	rind
¼ cup melted butter	4 to 5 cups flour
1 teaspoon salt	1 teaspoon vanilla

Dissolve the yeast in 1 tablespoon of warm water. Add to the orange juice, egg, butter, salt, sugar, grated rind, and 2 cups of the flour. Beat until smooth. Add 2 more cups flour or more, using just enough so that dough can be kneaded, and the vanilla extract. Knead dough until smooth and elastic. Place in a bowl, brush with butter, cover, and let rise until doubled. Put into 1 large loaf pan, well buttered, or 2 smaller glass pans. Let rise again until doubled, and then bake in a 350° oven for 45 minutes, or until done.

NOTE.   Remember that no sweet bread should have too much flour, as this makes a tough loaf. Use just enough flour to make a barely workable loaf, no more. Braided loaves, however, are an exception, as these always require more flour.

PAN DE HUEVO
(Egg Bread)

This sweet egg bread is very popular throughout the Spanish-speaking countries, where most breads are sweet and contain many eggs. In South

America this is considered a breakfast bread and is served with coffee or hot chocolate.

8 large eggs, separated	3 tablespoons water
½ cup sugar	½ teaspoon salt
¼ cup melted butter	4½ to 5 cups flour
1 cake yeast	

Beat the egg yolks with the sugar until light and fluffy. Add the melted butter, the yeast dissolved in the 3 tablespoons water, and the salt, and then fold in the stiffly beaten egg whites. Now, sprinkling 1 cup at a time over the egg mixture, carefully fold in 4 cups of the flour. Cover the bowl and let the dough rise until doubled. Punch the dough down and turn out onto a breadboard sprinkled with another ½ cup of flour. Knead the dough lightly, adding enough flour to make a nonsticky dough. But do not add too much flour, as these rolls must be soft. Roll the dough to a thickness of ½ inch and cut it into squares. Put the squares on a buttered cookie sheet and let rise again until doubled. Bake in a 400° oven for 15 to 18 minutes, or until done.

NOTE.   If desired—this is traditional—add 1 or 2 teaspoons anise seed to the dough.

PAN DULCE CHILEÑO

This sweet egg bread from Chile shows the Spanish influence. The rolls are very attractive. They may be served either frosted or plain. However we prefer brushing the unbaked rolls with cream and sprinkling with Anise Sugar.

⅔ cup scalded and cooled milk	½ to ⅔ cup sugar
2 cakes yeast	8 egg yolks
1 tablespoon sugar	1 teaspoon salt
1 cup flour	3 to 4 cups flour
½ cup butter	

Combine the first 4 ingredients, beating thoroughly. Cover and let rise until light and bubbly. Then stir down. Cream the butter and ½ to ⅔ cup sugar and then add the egg yolks, beating until blended. Stir this mixture into sponge along with the salt and 2 cups flour. Beat thoroughly.

Add just enough more flour to make a dough that can be kneaded. When dough has been kneaded until smooth, put it into a buttered bowl, brush dough with soft butter, cover, and let rise until doubled. Then punch down and shape into small braided rolls. Place on buttered cookie sheets and let rise until doubled. Brush with cream and sprinkle with plain sugar or Anise Sugar. Bake in a 375° oven until done, about 25 minutes.

POTATO-RAISIN BREAD

The potatoes make a moist, beautifully textured bread that keeps well. It's a delicious bread, not overly sweet, which makes good toast.

1½ cups hot mashed	2 cakes yeast
potatoes	⅓ cup warm water
½ cup soft butter	6 cups flour
⅓ cup sugar	⅓ cup golden raisins
½ teaspoon salt	⅓ cup chopped nuts
1 cup scalded sweet cream	

Combine the hot mashed potatoes, butter, sugar, and salt. Stir until the butter is melted. Add the scalded sweet cream and let cool. Dissolve the yeast in the warm water and add to the cooled potato-cream mixture. Stir in 3 cups of the flour and beat until smooth. Gradually blend in the rest of the flour. Stir in the raisins and nuts. Turn the dough out onto a lightly floured board. Knead well. Place in a buttered bowl, cover, and let rise until doubled. Punch the dough down and turn out onto a floured board again. Shape into 2 loaves and place in buttered loaf pans. Cover and let rise again. Brush the loaves with soft butter. Bake in a 400° oven for 10 minutes, then reduce heat to 350° and bake another 45 minutes.

NOTE.   For a treat that the children will love, shape the dough into fancy shapes, brush with soft butter, and sprinkle with sugar before baking. Bake the rolls at 400° for about 20 minutes.

POTICA

This rich bread-cake from Yugoslavia is similar in many ways to the sweet breads of neighboring Hungary and Austria. The dough could be used in the variations given with other recipes, and almost any desired filling could be used. The Raisin Filling and Nut Filling are traditional, but a Poppy-Seed Filling, or brown sugar and cinnamon, or a stiff jam combined with chopped nuts could also be used.

1½ cups scalded milk, sweet cream, or sour cream	6 to 6½ cups flour
¾ to 1 cup sugar	1 cup sweet butter, melted
2 cakes yeast	4 eggs, or 8 egg yolks
	2 teaspoons salt

Pour the scalded milk, cream, or sour cream over the sugar. Stir to dissolve the sugar, then, when cooled to lukewarm, stir in the yeast. Add 3 cups flour and beat well. Cover and let rise until sponge is full of bubbles. Then stir in the butter, whole eggs or egg yolks, salt, and 3 more cups of flour (or more if needed). Beat well. Cover and let rise again until doubled. Divide into 2 parts and turn out onto a floured board. Roll to a thickness of ¾ inch. Spread with filling and roll as for a jelly roll. Fit into a buttered tube pan. Cover and let rise again until not quite doubled. Bake in a 350° oven for 45 minutes to 1 hour, or until browned and done. Glaze with a very light frosting.

NOTE. This dough is so rich that you can refrigerate it for several days and use as needed. Refrigerate after the first rising, brushing the top of the dough with softened or melted butter first. As the dough rises in the refrigerator, punch it down. When ready to use, let the dough come to room temperature first; this will take about 1 hour. From this point on follow the recipe.

RAISIN FILLING. Cream ⅓ cup butter and 3 egg yolks. Add the grated rind of 1 large lemon. Beat 3 egg whites until stiff, gradually adding ¾ cup sugar. Fold into the butter mixture and then add 2 cups golden raisins and if desired 1 teaspoon cinnamon.

NUT FILLING. Pour 1 cup scalded milk over 1½ pounds ground almonds or walnuts. Add ¼ pound butter and stir to melt the butter. Now add 1 cup sugar, 1 teaspoon vanilla extract, the grated rind of 1 lemon or 1 tablespoon rum, 1 egg yolk, and 4 egg whites, stiffly beaten.

CHOCOLATE FILLING. Combine 1 cup golden raisins, ½ pound chopped walnuts, ¼ cup bitter chocolate, grated, and ½ cup honey.

RAISIN-BRAN BREAD

Those who enjoy a heartier sweet bread will especially like this one. Very good for the children too.

1 cup scalded milk or boiling water	3½ cups flour
¼ cup butter	1 teaspoon salt
¼ cup molasses	½ teaspoon soda
1 cake yeast dissolved in ¼ cup warm water	½ cup brown sugar
1½ cups bran flakes or raisin-bran flakes	½ cup raisins
	½ cup chopped nuts
	½ cup chopped dates

Pour the scalded milk or boiling water over the butter and molasses. Let cool to lukewarm. Stir the dissolved yeast into the cooled liquid. In a large bowl blend the dry ingredients and the fruits and nuts. Pour the liquid mixture over the dry ingredients and blend well. The dough should be firm enough to knead but not stiff. Knead on a lightly floured board. Place in a buttered bowl, brush dough with butter, cover, and let rise until doubled. Punch down and shape into a loaf. Place in a buttered large loaf pan. Let rise again until doubled. Bake in a 350° to 375° oven for 1 hour, or until done. Brush the hot loaf with butter.

VERONA BREAD

This is the Italian Pandora de Verona; traditionally, after folding and rolling with only butter between layers, it is baked in a tube pan. We thought that the dough might lend itself to variations and with a bit of experimenting came up with a few.

1 cake yeast, dissolved in 2 tablespoons water	1 teaspoon vanilla extract, or grated rind of 1 lemon
2½ cups flour	7 egg yolks, or 4 whole eggs
¼ cup soft butter	¾ cup cold butter
½ teaspoon salt	sugar
	almonds

Combine the first 6 ingredients in the order listed. Blend into a dough and knead. Place in a bowl, brush with a small amount of butter, cover, and let rise until doubled. When dough has doubled, punch it down and place it on a floured breadboard. Roll the dough out into a long rectangle and sliver ¼ cup cold butter over it. Fold the dough over the butter and roll it out again into a long rectangle. Sliver another ¼ cup cold butter over dough and repeat the folding and rolling. Do this one more time, using ¾ cup butter in all, and folding and rolling 3 times. Now fold the dough once more (making 4 times in all), folding both ends toward the middle so they overlap. Place dough in a well-buttered, sugared 9- by 13-inch pan. Brush the top of the dough with more butter and sprinkle with sugar and slivered blanched almonds. Cover pan and let dough rise again until doubled. Bake in a 350° oven for 35 to 45 minutes, or until done. Cut into squares and serve.

NOTE. If desired, the sugar and almonds may be omitted and the top just brushed with butter. In this case the bread should be frosted when done.

FILLED VERONA BREAD. After the third rolling, spread the center of the rectangle with very thinly sliced apples. Sprinkle with sugar, cinnamon, and chopped nuts. Fold both sides over the middle, overlapping the ends and covering the filling. Place, upside down, in pan. Frost bread while warm and sprinkle thickly with chopped nuts.

NOTE. Chopped dates may be used in the filling. Or cooked and drained prunes, chopped, with a little sugar and grated lemon rind or orange rind. The dough also lends itself well to rolling, jelly-roll fashion, around any desired filling. Bake in a shallow buttered pan. Frost and decorate with nuts and candied cherries.

WHOLE-WHEAT EGG BREAD

This is a fine light bread. The filling may be omitted, and the raisins and nuts added to the dough. Dates may be used in place of the raisins, with grated lemon rind or orange rind substituting for the cinnamon. Spread with a lemon or orange glaze after baking.

4½ cups whole-wheat flour
1½ teaspoons salt
2 cakes yeast
⅓ cup honey
⅓ cup warm water
1⅓ cups hot water
⅓ cup soft butter
3 eggs

½ cup skim-milk powder
¼ teaspoon powdered clove
melted butter
brown sugar
cinnamon
raisins
chopped nuts

Combine the flour and salt and set aside. Dissolve the yeast and the honey in the warm water. Pour the hot water over the butter and stir until dissolved. Beat in the eggs and the yeast. Now, beat in 2 cups of the flour and beat until smooth. Add the skim-milk powder and cloves and beat again until smooth. Add the remaining 2½ cups flour and stir to mix thoroughly. Cover and let rise. When well risen (about 1½ hours), punch down and turn onto a floured board. Divide in half and pat each half into an oblong shape. Spread with melted butter, brown sugar, cinnamon, raisins, and/or chopped nuts. Roll as for a jelly roll and place each roll, seam side down in a buttered 8-inch loaf pan. Cover with a clean cloth and let rise until doubled, about 1 hour. Bake in a 350° oven until done, about 45 minutes. If bread seems to be browning too quickly, reduce heat to 325°.

12. *Miscellaneous Breads*

This final chapter includes various recipes which didn't fit in any other chapter but are too good and too useful to leave out. I am sure that there are still some good cooks who would like—if only occasionally—to try their hand at homemade crackers, rusks, and pretzels. Batter breads and filled breads are grouped here for the convenience of housewives who use them often. And today no apology is needed for providing a recipe for a homemade mix.

HOMEMADE MIX

This simple mix, which will keep for 2 months, can be used to make biscuits, pancakes, muffins, and some coffee cakes.

9 cups sifted white flour, or
8 cups unsifted whole-wheat
flour
1 tablespoon salt

¼ cup baking powder
1½ to 2 cups margarine
or shortening

Combine the dry ingredients in a large bowl. Cut in the margarine or shortening as for pastry. When the mix is thoroughly blended store in a canister or plastic container. In cold weather this will keep on the shelf; in hot weather it is best to keep the mix refrigerated even when shortening is used.

BISCUITS. Use 2 cups mix, 1 large egg, and ½ cup milk. Make as usual and bake in a 400° oven for 12 to 15 minutes.

NOTE. If desired, the dough may be made a little more moist and some grated Cheddar cheese blended into it.

COFFEE CAKE. For 1 pan of coffee cake use 2 cups mix, ½ cup sugar, 1 large egg, ¾ cup milk, and 3 tablespoons melted butter. Put into a pan and spread with any topping listed with Basic Coffee Cake (pages 176-77). The dough could also be used as the basis for baking-powder Kuchen, using toppings listed with Kuchens (pages 203-204).

MUFFINS. Use 3 cups mix, ¼ cup sugar, 1 cup milk, and 1 egg. Mix as for muffins and spoon into pans. Bake in a 425° oven for 20 minutes.

MUFFIN VARIATIONS. Add 5 or 6 slices of bacon, cooked crisp and crumbled. Or blend into batter 1 cup blueberries and ¼ cup sugar. Or blend into batter 1 cup fresh cranberries, chopped, and ⅓ cup sugar. The variations listed with the Basic Muffin Recipe (pages 23-26) may also be used.

PANCAKES. Use 1½ cups of mix, 1 tablespoon sugar, ½ cup milk, and 2 large eggs. Mix and bake as usual.

PANCAKE VARIATIONS. Use 1 large egg and ¾ cup 7-UP as liquid, omitting the milk. Very good. Or add ½ cup blueberries, or 1 cup peeled, cored, and chopped apples. Variations listed under Pancakes (Chapter 7) may also be used.

CAMPING TRIP NOTE. To use the mix on camping trips, add 2 cups skim-milk powder to the basic recipe and use water as the liquid.

YEAST PANCAKES. Combine ½ cup warm water and 2 cakes yeast. Stir in 2 cups mix, 1 cup milk, and 1 egg. Beat until smooth. Bake as usual.

FLAT BREAD

All the Scandinavian countries have a version of Flat Bread, which may be called Spisbrod, Knakkebrod, or Flatbrod. Most of these are a form of heavy cracker, quite unlike our idea of bread. They use a variety of hearty flours such as barley flour, oat, rye, graham, or whole wheat. Sometimes the dough is rolled very thin and cut into circles with a hole in the middle. Baked and dried, they are stored by being strung on lines. Sometimes, as in this recipe, the dough is rolled thicker and the bread eaten fresh as a dinner bread.

3 cups flour—rye, whole-wheat, barley, or a mixture	1 tablespoon baking powder
1 teaspoon salt	1¼ cups evaporated milk
1 tablespoon brown sugar	1 large egg
	¼ cup melted butter

Combine the dry ingredients and stir in the liquid ingredients. Turn the dough onto a floured breadboard and knead lightly. Pat or roll it into a large circle about ½ inch thick. Place on a buttered cookie sheet and bake in a 425° oven for 15 minutes, or until done.

NOTE. Buttermilk or sour milk may be used instead of evaporated milk. Add ½ teaspoon soda and use only 2 teaspoons baking powder.

AMERICAN FLAT BREAD

This excellent breakfast bread is very similar to Scones in ingredients and proportions of ingredients. It is easily made and worth trying. It goes very well with breakfast or with a light lunch.

2½ cups flour	1 tablespoon sugar
2 teaspoons baking powder	½ teaspoon soda
1 teaspoon salt	1 cup buttermilk

Sift the dry ingredients and stir in the buttermilk. Work mixture until well blended and then put it into a buttered 8-inch square pan. Bake in a 425° oven for 25 minutes, or until browned and done. If desired a criss-cross pattern can be cut into the top of the dough before it is baked.

GRIDDLE SCONES

Too good to be forgotten, these scones are a family treat. For sweet scones, increase the sugar to 2 or 3 tablespoons and add a cup of raisins.

2 cups flour	1 teaspoon soda
½ teaspoon salt	⅓ cup butter
1 teaspoon baking powder	1 cup sour cream
1 tablespoon sugar	1 large egg

Sift the flour, salt, baking powder, sugar, and soda into a bowl. Add the butter, cutting it into the flour mixture as for biscuits or pastry. Now add the sour cream and the egg, and blend into the dough until it is well moistened. Turn out onto a floured board and knead lightly, just enough to hold ingredients together. Pat the dough out and cut it into rounds. Bake on a hot griddle until risen and browned on the bottom, then turn scones over, and bake until done. The baking time will be about 15 minutes. Serve hot.

LEBANESE ZAHTAR BREAD

Zahtar is available at stores that sell Middle Eastern products. Or, if you can obtain powdered sumac, you can make your own, using ½ cup each toasted sesame seed, crumbled leaf thyme, and powdered sumac. Store in spice jars. Add 1 or 2 tablespoons of the mixture to the flour for breading fish or chicken. Commercial Zahtar omits the sesame seed, but we like to include it.

Use any nonsweet bread or roll dough, or a hot-roll mix. After the dough has risen once, press it into buttered pie pans, or a buttered pizza pan. The dough should be thin. Brush the top of dough liberally with oil and sprinkle generously with Zahtar. Don't let this spicy bread rise, but bake it immediately in a 400° oven for approximately 20 to 30 minutes, or until the bread is browned and done.

SPIRAL BREAD

Spiral Breads are so good, and so easy to make with either a bread dough or a hot-roll mix, that they are becoming more and more a part of our American cuisine. In each case, let the dough rise once. Then punch the dough down and turn it out onto a floured breadboard. Roll it out into a rectangle, brush with beaten egg, and then spread with any desired filling. Roll the dough as for a jelly roll and place in a buttered loaf pan. Let it rise again, brush with butter or beaten egg, and bake in a 375° or 400° oven until done, 45 to 60 minutes.

FILLINGS

CARAWAY CHEESE. Combine 1 cup grated Cheddar cheese, 2 teaspoons caraway seed, 2 tablespoons mayonnaise, and 2 tablespoons soft butter.

CHEESE-ONION. Combine 1 cup grated Cheddar cheese, ½ cup minced sautéed onion, and ½ cup toasted sesame seed. Or use 1 small can ripe olives, drained and sliced, instead of the sesame seed.

COTTAGE-CHEESE. Combine 1 cup drained cottage cheese, 1 tablespoon melted butter, and 2 tablespoons Zahtar.

HERB. Blend ⅓ cup soft butter with ¼ cup chopped parsley and 2 tablespoons minced green onions.

MAYONNAISE-ONION. Combine equal parts of mayonnaise and chopped green onions, seasoned with a bit of black pepper.

PARMESAN-GARLIC. Combine ¼ cup soft butter, ½ cup grated Parmesan or Romano cheese, and 1 clove of garlic, crushed.

NOTE.   Several of the Fillings for Hot Rolls (page 90) can also be used in Spiral Breads. It's fun to think up your own fillings. Using a sweet filling is an old idea, but the cheese, onion, and what-have-you fillings are a new and very good idea.

RUSKS

Rusks, which when twice-baked are Zwieback, until recent times were always home-baked. The rusks, actually light, sweet, biscuit-type rolls, were usually eaten fresh and those not eaten were then rebaked and stored. Several old cookbooks suggest soaking 4- or 5-day-old Rusks in cold milk until they are softened, then taking them out of the milk and serving them with melted butter as a breakfast dish.

1 cup soft butter	1 teaspoon soda
2 cups sugar	1 teaspoon vanilla extract
3 large eggs	¼ teaspoon salt
¾ cup sour cream	3 to 4 cups flour
1 cup chopped walnuts	

Cream the butter and sugar and add the eggs. Stir in the sour cream, walnuts, soda, vanilla extract, and salt. Add the flour gradually, using just enough to make a biscuit-type dough. Roll the dough out and cut it into rounds with a biscuit cutter, preferably a large one about 2½ inches in diameter. Bake in a 425° oven for 15 to 20 minutes, or until browned and done. Remove from oven, split open, return to the oven, cut side up, and brown.

NOTE.   If desired you can return the rusks to a 250° oven, let them bake for 10 minutes and then turn off heat and leave the Rusks in the oven until dry and crisp.

HOMEMADE CRACKERS

At one time all crackers were homemade, but today only a few dedicated cooks make them. Well worth an occasional try, the two recipes presented are typical. Soufflé Crackers, very popular just a few years ago, are ideally homemade, as the packaged kind are usually too thin.

2 cups flour   ¼ cup butter
1 teaspoon salt   ½ cup milk
½ teaspoon baking powder   1 large egg

Sift the flour, salt, and baking powder into a bowl. Cut in the butter until very fine. Add the milk and egg and mix to make a stiff dough. Knead thoroughly and then roll the dough very thin. Cut into squares or rounds and place on lightly buttered cookie sheets. Prick the crackers with a fork and then bake in a 400° oven for 10 minutes, or until very lightly browned. If desired, crackers may be sprinkled with coarse salt.

SODA CRACKERS.   Follow the basic recipe, but substitute sour milk for sweet milk, omit the baking powder, and add ½ teaspoon soda.

SOUFFLÉ CRACKERS.   Follow either of the preceding recipes, but roll the dough a little thicker than usual. Bake and let dry thoroughly. Preferably using crackers that are several days old, soak the crackers in ice water until they swell. (Do this in a shallow pan, using just enough ice water barely to cover the crackers.) With a spatula, lift the crackers out of the ice water, drain, and place on buttered cookie sheets. Dot each cracker with a bit of cold butter and bake in a 450° oven until puffy and a golden brown, about 20 minutes.

NOTE.   Any of the cheese mixtures presented as fillings for dinner rolls (see pages 90; 100) may be spread on crackers and heated in the oven, just until melted.

CHEESE WAFERS

Excellent with soup, salad, or as nibblers with a fine dry sherry.

½ pound aged Cheddar, grated   ⅛ teaspoon dry mustard (op-
½ cup butter   tional)
½ teaspoon salt   ⅛ teaspoon paprika (op-
1¼ cups flour   tional)

Combine all ingredients and work together until smooth. Shape into a roll and wrap in waxed paper. Chill. Slice as for refrigerator cookies and place on buttered cookie sheets. Bake in a 350° oven for 10 minutes, or until lightly browned and done. If desired, the wafers may be brushed with egg white and sprinkled with poppy seed, sesame seed, celery seed, or more grated cheese, before baking.

PRETZELS

There is a special knack to the shaping of Pretzels, which is acquired only by experience. Old-time pretzel makers dipped the pretzels into a lye solution. These pretzels are good, and not too difficult to make. A real treat in this ready-made age.

1 cake yeast	4 cups flour
1½ cups warm water	1 large egg, beaten
1 teaspoon salt	coarse salt
1 tablespoon sugar	

Dissolve the yeast in the warm water. Add the salt and sugar. Blend in the flour and knead the dough until smooth. As soon as the dough is kneaded, cut it into small pieces and roll the pieces into ropes. Twist the ropes into the traditional pretzel shapes and place the pretzels on paper-lined cookie sheets. Brush pretzels with the beaten egg and sprinkle generously with coarse salt. Bake immediately in a 425° oven for 12 to 15 minutes, or until browned. These do not keep long.

HARD PRETZELS. Follow the preceding recipe, decreasing water to 1¼ cups and adding ¼ cup melted butter. Make pretzels smaller and bake until well browned. These pretzels keep well.

BATTER BREADS

Batter breads as such were developed within the past 15 years. However, many old cookbooks give at least one recipe for a no-knead bread or coffee cake, and these were certainly the forerunners of modern batter breads. Batter breads don't have the fine texture of a well-kneaded loaf of bread, and the variations with a dominant flavor, such as Italian Pepper Bread or Cheese Batter Bread, are better than the plain versions. These are truly fine breads, and much enjoyed.

QUICK BATTER YEAST BREAD

2 cakes yeast	2 teaspoons salt, (part garlic
¾ cup warm water	salt may be used)
2 cups scalded and cooled milk	3 tablespoons soft butter
3 tablespoons sugar	6½ cups flour

Dissolve the yeast in the warm water. Add the cooled milk, sugar, salt, butter, and half of the flour. Beat until smooth. Add the remaining flour and beat thoroughly. Cover the bowl and let rise until doubled. In batter breads more yeast is used, so the rising times are greatly shortened. This rising will take no more than 30 or 40 minutes. Stir dough down and beat for a minute longer. Pour the batter into 2 buttered 8- by 4-inch loaf pans and spread evenly. Let rise again until batter reaches the tops of the pans, about 30 minutes. Bake in a 375° oven for 40 to 50 minutes. Brush with butter and cool the loaves on a rack.

NOTE. Remember never to let batter breads rise above the tops of the pans. They are very light, and if they rise too high the bread will fall during the baking.

VARIATIONS

As with any basic dough, many interesting and delicious changes may be made. Following are a few of our favorites.

BATTER BREAD WITH ONIONS. Spread batter in 2 buttered 9- by 13-inch pans. Brush the top with melted butter and spread with minced onions that have been sautéed in butter until golden. Sprinkle with poppy seed or sesame seed. Bake breads in a 375° oven approximately 30 minutes, or until browned and done.

OLIVE-CHEESE BATTER BREAD. Spread dough in 2 buttered 9- by 13-inch pans. Brush the tops with melted butter. Sprinkle liberally with a mixture of 2 cups grated sharp Cheddar cheese, ½ cup finely minced onion, and 1 can sliced black olives, well-drained. Bake in a 375° oven for about 30 minutes, or until done.

FRANKFURTER BREAD. Spread dough in 2 buttered 9- by 13-inch pans. Lay whole frankfurters over the dough, spacing them. Sprinkle the top of the dough with grated cheese. Let rise until doubled and bake as in basic recipe. If desired the frankfurters may be sliced and stirred into the dough. This is an especially good picnic bread.

WHOLE-WHEAT BATTER BREAD. Use ¼ cup brown sugar in place of 3 tablespoons white; increase butter to ¼ cup. Decrease total liquids to 2⅓ cups and add 2 large eggs to dough. Use 3 cups whole-wheat flour in place of as much white flour.

GARDEN BATTER BREAD. To the basic recipe add ⅓ cup grated fresh carrot, 2 tablespoons grated celery, 3 tablespoons grated onion, ½ to ¾ teaspoon crumbled dried sage, and ¼ teaspoon dried thyme.

ONION BATTER BREAD

The onion-soup mixes must certainly rate as one of the greatest contributions the testing kitchen has made to the home kitchen. I for one wouldn't be without them. You'll love the flavor in this bread.

2 cakes yeast	3 tablespoons soft butter
2 cups lukewarm water	1 package onion-soup mix
2 tablespoons sugar	4½ cups flour
1 teaspoon salt	

Dissolve the yeast in the water, with the sugar. Add the salt, butter, onion-soup mix, and 3 cups of the flour. Beat for 2 minutes. (I always use a wooden spoon.) Then add the rest of the flour and beat until very well blended. Cover the bowl and let rise until doubled, about 30 minutes. Stir down and pour into a well-buttered 1½-quart casserole. Cover and let rise again until doubled or until the batter reaches the top of the pan. Bake in a 375° oven for 50 to 55 minutes, or until browned and done. Turn out onto a rack and brush the top with melted or softened butter.

HERB BATTER BREAD. In the preceding recipe omit the onion-soup mix and use instead one or two herbs of your choice. We enjoy a combination of 2 teaspoons caraway seed, ¼ teaspoon ground nutmeg, and ½ teaspoon poultry seasoning or crumbled leaf sage. Bake as in preceding recipe. Delicious!

CHEESE BATTER BREAD

This is an easy bread with a fine, old-fashioned, *honest* flavor. I use a sharp Cheddar, but you may use a mild Cheddar or a Monterey Jack, if you prefer.

4 cakes yeast	4 large eggs
3 cups water, lukewarm	10 cups flour
¼ cup sugar	4 cups grated cheese
1 tablespoon salt	⅓ cup caraway seed

Dissolve the yeast in the lukewarm water, in a large bowl. Stir in the sugar, salt, eggs, and half the flour. Beat thoroughly for about 2 minutes, or until the dough is smooth. Now add the grated cheese, caraway seed, and the rest of the flour. Beat until thoroughly blended. Cover with a clean cloth and let rise until doubled, about 30 minutes. Stir down and pour into 3 greased loaf pans; cover and let rise again just until the batter reaches the top of the pan. Bake in a 375° oven for 1 hour. Turn out onto a rack, brush with soft butter, and cool. Makes 3 large loaves.

NOTE.   This bread may be baked in 10-ounce individual deep-dish pie dishes or loaf pans. Half the dough will fill 8 to 10. They make wonderful individual party loaves. Bake in a 375° oven for 20 to 25 minutes.

WHEAT-GERM–RYE BATTER BREAD

A very good pumpernickel-type bread. Let it set several hours, or preferably overnight, before cutting. As with any of the heavier breads, it is best cut into thin slices. I always include this bread in the variety of breads that I serve with buffet dinners.

1 cake yeast	2 teaspoons salt
⅓ cup warm water	2¼ cups rye flour
¼ cup brown sugar	1½ cups wheat germ
1½ cups hot water	1 tablespoon caraway seed
¼ cup butter	

Combine the yeast, warm water, and brown sugar. Let stand until foamy. Combine the hot water, butter, and salt and stir until butter is dissolved; by then the water should have cooled to lukewarm. Combine with the yeast mixture and add the rye flour. Beat well, then stir in the wheat germ and caraway seed and beat again. Cover with a towel and set in a warm place to rise. The batter will take approximately 1½ hours to rise, a little longer in winter and not quite so long in summer. When it has risen, beat the dough down with a spoon. Turn into a well-buttered loaf pan and spread smoothly. Cover with a towel and let rise until batter just reaches the top of the pan. Put pan in an oven preheated to 300° and then raise the temperature to 350°. After 20 minutes, turn the heat down to 325° and finish baking. The total baking time is 45 minutes. At the end of that time, turn the heat off and leave the bread in the oven for 5 minutes, before removing it to a rack to cool.

ITALIAN PEPPER BREAD

This is a wonderful Italian bread, traditionally not a batter recipe but a hard-crusted loaf. The variations are as uniformly good as the basic recipe.

1½ cups hot water	1 large egg
1 teaspoon salt	5 cups flour
3 tablespoons sugar	1 teaspoon freshly ground
2 tablespoons bacon fat	black pepper
2 cakes yeast	½ teaspoon dried sweet basil
½ cup warm water	¼ cup crumbled bacon

Combine the hot water, salt, 2 tablespoons of the sugar, and the bacon fat. Cool. Add the yeast and the remaining 1 tablespoon sugar to the warm water and stir to dissolve. Combine the mixtures and add the egg, flour, pepper, and basil. Beat for 2 or 3 minutes, or until mixture is smooth. Now stir in the crumbled bacon. Cover the batter and let rise until doubled. Stir down and beat for 2 minutes longer. Pour batter into 2 greased 8- by 4-inch loaf pans. Cover and let rise again until batter is just barely to the tops of the pans, or a little below. Bake in a 400° oven for 40 minutes, or until done.

VARIATION. If desired, and this is very good, use 1½ cups whole-wheat flour to replace the same amount of white flour, and add ¼ teaspoon coriander.

PARMESAN-CHEESE BATTER BREAD. Omit the sweet basil and use 1 teaspoon dried oregano. Decrease the flour to 4½ cups and add ½ cup grated Parmesan or Romano cheese. The pepper and the bacon may be used or not, as desired.

NO EXCUSE QUICK BREAD

1 cake yeast
1 quart warm water, milk, whey, or potato water
1 teaspoon honey or molasses or sugar

3 pounds freshly ground whole-wheat flour
½ cup sesame, soy, or other oil

Everything should be comfortably warm. Mix the yeast into a little of the liquid, with the honey. Set aside until it bubbles. Combine flour and salt and gradually stir into the yeast mixture with the rest of the liquid. Add the oil. This dough will be considerably moister than the usual bread dough. Spoon into 3 greased loaf pans, and set in a warm place to rise almost to the tops of the pans. Bake in a 375° oven for 45 to 60 minutes, or until done, but be sure to give it plenty of time. Turn out of pans at once to cool.

All life moving to one measure—daily bread.
—W. W. GIBSON

RAISIN BATTER BREAD

2 cups lukewarm water
2 cakes yeast
3 large eggs
7 cups flour, part whole-wheat
1 tablespoon grated orange rind

⅔ cup white sugar or brown
  sugar
2 teaspoons salt
1 teaspoon cinnamon or ginger
½ cup soft butter
1 cup raisins

Pour the water into a large bowl and add the yeast. Stir to dissolve. Mix the dry ingredients together. Add the eggs and half of the dry ingredients to the dissolved yeast. Stir in the soft butter and beat thoroughly for 2 or 3 minutes, or until mixture is smooth. Now add the rest of the dry ingredients and beat until batter is smooth and thoroughly mixed. Stir in the raisins. Cover the bowl and let the batter rise until doubled. Butter 2 loaf pans, either 8 by 4 inches or 9 by 5 inches. Pour the batter into the loaf pans and let rise until batter just reaches the tops of the pans. Bake in a 375° oven for 40 to 50 minutes, or until done. Frost the loaves with an Orange Glaze.

SOUR-CREAM BATTER ROLLS

This recipe makes 2 dozen delicious rolls, wonderful for the holiday season, when I use part candied red cherries and part candied green pineapple.

1 cup sour cream
1 cup sugar
1 teaspoon salt
⅓ cup soft butter
2 cakes or 2 packages yeast
⅓ cup warm water
3 large eggs
4 cups flour

½ cup slivered, toasted
  almonds
½ cup chopped candied cherries or pineapple
2 tablespoons rum or brandy
½ cup slivered blanched
  almonds

Bring the sour cream just to a boil. Combine ½ cup of the sugar, the salt, and the butter, and stir in the hot sour cream. Set aside to cool. When mixture has cooled, dissolve the yeast in the warm water and then stir into the sour-cream mixture. Add the eggs and half of the flour. Beat well. Now add the rest of the flour, the toasted almonds, candied fruit, and rum or brandy. Stir until thoroughly blended. Spoon the batter into well-buttered muffin tins, filling them no more than half full. Cover and let the batter rise until barely doubled. Now blend the slivered, blanched almonds with the remaining ½ cup sugar. Sprinkle on the tops of the rolls. Bake in a 400° oven for 20 minutes, or until browned and done. Remove from pans immediately and serve hot.

ORANGE TEA ROLLS

This is a rich batter roll recipe, which takes only 2 hours from mixing bowl to table.

1¾ cups milk	TOPPING
¾ cup sugar	⅓ cup butter
1 teaspoon salt	1⅓ cups orange juice
1 tablespoon grated orange	1 cup sugar
rind	1 tablespoon grated orange
¾ cup butter	rind
2 cakes yeast	6 rose-geranium leaves,
3 large eggs	minced, or 1 teaspoon
5 cups flour	vanilla extract

Combine the first 5 ingredients in a saucepan. Heat until the butter melts and the milk is scalded. Let cool to lukewarm, then stir in the yeast. Beat in the eggs and half the flour. Beat for a minute or two, or until mixture is smooth. Now beat in the rest of the flour. Cover and let batter rise until doubled. While it is rising make the topping. Combine the butter, orange juice, sugar, and orange rind in a saucepan, and heat and stir for several minutes. Add the rose-geranium leaves or vanilla extract. Pour this syrup into approximately 2 dozen muffin tins. Stir the batter down and spoon it into the muffin tins, filling them no more than half full. Cover and let batter rise until it reaches the tops of the tins. Bake in a 350° oven until browned and done, about 20 minutes. Turn out of tins immediately and serve hot.

DESSERT BREAD

This delicious buttery bread is good with, or without, the addition of chopped walnuts and raisins. The Danes make a very similar bread, using 1½ teaspoons ginger and omitting the vanilla extract.

1 cup scalded milk	grated rind of 1 large lemon
½ cup butter	1 teaspoon salt
½ cup sugar	4 cups flour
1 cake or 1 package yeast	½ cup each chopped walnuts
¼ cup warm water	or slivered almonds, and rai-
2 large eggs	sins (optional)
2 teaspoons vanilla extract	

Pour the scalded milk over the butter and sugar. Let cool to lukewarm. Dissolve the yeast in the water and add to the cooled milk mixture. Stir in the eggs, vanilla extract, lemon rind, salt, and half the flour. Beat thoroughly. Stir the remaining 2 cups of flour with the nuts and raisins, if used, and add to the batter; otherwise just stir the flour into the batter. Beat until thoroughly blended. Cover the bowl and let the dough rise until doubled. When doubled, punch the dough down and let it rise again. After the second rising, stir the dough down and pour into a well-buttered 1½-quart casserole. Let dough rise again until just doubled. Brush the risen loaf with cream and sprinkle with sugar. Bake in a 350° oven for 30 to 40 minutes, or until well browned and done.

ORANGE-APRICOT COFFEE BREAD

A delicious, and very easy, coffee cake. A variety of toppings may be used, but the marmalade topping is our particular favorite.

2 cakes yeast	4 egg yolks (or 2 whole eggs)
½ cup sugar	2 tablespoons grated orange
1½ cups warm water	rind
1 teaspoon salt	4½ cups flour
⅓ cup soft butter	

Dissolve the yeast and sugar in the warm water. Add the salt, butter, egg yolks (or whole eggs), grated orange rind, and half the flour. Beat thoroughly. Stir in the rest of flour and beat until well blended. Cover batter and let rise until doubled. Stir the batter down and pour into a well-buttered 9- by 13- by 2-inch pan. Brush the top of batter with melted butter and spread with topping. Let rise until doubled, and bake in a 375° oven for 35 to 40 minutes, or until browned and done.

ORANGE-APRICOT TOPPING. Combine ¼ cup each orange marmalade, apricot preserves, and melted butter, and 1 cup shredded coconut. Spread on coffee cake and sprinkle with 1 tablespoon sugar, or with ½ cup slivered blanched almonds.

STREUSSEL TOPPING. Combine 1 cup flour, ½ cup sugar, 1 tablespoon grated orange rind, and ⅓ to ½ cup melted butter. Rub together to form large crumbs. Sprinkle on top of coffee cake.

FILLED BREADS

In this category fall the savory Pizzas, Pissaladières, and Pasties that are made the world over. Most countries include a meat- or vegetable-filled pastry in their cuisine, and many times the only difference is in the name. The Russian Piroshki, the Polish Pierogi, and the German Beurek are all meat- or vegetable-filled sandwiches, with only a slight difference in fillings. The Russians are apt to use fish, the Germans to include their beloved cabbage, and Polish housewives to use ham or cabbage. The Armenians make a Piroshki using a lamb filling, and also a meat cake very similar to the Lebanese Sfeeha. The Cornish Pasty, made famous by the miners of Cornwall, England, comes in any size from a triangular individual cake to large dinner-sized pasties that will feed two or three people.

Some nationalities use a flaky pastry to enclose the savory filling. Thus Strudel might be apple, cherry, cheese, ham, or cabbage, and the Greeks use the popular Phyllo Sheets to enclose various fillings.

All the Spanish-speaking countries eat Empanadas, a flaky pastry filled with bits of meat, chicken, seafood, and/or olives, and served as an appetizer. And in Russia and Poland flaky Piroshkis and Pierogis are made as appetizers. Since the Tortilla is Mexico's bread, Tacos and Enchiladas both classify as filled breads.

The most popular of all filled breads are the various Pizzas, and next the German Onion Kuchen, a wonderful snack, appetizer, or what-have-you, when prepared properly.

Most filled breads are excellent picnic food and good lunch-box fillers, a welcome change from the ubiquitous sandwich. Some of them can be served with soup for lunch or supper. With a salad, or antipasto, and beer or wine, a Pizza or Pissaladière makes a complete meal.

Many more wonderful recipes and variations could be added if space permitted. Except for Sfeeha and Fatayir, which are included for admittedly sentimental reasons as fond memories of my childhood and also for the benefit of all second-generation Lebanese, the recipes in this section were chosen because of their particular appeal to American tastes.

Some of the following recipes may be made with refrigerated canned biscuits; all of them may be made with a hot-roll mix, or with any roll or bread dough. With a bowl of refrigerated dough on hand, you always have the makings of some kind of delicious filled bread.

CHEESE-FILLED BREAD

This filled bread is put together in a slightly unusual manner. For convenience a hot-roll mix may be used. However, Refrigerator Roll dough made up once or twice a week and kept on hand is just as simple and much cheaper.

If a hot-roll mix is used, make it up according to the instructions, but use 2 eggs instead of the 1 egg called for. Let the dough rise once. Then punch it down and roll the dough into a rectangle (this is best done right on a buttered cookie sheet). The dough, when rolled, should be about ¼ inch thick. Spread the center of the dough with a thin coating of mayonnaise and then sprinkle with minced green onions. Over the onions, overlap slices of Cheddar or Jack cheese. Sprinkle with a small amount of crumbled oregano and drizzle with a very little olive oil. Now fold the ends of the dough over just to cover the ends of the filling—do *not* fold the ends all the way over. Pull the sides of dough up and over the filling.

Overlap the dough on top and seal the edges. Carefully flip the loaf over so that the seam side is on the bottom. Slash the top in several places and brush with beaten egg. Bake in a 400° oven until done, about 30 to 35 minutes. Slice and serve hot.

SFEEHA
(LaHm-BI-AjIn)

This is a delicious meat pastry bearing a vague resemblance to Pizza. The pastries can be reheated easily in a water-sprinkled paper bag in a 350° oven and are especially good on picnics, hot *or* cold. This and Fatayir, which follows, may seem difficult but they are well worth making, if only on special occasions. My grandmother, a typical old-country cook who never measured a smidgen, made Sfeeha and Fatayir as special treats, and I spent many an hour in her kitchen with pad and pencil in an attempt to learn *her* way with Lebanese foods.

1 cake yeast	¼ cup sugar
1½ cups warm water	1½ teaspoons salt
¼ cup melted butter	Filling
5 cups flour	

Dissolve the yeast in ¼ cup of the warm water. Combine the rest of the warm water, the butter, flour, sugar, and salt, and add the dissolved yeast. Blend well. Turn the dough out on a floured board and knead. Place the dough in a bowl, brush the top with melted butter, cover, and let rise until doubled. Punch down and then pinch off pieces of the dough. Flatten the pieces with your hands, or else, using a rolling pin, roll the pieces into 5-inch rounds. Put the rounds on buttered cookie sheets and spread each to the edges with Filling. Bake in a 450° oven just long enough to brown the dough—about 15 to 20 minutes, no longer.

FILLING.   Combine 2 pounds ground lean lamb, 2 large onions, minced, and ½ cup pine nuts. Brown this mixture in ⅓ cup butter or oil. Remove the pan from the heat and stir in ¼ cup lemon juice, 1 teaspoon salt, and ¼ teaspoon each pepper, cinnamon, cloves, and nutmeg. Cool the mixture before using.

NOTE. This Lebanese pastry may be made with a hot-roll mix, or with refrigerated canned biscuits. I would not recommend using beef in this recipe. A very few Lebanese recipes are equally delicious with either lamb or beef, but this one requires lamb.

FATAYIR
(Lebanese Spinach Rolls)

Similar to Cornish Pasties, these Lebanese "pies," make wonderful additions to the lunch box or the picnic basket. Like Sfeeha, Fatayir may be made with a hot-roll mix, or with refrigerated canned biscuits.

1 cake yeast	1 tablespoon salt
2 cups warm water	¾ cup melted butter
5 cups white flour	Filling
1½ cups whole-wheat flour	

Dissolve the yeast in the warm water. Sift the dry ingredients and add to the yeast mixture with the melted butter. Knead the dough. Place in a bowl, brush the top with butter, cover, and let rise until doubled. Meanwhile, make the Filling. Punch the dough down and roll it out to a thickness of ⅛ inch. Cut into 5-inch squares. Put some of the Filling on each square, fold the dough over to make a triangle, and seal the edges. Place on buttered cookie sheets. Brush the pastries with melted butter and bake in a 450° oven for about 25 minutes, or until browned and done.

FILLING. Wash and drain thoroughly 4 pounds spinach and tear the leaves into small pieces. Combine leaves with 3 onions, minced, ½ cup each of pine nuts and olive oil, the juice of 3 lemons, and 1 tablespoon salt.

CHA SIU BOU
(Chinese Steam Buns)

Using a hot-roll mix, or any roll dough if you are making bread or rolls, these are not at all difficult to make. Traditionally they are a luncheon or teatime snack, but we find them good at any time, especially picnic time. You may make the filled buns in quantity and freeze them, then, when ready to eat, reheat the buns by steaming. Chopped, cooked chicken may be used in place of the beef.

Prepare 1 package hot-roll mix, following instructions on package, but use 2 eggs instead of the 1 egg called for. Let the dough rise. When doubled in bulk, punch the dough down and knead gently on a floured board. Pinch off pieces of dough the size of a small egg and pat into 3-inch rounds. Spoon 1 or 2 tablespoons Filling on each circle of dough. Pull the edges up and over the Filling, forming a sacklike piece of dough. Pinch the edges together. Place each bun, seam side down, on a square of waxed paper or aluminum foil. Cover the buns and let them rise for 10 or 15 minutes. Then set the buns, on the paper, on a steamer rack and steam them for 12 to 15 minutes, or a little longer. When done the buns will have a glazed look, like Bagels. If you don't have a regular steamer, place the buns on a trivet over boiling water.

Any nonrich bread or roll dough may be used. If you are a traditionalist, make the dough in the usual manner with 4 cups of flour, ½ teaspoon salt, 1 cake yeast, 1 tablespoon sugar, 2 tablespoons peanut oil or soy oil, and 2 cups warm water. Let rise. Then turn out onto a floured board and roll into a long, fairly thick rope. Cut into 1-inch lengths and roll or pat each length into a 3-inch round.

FILLING. Although the Chinese often use halved Chinese sausages, the traditional filling is barbecued pork or chicken, very finely minced. For this filling use 1 teaspoon sugar, ¼ cup peanut oil, soy oil, or sesame oil, ¼ cup soy sauce, 1 pound barbecued pork or chicken, 1 teaspoon minced fresh ginger, and ¼ cup finely minced onion, or green onion. Combine ingredients thoroughly. However, the filling doesn't have to be this complicated to be good. We use 1 cup of any leftover meat, although pork or chicken is preferable, 3 green onions, minced, 1 tablespoon soy sauce, and 2 teaspoons sugar. We have, however, used frankfurters that were either halved or cut into thirds; or thick slices of Polish sausage; or a sweet filling made with 1 cup chopped dates, ⅓ cup each chopped nuts and orange marmalade, and the grated rind of 1 orange. It is the steaming that makes these buns so different, and so delicious. In any case, the buns are best served hot and are so good that almost any quantity made will disappear quickly.

CORNISH PASTIES

"Pasty" rhymes with "nasty," but these meat-filled pastries, brought to this country by the Cornish miners, are delicious and hearty, good for lunch box or picnic. Traditionally the crust is made with suet, which is now available in big city markets the year round. For those who would like to try the traditional crust, use the following ingredients and assemble them as for pie crust: 2 cups suet, ½ cup lard, 3 cups flour, 1 teaspoon salt, 2 teaspoons baking powder, and enough water to bind ingredients together.

A hot-roll mix, made following instructions but using 2 eggs instead of 1, may be used, as may refrigerated canned biscuits, or any pie-crust recipe.

Traditional filling recipes use round steak and potatoes, and traditionally the filling is not cooked first; the pastries are baked, in a slow oven, for several hours. The result is a delight for the meat-and-potatoes man. Our favorite filling uses 1 pound round steak, diced; 1 cup lean pork steak, diced; 2 large potatoes, diced; 1 large onion, minced; salt and pepper. I sauté the filling in butter, over a medium heat, until the meat and potatoes are done.

Roll the dough out and cut into squares. In the center of each square put approximately ⅓ cup filling. The amount depends on the size of the squares, but the pasties should be well filled. Fold the dough over, forming a triangle, and seal the edges securely. Place on buttered cookie sheets, brush with butter, and bake in a 350° oven for about 30 minutes, or until pasties are done. Some cooks slash the tops of the pasties and insert a little cream.

PISSALADIÈRE

A non-rich crusty bread or roll dough should be used for this. A French Bread dough is ideal, but a hot-roll mix will do. Line an oiled pizza pan with a very thin layer of dough (no thicker than ⅛ inch). Make a rim around the edges to hold in the filling.

Cook 6 large thinly sliced onions, 2 mashed cloves of garlic, and any desired amount of anchovies in olive oil until the onions and garlic are quite soft. Start out with a small amount of anchovies until you know by taste how much you like. Mash the anchovies into the oil. Traditionally, whole anchovies are laid across the onions just before baking, but we find that this is just too much anchovy. Cool the onion mixture before spreading it over the dough. Spread sliced ripe olives over the onions, or blend them in with the onions. Bake immediately in a 375° to 400° oven for 20 to 25 minutes, or until crust is browned. Serve hot.

ONION KUCHEN

For this delicious pastry you can use a biscuit mix, any nonsweet baking-powder dough, or a yeast dough. Spread the dough in a buttered 10-inch pie pan, an 8- or 9-inch square pan, or an oblong pan. The ingredients for the filling can only be given approximately, as the filling may be as thick, or as thin, as you wish, but there should be a lot of onions. If you use a pie pan, or a square pan, you will need about 4 or 5 large onions, sliced very thin. We prefer the onions sliced into rings, but some people prefer to chop them. Sauté the onions in butter or oil until golden but not browned. Cool the onions, then spread them over the dough. Now, for each pan of Kuchen, beat ¾ to 1 cup of sour cream with 2 or 3 egg yolks. Season with black pepper, and with caraway seed if desired. Pour this over the onions. Or—and many German cooks do it this way—carefully blend the onions and the sour-cream mixture together, and spoon over the dough. Bake in a 375° oven for approximately 35 minutes, or until crust is browned and done. If desired, the top may be browned under the broiler. Serve hot.

NOTE. Many German cooks add thinly sliced apples to the onion mixture, sautéing the apples with the onions.

PIZZA

My favorite Pizza dough, made the same way as any bread dough, uses 5 cups flour, ½ teaspoon salt, ½ teaspoon black pepper, ¼ cup oil (olive oil is preferable), 1 cake yeast, and 1¼ cups warm water. Any hard-crusted bread dough may be used, or a hot-roll mix, but do add the black pepper to the dough as this is an important touch. When the dough has risen once, divide it into 2 parts and stretch each part to fit an oiled pizza pan. Spread with desired filling and bake immediately in a 400° oven until done, about 30 minutes or more, depending on the size of the Pizza, and on the filling.

FILLING. The preferred sauce for Pizzas is a homemade tomato sauce simmered for about 30 to 45 minutes. I use 2 crushed cloves garlic; several anchovies, mashed into the oil so that there is only a faint flavor of anchovy; tomato sauce or purée; salt, pepper, and sweet basil. Peperoni or hot or sweet Italian sausage may be added to the sauce. Spoon a little of the sauce over the Pizza crust, spread liberally with grated Mozzarella, and then spoon more sauce over the cheese. Sprinkle the top with grated Parmesan or Romano cheese and some crumbled oregano. Bake. The addition of mushrooms, anchovy pieces, or larger quantities of peperoni or sausage changes the character of the Pizza.

FILLED ONION PIZZA

This Italian specialty is another delicious way of preparing Pizza.

Spread half the dough over the oiled pizza pan. Cook a large quantity of thinly sliced onions (4 or 5 for each Pizza) in olive oil until soft but not browned. Salt and pepper the onions, cool them, and then spread over the dough. Cover the onions with a thin layer of sliced ripe olives and then cover the filling with the other layer of dough. Pinch the edges to seal. Bake in a 375° oven about 45 minutes.

FILLED CHEESE PIZZA

Combine 1 pound Ricotta; 2 large eggs; ¼ cup grated Parmesan or Romano; ½ pound Mozzarella, grated; and as much Italian sausage as desired, first cooked until done and then sliced. Pour this onto the yeast crust and cover with the other half of the dough. Slash the top in several places and bake in a 375° oven until done, about 45 minutes. With a salad and beverage, this, or any Pizza, makes a meal,

PIZZA ROLLS

Use a hot-roll mix or a roll dough. Roll the dough thinly and cut into rounds with a 3-inch biscuit cutter. Place rounds on an oiled cookie sheet and brush the dough with olive oil. Top each round with a thin slice of tomato, then with several onion rings and sliced ripe olives, and top off with grated Mozzarella. Sprinkle with olive oil and then with grated Romano or Parmesan cheese and crumbled oregano. Let rise about 20 minutes and then bake in a 450° oven until browned and done.

BEUREK

Use a hot-roll mix and prepare it as directed, but use 2 eggs in the dough. Let the dough rise once and then roll it out to a thickness of ⅛ inch. Cut into 5-inch squares. In the center of each square place some of the Filling. Draw the edges up and over the filling and pinch together. Place the squares seam side down on buttered cookie sheets and let rise about 20 minutes. Bake in a 400° oven for 15 to 20 minutes, or until browned and done.

FILLING. Simmer 2 cups chopped cabbage and 1 onion, minced, in butter until tender. Cover the pan and the vegetables will steam tender. Add 1 cup of ground cooked meat, salt, pepper, and a little cream or bouillon to moisten.

RUSSIAN COULIBAC

This is very similar to Beurek. The dough is usually richer, but a hot-roll mix will do. Roll the dough into a large square. Use the filling for Beurek, adding 4 chopped hard-cooked eggs. Place all of the filling in the center of the dough. Lap the edges of the dough over the filling and seal. Turn upside down on a buttered cookie sheet. Let rise about 20 minutes and then bake in a 350° oven for 1 hour, or until done. Cut into squares and serve with gravy.

Index

295

Pizza (continued)
  rolls, 294
Plain kuchen dough, 202–203
Polish hola, 253
Pope ladies, 56–57
Popovers, 35–38
  baking, 35–36
  basic recipe, 36
  variations, 37
Poppy-seed filling, 224, 254
Portuguese
  bread, 66–67
  Easter, 245
  malsadas, 121–122
  sonhos, see French doughnuts
Potato
  biscuit, 14
  bread
    garlic, 77
    -raisin, 265
    refrigerator, 77–78
    triple-rich, 78
    whole-wheat, 79
  -chocolate loaf, 169–170
  -cornmeal muffins, 33
  -flour muffins, 34
  hotcakes, sourdough, 151
  muffins, 33
  pancakes, 138
  scones, 22
  water, in breads, 2
Potica, 265–66
Pretzels, 277
Provincial coffee cake, 184
Prune
  coffee cake, 180
  schnecken, 230
  filling, 224
  nut bread, 170
Pumpernickel, 82–83
Pumpkin, nut bread, 158
  rolls, 103
Puris, 110–11

Quick batter yeast bread, 278–79
Quick breads
  barbecue, 50
  bran brown, 49
  caraway-seed, 48
  cheese wine, 47
  hot, 46–47
  Irish soda, 48
  steamed molasses, 49
  See also Baking powder tea breads
    and coffee cakes; Batter breads;
    Biscuits; Bannocks; Cornbreads;
    Muffins; Scones
Quick cake, 177–78
Quick loaf bread, 60

Raised cornmeal bread, 68
Raisin
  bread
    batter, 283
    -bran, 267
    carrot-, 161
    Greek, 258
    -nut, 163
    filling for potica, 266
Ready-to-serve rolls, homemade, 98
Refrigerator
  bran muffins, 29
  potato bread, 77–78
  rolls, 101
  rich, 225–26
  whole-wheat, 102–103
  -type sour-cream sweet rolls, 230–31
Relish spread, 53–54
Rhubarb kuchen, 205
Rice
  bread, 79
  hotcakes, 138
  muffins, 25
  polish, 5, 60, 84, 130
  waffles, 142
Rich
  bran rolls, 99
  German coffee braid, 234
  kuchen dough, 201
  popovers, 37
  refrigerator rolls, 225–26
  sour-cream biscuits, 19
  sour-cream dough, 209
  tea biscuits, 16
Rogelach, 207
Rohrnudeln in der auflaufform, 215
Rolls, 89–104
  bagels, 91–92
  bran, 102
  buckwheat, 94
  buttermilk herb, 94
  carrot, 103
  cheese, 102
  coconut, 102
  corn, 102
  cream, 95
  croissants, 96
  crust on, 89
  crusty French dinner, 97
  dinner seed, 95
  fillings for hot, 90–91
  frankfurter, 100
  freshening stale, 8
  Grape-Nuts, 104
  herb, 102
  homemade ready-to-serve, 98
  honey, 97
  Italian, 99
  orange tea, 284
  pizza, 294